The City of Dickens

THE
City of Dickens

ALEXANDER WELSH

And I John saw the holy city,
new Jerusalem, coming down from
God out of heaven, prepared as
a bride adorned for her husband.
—Revelation

CLARENDON PRESS · OXFORD

Oxford University Press, Ely House, London W.1

GLASGOW NEW YORK TORONTO MELBOURNE WELLINGTON
CAPE TOWN IBADAN NAIROBI DAR ES SALAAM LUSAKA ADDIS ABABA
DELHI BOMBAY CALCUTTA MADRAS KARACHI LAHORE DACCA
KUALA LUMPUR SINGAPORE HONG KONG TOKYO

ISBN 0 19 812008 7

© OXFORD UNIVERSITY PRESS 1971

First published 1971
Reprinted 1973

PRINTED IN GREAT BRITAIN
BY FLETCHER AND SON LTD, NORWICH

FOREWORD

THE means of expressing value and purpose in fiction vary, and are especially difficult to isolate in the case of Dickens, whose positive values were vague compared with the sharpness of his attack on things he disliked. The means include statement and dialogue, the manipulation of settings and outcome of actions, the endowment of certain characters with special virtues, and often strained uses of metaphor. Nor are such positive expressions rightly interpreted by the reader except against the background of whatever is condemned or repudiated in the novel. The most obvious expressions of value in Dickens are devoted to the celebration of home, and are delivered in almost religious tones. But to remark that Dickens and other Victorians were officially or even spontaneously in love with home life does not explain very much; and a reason for taking novels seriously is presumably that they will help explain as well as illustrate love affairs. My dictionary gives the first definition of *home* as one's dwelling place or that of one's family; but the second, as one's abode after death.

The worship of hearth and home that culminates in the nineteenth century, and which importantly survives in our own lives, is not fully explicable without the pressures that the modern city has brought to bear upon it. In this book I have treated the city of Dickens both as an historical reality and as a metaphor that provides a context for values and purposes expressed by the English novel. I am not contending that this city everywhere controlled the nineteenth-century imagination or became the sufficient cause of Dickens's achievement. But as a metaphor it is instructive, because a hundred years ago it still reflected the Christian tradition of two cities. That tradition supposed that the earthly city must contain its own antithesis; it also, in some degree, served as a model of discrimination between good and bad, favoured and unfavoured characters in the novel.

In the first part of the book I have recalled the conventional way of describing the city in literature and suggested how this was modified by historical change in the nineteenth century. Neither satire nor the advent of the modern city furnishes a very hopeful prospect of human life, however; death is the only end of existence prophesied by either. The absence of a political remedy for the city's ills makes the prospect even bleaker. The city so envisioned corresponds well enough with the Christian idea of the city of destruction, from which one hoped eventually to escape; and in the second part I have shown how some of Dickens's themes mirror the religious conviction that some individuals are not necessarily a part of this city but perhaps destined for a better place. This analysis encounters obvious difficulties. For one thing, it makes out Dickens's position to be generally a Puritan one, and he himself might not accept that without a protest. For another, the ultimate destination of the Christian wayfarer, the City of God, is not a self-evident proposition in the nineteenth century. But these same difficulties lead to a new line of attack in the third part, in which I examine the Victorian readiness to make a heaven of hearth and home, and the ambition of the novel virtually to impose its own religious construction of reality. The prominence of the heroine in this domestic idyll confirms the antithesis of the hearth to the actual and earthly city, and may suggest to some readers an unexpected resemblance between calm Victorian angels and the more fervidly imagined females of European romanticism. Though I have stressed some neglected aspects of Dickens's work for their own sake, the argument in all three parts moves as nearly as possible along this speculative path. The generalizations offered in the last chapter are not intended to oppress the variety of the English novel, but to show how the extravagances of Dickens relate to a literary form that is, after all, more coherent and capable of definition in late eighteenth- and nineteenth-century England than elsewhere.

The first part of the book draws heavily on Dickens's journalism and incidental writings; the second, on the juncture—or disjuncture—of his values and his fictions; and the third, more and more closely on the contrivances of the novels themselves. This descent into the novel is not always as smooth as I could wish, but I hope it suggests some of the dimensions of the relation of literature to life. The only advantage novels have over real life is that they are not real, yet they persistently pretend to reality. In one way or another they exploit their freedom from reality in order to give shape to experience, or to bundle off a portion of reality from the whole of it. Even at the perceptual level, as E. H. Gombrich has shown, art manipulates forms in which experience comes already packaged. At the thematic level the interdependence of literary and other forms should be more obvious. Traditional novels do not encounter life as a stream of particles or discrete moments, but life as it is already construed by earlier literature, by science and morality, by religion, and by attitudes of every kind. They may very well incorporate fancies that seem to have no relation to life. Literary critics have wished just as often as historians that they might see the reality that lies behind a fiction or a history, but we can no more 'see' the city of Dickens than we can see our own cities with eyes alone.

A number of beneficent institutions have contributed to this book. I am specifically indebted to the journal *Victorian Studies* for an invitation to the symposium on the Victorian city at Indiana University in 1967 and for permission to reprint that portion of Chapters I and II that appeared in the journal in 1968. To Yale University I am indebted for a Morse Fellowship that enabled me to undertake a study of Dickens, and to the University of Pittsburgh for assistance in the preparation of the manuscript and illustrations. Dickens scholarship, editing, and criticism have become an institution in their own right, and though it would be misleading for me to try to summarize my debt to that institution here, I seriously feel the impossibility of writing this book without it. I am also warmly grateful to the individuals who have helped me: Ross Dabney vigorously read and debated each chapter as it was written; Charles Crow, Donald Fanger, and Philip Collins read the completed draft and made numerous suggestions that have found their way into the final revision and the notes; Katharine Welsh studied and commented on every stage of the work and performed much of the necessary tracing of quotations and other tasks.

Finally, I wish to dedicate the book to four persons for whom in different ways it was conceived and planned, but who died before it could be completed: my father and mother, Stephen W. Reed, and David Owen.

London, March 1970   **A.W.**

CONTENTS

LIST OF PLATES

ABBREVIATIONS USED IN THE NOTES

VOLUMES of the New Oxford Illustrated Dickens (London, 1947–58) are designated by initial letters:

BH	*Bleak House*	*MHC*	*Master Humphrey's Clock*
BR	*Barnaby Rudge*	*NN*	*Nicholas Nickleby*
CB	*Christmas Books*	*OCS*	*The Old Curiosity Shop*
CS	*Christmas Stories*	*OMF*	*Our Mutual Friend*
DC	*David Copperfield*	*OT*	*Oliver Twist*
D&S	*Dombey and Son*	*PP*	*Pickwick Papers*
GE	*Great Expectations*	*RP*	*Reprinted Pieces* (with *UT*)
HT	*Hard Times*	*SB*	*Sketches by Boz*
LD	*Little Dorrit*	*TTC*	*A Tale of Two Cities*
MC	*Martin Chuzzlewit*	*UT*	*The Uncommercial Traveller*
MED	*The Mystery of Edwin Drood*		(with *RP*)

The following short titles are also used in the notes:

Collected Papers. Collected Papers, 2 vols., The Nonesuch Dickens (London, 1937).

Coutts Letters. Letters from Charles Dickens to Angela Burdett-Coutts, 1841–1865, ed. Edgar Johnson (London, 1953).

Letters. The Letters of Charles Dickens, ed. Walter Dexter, 3 vols., The Nonesuch Dickens (London, 1938).

Speeches. The Speeches of Charles Dickens, ed. K. J. Fielding (Oxford, 1960).

FORSTER. JOHN FORSTER, *The Life of Charles Dickens*, 2 vols., Everyman's Library (London, 1927).

Part One

THE METROPOLIS

Cityful passing away, other cityful coming, passing away too: other coming on, passing on. Houses, lines of houses, streets, miles of pavements, piled up bricks, stones. Changing hands. This owner, that. Landlord never dies they say. Other steps into his shoes when he gets his notice to quit. They buy the place up with gold and still they have all the gold. Swindle in it somewhere. Piled up in cities, worn away age after age. Pyramids in sand. Built on bread and onions. Slaves. Chinese wall. Babylon. Big stones left. Round towers. Rest rubble, sprawling suburbs, jerrybuilt, Kerwan's mushroom houses, built of breeze. Shelter for the night.

No one is anything.

—JOYCE, *Ulysses*

1

THE CITY OF SATIRE

W HEN the ghost of Christmas Present reveals to Scrooge the allegorical figures of Want and Ignorance, he gestures with his arm 'towards the city'.[1] The gesture is made as a matter of course. Today we are resigned prisoners of the Spenglerian world city; and Lewis Mumford, our chief partisan of the city as a way of life, has sensibly argued that we have produced, in the hydrogen bomb, the final anti-city weapon and strategy. Spengler placed the transition from meaningful 'culture' in the West to encrusted 'civilization' at the end of the eighteenth century; and Mumford reserves his bitterest criticism of the city for the nineteenth and twentieth centuries. Charles Dickens lived through and reacted to an experience of the city that is in many respects continuous with our own.

A problem immediately arises of determining what this city is like, or even what it looks like. For a small city it might be possible to climb to a hilltop and view all of it at once: but the result would still be only a view, and the view itself would be the result of preconceptions and interpretations of what is there. A description based on the view will introduce other distortions of the scene, some conventional and some experimental. Viewing and describing are a process of continual modification, from moment to moment and from generation to generation of time. This process takes place quite naturally; a strain is more likely to be felt when the question arises of what the city means, of the significance of the pictures. The significance changes more variously and abruptly, until the modifications are so attenuated that they can no longer be tested against the kind of objective stimuli received on hilltops. It is at that stage, perhaps, because of the need to simplify once again, that the conservative tendency of interpretation reasserts itself, as in the construction of figures of Want and Ignorance in the city.

[1] *A Christmas Carol, CB,* p. 57.

History affords ample evidence of this process. Modern scientific descriptions of the city pretend to owe more to direct observation than to past interpretations; the city is conceived as a set of interrelated problems in contemporary finance, engineering, politics, and psychology, and the persons responsible for the analysis of these problems are called 'city planners', as if they dealt only with the future. But the description of some of the problems is ancient, and is especially to be found in the kind of literature called satire. The dirt, crime, and disease in the city, the private interest or indifference, the corruption of public interest, were for a long time favourite subjects of satire, which consequently developed certain conventions for describing cities. Even city planners borrow from these conventions, and poets and painters have resorted to them freely. Yet conventions also break down, overlap with new interpretations, and sometimes give way. To describe Dickens's description of the city is to study this process. He began with certain conventions of satire and modified them according to the experience of his time. Nor was his description confined to views of the city. He worried about what went on there, and the old ways of grasping what went on were confounded by historical change.

Boswell remarks that the imitations of Juvenal's third satire by Johnson, Boileau, and others 'prove, that great cities, in every age, and in every country, will furnish similar topicks of satire'.[2] And so it seems. Even engineering problems of the city have been exposed by satirists. The defective and malodorous sewer formed by the Fleet River in London figured in the satires of Pope and Swift; and John Gay's *Trivia* described a London traffic jam in the early eighteenth century:

> Forth issuing from steep Lanes, the *Collier's* Steeds
> Drag the black Load; another Cart succeeds,
> Team follows Team, Crouds heap'd on Crouds appear,
> And wait impatient, 'till the Road grow clear.
> Now all the Pavement sounds with trampling Feet,
> And the mixt Hurry barricades the Street.
> Entangled here, the Waggon's lengthen'd Team
> Crack the tough Harness; Here the pond'rous Beam
> Lies over-turn'd athwart; For Slaughter fed,
> Here lowing Bullocks raise their horned Head.

[2] *The Life of Samuel Johnson*, 2 vols., Everyman's Library (London, 1906), I, 65.

New Oaths grow loud, with Coaches Coaches jar,
And the smart Blow provokes the sturdy War . . .[3]

As for the arbitration of taste, the moral certainty, the apocalyptic vision proffered by Mumford and many lesser critics of the city, it may be said that these qualities also belong to the genus satire. For all its historicism, *The Decline of the West* is to some extent a satire of megalopolis; the corruption of money and the contrast of city and country are its familiar themes. Satire concentrates on the correctable but uncorrected faults of man in society, stressing the degree to which human practice falls short of human ideal. Since, in William Cowper's words, 'God made the country, and man made the town',[4] the town affords the better target for an attack on human failure. The crowding, contrasts, and changes of the city provide the satirist with the image of moral confusion that he requires.

Dickens wrote novels that are bursting with people and things, and within the novels he used studied descriptions of crowded people and things as a stock image of the city. In *Martin Chuzzlewit* he summarized the scene near the Monument in London with the phrase, 'this crowd of objects'. The description includes a 'forest' of man-made spires, a 'wilderness' of architectural detail, and 'smoke and noise enough for all the world at once'.[5] The imagery should be compared with this stanza from Byron's *Don Juan*:

> A mighty mass of brick, and smoke, and shipping,
>   Dirty and dusky, but as wide as eye
> Could reach, with here and there a sail just skipping
>   In sight, then lost amidst the forestry
> Of masts; a wilderness of steeples peeping
>   On tiptoe through their sea-coal canopy;
> A huge, dun cupola, like a foolscap crown
> On a fool's head—and there is London Town![6]

The crowding of the city affords contrasts, and Dickens exploited any and every contrast that the city made available to him. In *Oliver Twist*, at the melodramatic encounter of Rose

---

[3] *Trivia: or the Art of Walking in the Streets of London*, ed. W. H. Williams (London, 1922), Bk. III, ll. 25–36.
[4] *The Task*, Bk. I, l. 749.
[5] *MC*, ch. ix, p. 130.
[6] Canto X, lxxxii.

Maylie and Nancy on London Bridge, he pauses to describe the poor who cross and recross the river in search of shelter: 'Midnight had come upon the crowded city. The palace, the night-cellar, the jail, the madhouse: the chambers of birth and death, of health and sickness, the rigid face of the corpse and the calm sleep of the child: midnight was upon them all.'[7] The same contrasts of wealth and poverty, virtue and vice, housed and houseless, day and night, organize for Dickens the passage in *Master Humphrey's Clock* that served as a transition between *The Old Curiosity Shop* and *Barnaby Rudge*:

> The day begins to break, and soon there is the hum and noise of life. Those who have spent the night on doorsteps and cold stones crawl off to beg; they who have slept in beds come forth to their occupation, too, and business is astir. . . . The streets are filled with carriages, and people gaily clad. The jails are full, too, to the throat, nor have the workhouses or hospitals much room to spare. The courts of law are crowded. . . . So, each of these thousand worlds goes on, intent upon itself, until night comes again,—first with its lights and pleasures, and its cheerful streets; then with its guilt and darkness.[8]

In the early novels, not only the stock contrasts of satire, but the way they are dropped in place, show that the discovery of a world, or even a 'thousand worlds', in the city is older than megalopolis, older than conurbation, older than Dickens. It may be said to have been a literary discovery. Phrases like 'curious to observe', 'a strange procession', and 'the shifting scene' betray the following description of London in *Nicholas Nickleby* as a set piece:

> Streams of people apparently without end poured on and on, jostling each other in the crowd and hurrying forward, scarcely seeming to notice the riches that surrounded them on every side; while vehicles of all shapes and makes, mingled up together in one moving mass like running water, lent their ceaseless roar to swell the noise and tumult.
>
> As they dashed by the quickly-changing and ever-varying objects, it was curious to observe in what a strange procession they passed before the eye. Emporiums of splendid dresses, the materials brought from every quarter of the world; tempting stores of everything to stimulate and pamper the sated appetite and give new relish to the oft-repeated feast; vessels of burnished gold and silver, wrought into every exquisite form of vase, and dish, and goblet; guns, swords, pistols, and

---

[7] *OT*, ch. xlvi, p. 348.   [8] *MHC*, ch. vi, pp. 108–9.

patent engines of destruction; screws and irons for the crooked, clothes for the newly-born, drugs for the sick, coffins for the dead, churchyards for the buried—all these jumbled each with the other and flocking side by side, seemed to flit by in motley dance like the fantastic groups of the old Dutch painter, and with the same stern moral for the unheeding restless crowd.

Nor were there wanting objects in the crowd itself to give new point and purpose to the shifting scene. The rags of the squalid ballad-singer fluttered in the rich light that showed the goldsmith's treasures; pale and pinched-up faces hovered about the windows where was tempting food; hungry eyes wandered over the profusion guarded by one thin sheet of brittle glass—an iron wall to them; half-naked shivering figures stopped to gaze at Chinese shawls and golden stuffs of India. There was a christening party at the largest coffin-maker's, and a funeral hatchment had stopped some great improvements in the bravest mansion. Life and death went hand in hand; wealth and poverty stood side by side; repletion and starvation laid them down together.[9]

When a satirist wishes to ridicule the vanity of human wishes, he sketches an individual like Mrs. Nickleby; when he wishes to preach the vanity of mortality, he reduces the created world to the streets of the city. As in the night scenes in *Oliver Twist* and *Master Humphrey's Clock*, darkness accentuates the differences among men and yet enforces the same 'stern moral' for all engaged in the dance of death. The levelling carried out by the 'jostling' people and 'jumbled' objects is not democratic but ironic. Frequently, like other Victorians, Dickens pointed to the levelling possibilities of class revolution; but more often he warned of the levelling by death and fortune traditionally threatened by satirists.

The passing of time is more perceptible in the city than in the village. In the city fields continually give way to new buildings, old buildings to new tenants. Fire and demolition begin the process all over again. The physical surface of the city is constantly changing. Dickens had little historical imagination; but he had the city-dweller's experience of architectural change. His sense of history was that of the city and of satire. 'Shops and their Tenants' and 'Gin-Shops' in *Sketches by Boz* are merely the first of his glances at the misfortunes of business enterprise and the 'epidemics' of architectural fashion. The unlimited, changing face of the city expresses the uncertain fate of its inhabitants;

[9] *NN*, ch. xxxii, pp. 408–9.

and the theme of mutability joins that of congestion and contrast. Covent Garden, for example, with its complicated history of architectural and theatrical success, estate planning and produce marketing, fire and decay, is described as it might appear to Little Dorrit, not for its historical interest, but from the satiric point of view:

Courtly ideas of Covent Garden, as a place with famous coffee-houses, where gentlemen wearing gold-laced coats and swords had quarrelled and fought duels; costly ideas of Covent Garden, as a place where there were flowers in winter at guineas a-piece, pine-apples at guineas a pound, and peas at guineas a pint; picturesque ideas of Covent Garden, as a place where there was a mighty theatre, showing wonderful and beautiful sights to richly-dressed ladies and gentlemen, and which was for ever far beyond the reach of poor Fanny or poor uncle; desolate ideas of Covent Garden, as having all those arches in it, where the miserable children in rags among whom she had just now passed, like young rats, slunk and hid, fed on offal, huddled together for warmth, and were hunted about (look to the rats young and old, all ye Barnacles, for before God they are eating away our foundations, and will bring the roofs on our heads!); teeming ideas of Covent Garden, as a place of past and present mystery, romance, abundance, want, beauty, ugliness, fair country gardens, and foul street-gutters; all confused together.[10]

In the apostrophe to the ruling classes the impatient voice of the satirist breaks the thought of the heroine, who in this passage is only a thinly disguised *persona* for the satirist in any case. The interruption that must seem a tactical blunder to the realist and a sin of point-of-view to the artist, is here a deliberate device. By such abrupt changes of style the satirist intends to jar his audience into wakefulness.

To compare the rich to the poor, the clothed to the naked, the stuffed to the starving in satire implies not only the mortality of man, but his animality as well. One means of reducing man to animal is to stress his digestive functions, and there are many individual gluttons in Dickens. But the market of a great city displays the carnivorousness of man generally, and its blood and guts and smells are a favourite subject with satirists. The dens and lairs of human beings in *Oliver Twist* are matched by the pens of the animals in Smithfield. The long description of

[10] *LD*, Bk. I, ch. xiv, p. 166.

Smithfield in the novel is developed by means of a satiric catalogue of the filth, steam, fog, and stench, the men and animals, the noise and crush of the market. This 'stunning and bewildering scene, which quite confounded the senses', is another set piece of the young Dickens, but it nevertheless anticipates the cry of Fagin, 'What right have they to butcher me?'[11] In *Great Expectations* Pip describes Smithfield more economically as 'all asmear with filth and fat and blood and foam', and in the next paragraph records his first encounter with Newgate Prison and its gallows.[12]

The image of the city that stresses crowding, contrast, and change, the synecdochic image of the city as a market, fair, or sewer, the opposition of town and country, are tenacious conventions of literature—so tenacious, in fact, that to some extent satiric conventions control even non-literary descriptions of the city. Much of our modern conception of the city, for example, is based on aerial photography, and one conjectures that balloon flights in the nineteenth century must have helped to erode the literary conception of the city. Henry Mayhew and J. Binny describe London as seen from a balloon in 1862; but though their experience is new, the account of what they saw is conventional:

> It was a wonderful sight . . . to behold that vast bricken mass of churches and hospitals, banks and prisons, palaces and workhouses, docks and refuges for the destitute, parks and squares, and courts and alleys, which make up London—all blent into one immense black spot—to look down upon the whole as the birds of the air look down upon it, and see it dwindled into a mere rubbish heap—to contemplate from afar that strange conglomeration of vice and avarice and low cunning, of noble aspirations and human heroism, and to grasp it in the eye, in all its incongruous integrity, at a single glance—to take, as it were, an angel's view of that huge town where, perhaps, there is more virtue and more iniquity, more wealth and more want, brought together into one dense focus than in any other part of the earth.[13]

The familiar themes of crowding and contrast suggest that satire taught these balloonists what to see before they left

---

[11] *OT*, ch. xxi, p. 153; ch. lii, p. 410. Cf. John Bayley, '*Oliver Twist:* "Things as they really are"', in *Dickens and the Twentieth Century*, ed. John Gross and Gabriel Pearson (London, 1962), pp. 58–62.

[12] *GE*, ch. xx, pp. 155–6.

[13] *The Criminal Prisons of London*, quoted by Asa Briggs, *Victorian Cities* (London, 1963), p. 53.

ground. When they see—or envision—the whole of London as 'a mere rubbish heap', they resort to a figure that Dickens was employing at about this time in *Our Mutual Friend*.

Dickens was a powerful satirist, perhaps the greatest of his time. To many occasions he brought the satirist's purpose of moral attack, and to all occasions he brought his unsurpassed eye for detail. George Eliot praised his 'power of rendering the external traits of our town population' and regretted the thinness of his treatment of character and emotion.[14] But rendering the external traits is the satirist's main business. Dickens was master of the surface of people and things, and the surface is important to the satirist not only for the rendering of his central symbol, the congested city, but because surface implies depth. The narrator of *Bleak House* need hardly tell us that the street mud is a 'kindred mystery' of the law.[15] The satirist is so caught up in the moral imperative of his task that he cannot mention the physical aspect of things without implying deeper significance. The variegation and cacophony of his surfaces imply some hidden moral disorder. The irony of appearance and reality is his favourite mode.

Still, as a novelist, Dickens's purpose was never exclusively satirical. He wrote to William Charles Macready in 1844 that *The Chimes* would cloud the eye of Sir Peter Laurie's philosophy 'with black and blue, but many a gentle one with crystal of the finest sort'. Only the latter effect is recorded when Dickens reports Macready 'undisguisedly sobbing and crying on the sofa' during the reading of that story.[16] A mixed and varied impact on his audience is highly desired by the satirist, but he should appeal primarily to scorn, secondarily to laughter, and only occasionally to sentiment. In the novels Dickens carefully intersperses satire with other matter. He was above all a humourist, and humour employs irony, incongruity, and even the clutter and disarray of the city without any intention of condemnation, but only of amusement. A case in point is an essay in *Household Words* in 1854 that describes the transformation of a run-down lower-middle-class part of London, evidently the

---

[14] 'The Natural History of German Life', reprinted in *The Essays of George Eliot*, ed. Thomas Pinney (London, 1963), p. 271.

[15] *BH*, ch. x, p. 135.

[16] 28 Nov. 1844, *Letters*, I, 646; to his wife, 2 Dec. 1844, I, 647–8.

district between Camden Town and Bloomsbury, during the construction of a railway terminus.

In a word, the Railway Terminus Works themselves are a picture of our moral state. They look confused and dissipated, with an air as if they were always up all night, and always giddy. Here, is a vast shed that was not here yesterday, and that may be pulled down to-morrow; there, a wall that is run up until some other building is ready; there, an open piece of ground, which is a quagmire in the middle, bounded on all four sides by a wilderness of houses, pulled down, shored up, broken-headed, crippled, on crutches, knocked about and mangled in all sorts of ways, and billed with fragments of all kinds of ideas. We are, mind and body, an unsettled neighbourhood. We are demoralized by the contemplation of luggage in perpetual motion.[17]

Dickens rather approves these signs of progress than otherwise; there is no kind of attack in the entire essay, which is one of his fine descriptions of nondescript London. Yet he calls attention to the clutter and change of scene that, for satire, represent moral chaos. He goes further and spells out the meaning that is always implicit in satire, that the physical scene is 'a picture of our moral state'. The conclusion of this essay is almost a humorous spoof on satire itself.

Moreover, satire becomes historically inadequate for coping with the nineteenth-century city. The would-be satirist must take up journalism, science, religion, or revolution, instead. Friedrich Engels plays briefly with a satiric theme in *The Condition of the Working Class in England in 1844*: he notes 'the hundreds of thousands of all classes crowding past each other' in the streets of London, their indifference, private interests, and loss of human qualities. But when Engels settles down to his detailed study of Manchester, he observes that rich and poor do not crowd past one another in cities but live in sharply segregated districts; that, as if by design, the slums of the poor are further obscured from sight and smell by the strips of commercial property that line the main thoroughfares of the city.[18] The true significance of crowding in the city is not the traditional contrast of types dear to the satirist, but the anonymous suffering of human kind.

Throughout his writings Dickens comments on the loneliness

---

[17] 'An Unsettled Neighbourhood', *Collected Papers*, I, 519.
[18] *The Condition of the Working Class in England in 1844*, trans. F. K. Wischnewetsky (London, 1936), pp. 23–4, 45–7.

of the city-dweller. 'Thoughts about People' in *Sketches by Boz*
begins: 'It is strange with how little notice, good, bad, or indifferent, a man may live and die in London. He awakens no
sympathy in the breast of any single person; his existence is a
matter of interest to no one save himself; he cannot be said to be
forgotten when he dies, for no one remembered him when he was
alive.'[19] In *Master Humphrey's Clock* where he writes of the
'worlds' within the city, he notes that each 'has its own inhabitants, each is distinct from, and almost unconscious of the
existence of any other'.[20] In *Barnaby Rudge* he compares the
state of being 'shelterless and alone in the open country' with
the greater agony and suffering of the same conditions in the
city.[21] In *The Old Curiosity Shop* he writes of those 'who live
solitarily in great cities as in the bucket of a human well'; and in
Bleak House Charley Neckett 'melt[s] into the city's strife and
sound, like a dewdrop in an ocean'.[22] Dickens knows nothing of
alienation in the philosophical sense of Marx and Engels, but he
understands that alienation is a common condition of urban man.
Walter Bagehot saw that Dickens's genius was 'especially
suited to the delineation of city life' for this very reason. 'London is like a newspaper. Everything is there, and everything is
disconnected. There is every kind of person in some houses; but
there is no more connection between the houses than between
the neighbours in the lists of "births, marriages, and deaths."'[23]

Ironically, when the alienation of the citizen from the city
becomes a general theme in literature, the satirist may lose his
office. The satirist is the classical type of the alienated man, but
he likes to imagine himself as isolated intellect, pitted alone
against the city. If everyone suffers alike from alienation, the
satirist will find it hard to maintain his detachment. To describe
alienation as the common modern experience requires something
closer to journalism. A good journalist, for better or worse,
gives a time and place to the anonymous activity that surrounds
us, and it was as a journalist that Dickens began to pursue
human anonymity through the streets of London.

[19] *SB*, p. 215.
[20] *MHC*, ch. vi, p. 108.
[21] *BR*, ch. xviii, p. 138.
[22] *OCS*, ch. xv, p. 116; *BH*, ch. xv, p. 217.
[23] 'Charles Dickens', in *Works*, ed. Mrs. Russell Barrington, 10 vols. (London,
1915), III, 84–5.

In 'A Small Star in the East', an article on London for *All the Year Round*, one can follow the progressive reduction of satire, through journalism, to pathos and religious hope. The considerably sophisticated method of the article may be seen to be anti-literary. Dickens repudiates a satiric account of East London in order to stress the utter reality of what he has witnessed. He begins with the same allegory from medieval satire, the Dance of Death, that he had used in the description of London in *Nicholas Nickleby*, and, in order to stress the moral, rejects the satiric embellishment:

I had been looking, yesternight, through the famous 'Dance of Death,' and to-day the grim old woodcuts arose in my mind with the new significance of a ghastly monotony not to be found in the original. The weird skeleton rattled along the streets before me, and struck fiercely; but it was never at the pains of assuming a disguise. It played on no dulcimer here, was crowned with no flowers, waved no plume, minced in no flowing robe or train, lifted no wine-cup, sat at no feast, cast no dice, counted no gold. It was simply a bare, gaunt, famished skeleton, slaying his way along.

In the slums of the city, in other words, death is not the ironic and unexpected leveller of men of all classes and characters but the starvation that slowly and predictably overcomes those who do not have enough to eat. The second paragraph preserves some of the stock literary ideas of the city—a wilderness or desert inhabited by a tribe—but adds the subjects of river pollution, the system of rental in slum housing, and what is now called structural unemployment:

The borders of Ratcliff and Stepney, eastward of London, and giving on the impure river, were the scene of this uncompromising dance of death, upon a drizzling November day. A squalid maze of streets, courts, and alleys of miserable houses let out in single rooms. A wilderness of dirt, rags, and hunger. A mud-desert, chiefly inhabited by a tribe from whom employment has departed, or to whom it comes but fitfully and rarely. . . .

The third paragraph seems to belong to satire again, since it calls attention to a particular irony and hits obliquely at politicians, a favourite target of Dickens's satire; but the irony is deliberately understated, the present reality implied to be far more cruel than the woodcuts of the dance of Death:

One grisly joke alone, methought, the skeleton seemed to play off here. It had stuck election-bills on the walls, which the wind and rain had deteriorated into suitable rags. . . . It adjured the free and independent starvers to vote for Thisman and vote for Thatman. . . . Surely the skeleton is nowhere more cruelly ironical in the original monkish idea!

The tendency to satire aroused by the thought of politicians is quickly submerged in the fourth paragraph by a reflection on their uselessness in the necessary task of 'devising employment useful to the community for those who want but to work and live; for equalising rates, cultivating waste lands, facilitating emigration, and, above all things, saving and utilizing the on-coming generations, and thereby changing ever-growing national weakness into strength'. And with this preamble Dickens knocks on the first of three different doors, giving us, in the classic manner of journalism, a summary of his interviews with the poor of East London. After the last of these interviews he remarks:

I could enter no other houses for that one while, for I could not bear the contemplation of the children. Such heart as I had summoned to sustain me against the miseries of the adults failed me when I looked at the children. I saw how young they were, how hungry, how serious, and still. I thought of them, sick and dying in those lairs. I think of them dead without anguish; but to think of them so suffering and so dying quite unmanned me.[24]

A satirist wants to keep his distance. In this article Dickens adopts the satirist's willingness to look at the lowest human kind but surrenders the satirist's detachment. Instead, his ability to move us depends on his skill in stripping away our own detachment. By lowering himself to the level of his subject he achieves pathos. By introducing, in the remainder of the article, two heroes and a sign of hope, he conveys a religious message. The 'Small Star in the East' of the title refers to a children's hospital founded in a former sail-loft in Ratcliff by a young surgeon and his wife. Their courage and sacrifice redeem the despair of monotonous death.

There is a felt pleasure in satire that is unacceptable in serious journalism. The professional journalist is ready to mount a public campaign for the 'improvement' of the city—as in the

[24] *UT*, pp. 319 ff.

stated purpose of Dickens's periodical, *Household Words*, 'which is the raising up of those that are down, and the general improvement of our social condition'.[25] The satirist, also, may set out to improve social conditions, but the satire itself affords him relief. Nothing affords the serious journalist relief except the chance to report that conditions to which he has earlier called attention have improved. There is no pleasure in journalism except reflected pleasure; it is not literature. 'The careless maintenance from year to year, in this capital city of the world, of a vast hopeless nursery of ignorance, misery, and vice: a breeding place for the hulks and jails: is horrible to contemplate'[26]—that sentence, from a letter by Dickens to the *Daily News* in 1846, is figurative but unmistakeably journalistic. And the same sort of language can be used in novels. Of the neighbourhood near Golden Square Dickens writes in *David Copperfield* that a building is 'decayed and dirty' but also that the floors are 'unsound and even unsafe', and he complains of the bad ventilation and 'common dust-heap'.[27] It is the language of the journalist or the inspector of slums. The city has become 'unsound and even unsafe'.

When Umbricius stands at the edge of Rome in Juvenal's satire, he has made a choice, the choice of exile.[28] But though a satirist or his *persona* can make this choice, the entire population of a city cannot. In the nineteenth century, as this or that condition of the city is seen, however dimly, to have some physical or quasi-physical cause, the possibility of choice diminishes. Individual moral choice seems hopelessly interwoven and dependent on other choices, many of them not moral at all. The moral indictment of humanity and the hope for a moral cure for its ills begin to falter.

[25] To Mrs. Gaskell, 31 Jan. 1850, *Letters*, II, 202.
[26] *Collected Papers*, I, 39.
[27] *DC*, ch. l, p. 717.
[28] E. C. Witke, 'Juvenal III: an Eclogue for the Urban Poor', *Hermes*, XC (1962), 248.

II

THE CITY AS A PROBLEM

T H E main cause to which we must attribute the high mortality is the
close packing and overcrowding which exists throughout the district.
. . . Overcrowding and disease mutually act and react upon each other.

The overcrowding of dwellings is one of the most frequent sources of
sickness and decay at all ages.

Perhaps there is no single influence to which a human being is exposed
more prejudicial to his health than overcrowding in rooms the air of
which cannot be perpetually and rapidly changed.

These statements concern the prime subject of satire, the
crowded city, yet clearly they are not composed by satirists; the
statements are not in the least ironic, and in so far as they denote
a scene or surface of the city, they imply a direct rather than
deceptive relation between the surface and the underlying
reality. Each statement bears heavily on a relation of cause and
effect; and each, while emphatic, carefully stops short of outright universality or certainty, employing forms of qualification
that may be thought to vitiate modern prose, but are the genuine
expression of inductive science. The statements were composed,
in fact, by three Medical Officers of Health, in three parishes of
London, in the years 1856–9.[1]

The pages of prose dedicated to this aspect of London multi-
plied several times over as a result of the Act of 1855 that
created the Metropolitan Board of Works, and required each
constituted vestry or district board to appoint one or more medical officers and to receive their reports. Earlier there were the
Poor-Law medical officers, but the first municipal officer was
appointed by Liverpool in 1847. Dr. John Simon, whose first
annual report brought him fame and notoriety overnight, was

[1] Quoted by Henry Jephson, *The Sanitary Evolution of London* (London, 1907),
p. 119. Jephson's book is largely a compilation of such reports: for statements on
'overcrowding' in the 1860s, see p. 175.

elected by the Corporation of the City of London in 1848.[2] Here
it is sufficient to note the use of a new term, 'overcrowding',
which, unlike mere 'crowding', implies the violation of a
standard. Satire, too, compares folly, vice, or degradation
against an implicit standard; but in the medical reports the standard intended is a measurable one. The number of cubic feet of
air necessary to each adult person has not yet been agreed
upon, to be sure, but that there exists such a quantity is assumed
by these reports and will be accepted in law (though still far
from acceptance in practice) in the Sanitary Act of 1866. Today
we take for granted a flood of statistics in any discussion of
social conditions; their use was more striking in the nineteenth
century, at the beginning of the deluge.[3] After 1855 the newly
empowered Medical Officers naturally stressed the statistics of
mortality, especially infant mortality; but the city was also examined in terms of the number of cubic feet of space per person
in dwellings, workshops, and classrooms, the number of miles of
sewers and the quantitative analysis of their contents, the number of dead in the churchyards and their estimated rate of decay.

For the true quantifying spirit of the day one may handily
turn to a report of Henry Austin, Dickens's brother-in-law, to
the General Board of Health in 1857:

In towns of rich and of poor population the quality of the sewage
may also materially differ. Speaking of the excess of animal food con-
sumed by the classes in easy circumstances, Professor Way says, 'the
nitrogen of this food is discharged in the fæces, which are probably
therefore much richer in this element than that of the working community.'. . . The value of the refuse of Belgravia would, no doubt, exceed that of Bethnal Green.[4]

If this last calculation were written by Swift, we would understand that the stated difference between the rich and the poor was
an ironic comment on their sameness. But Austin, the civil en-

---

[2] See Royston Lambert, *Sir John Simon, 1816–1904, and English Social Administration* (London, 1963), pp. 99–160.

[3] The first census was taken in 1801; the civil registration of births, marriages,
and deaths was introduced in 1837. The word 'statistics' itself is not much older
than the century; the Royal Statistical Society was founded in 1838, and by the mid-
century a number of the industrial towns had statistical societies of their own. See
Briggs, *Victorian Cities*, p. 99; also G. M. Young, *Victorian England: Portrait of an
Age*, 2nd ed. (New York, 1954), p. 56.

[4] *Report on the Means of Deodorizing and Utilizing the Sewage of Towns, Parliamentary Papers*, 1857 (Sess. II), xx, 458.

gineer, is genuinely concerned with the variance of sewage from place to place, and from day to day, in the city. It does not amuse him that those 'in easy circumstances' should produce a finer excrement; to an engineer, an irony is a problem to be solved. Since Austin is seeking a way to utilize the sewage systematically, the differences of Bethnal Green and Belgravia must be resolved. The problem of human waste has been quantified by the city, so to speak, before the engineer arrives on the scene to deal with it. For Charles Babbage, inventor of the calculating machine, science had outstripped satire. 'The wild imaginings of the satirists' were rivalled by the 'realities' of the nineteenth century: 'as if in mockery of the College of Laputa, light almost solar has been extracted from the refuse of fish; fire has been sifted by the lamp of Davy; and machinery has been taught arithmetic instead of poetry.'[5]

One critic has remarked that 'satire provides a statistical image of the world'[6]—but if so, surely this is one of the respects in which satire competes rather than joins with science. The rise of statistics may be an important factor in the general decline of satire during the nineteenth century. Satirists, in fact, have usually opposed the reduction of the human world to statistical terms—a stance that is well attested by certain famous passages in *Hard Times*, a novel that is also a product of the 1850s. What Dickens attacks, however, is the fallacious application of aggregate figures to individual cases. For example, the significance of a man's death to himself, his family and friends, is very large; in comparison, its significance as a single unit in a table of mortality is contemptible. The same logic regulates, and limits, the satire of statistics in *Hard Times*; it supplies the point of Sissy Jupe's refusal to answer M'Choakumchild's question about the percentage of persons 'drowned or burnt to death' at sea and the absurdity of Gradgrind's confidence in the duration of life:

> 'It is short, no doubt, my dear. Still, the average duration of human life is proved to have increased of late years. The calculations of various life assurance and annuity offices, among other figures which cannot go wrong, have established the fact.'

5 *On the Economy of Machinery and Manufactures*, 4th ed. (London, 1835), p. 390
6 Alvin Kernan, *The Plot of Satire* (New Haven, 1965), p. 200. I am also indebted to Kernan's earlier study, *The Cankered Muse* (New Haven, 1959), ch. i.

'I speak of my own life, father.'

'O indeed? Still,' said Mr. Gradgrind, 'I need not point out to you, Louisa, that it is governed by the laws which govern lives in the aggregate.'[7]

Dickens did not conduct an indiscriminate attack against statistics. Like most of his countrymen he admired, on the whole, the kind of investigation of the condition of England that was current and the way in which its results were tabulated. He admired, for example, Henry Thomas Buckle's *History of Civilization in England*, and Buckle's enthusiasm for statistics, if anything, exceeded that of Mr. Gradgrind.[8]

The greatest single factor affecting nineteenth-century views of the city was simply its size, and the statistics of increase readily confirmed what was palpable to the eye and measured by the feet of anyone born near the beginning of the century. From 1801 to 1841 London and its suburbs doubled in population to become a city of two and a quarter million persons—and the population was destined to double again in the next forty years. As a result of this growth, the word 'metropolis' took on connotations of pride mixed with anxiety. For the theoretical significance of population had changed, as well as the numbers. Malthusian pessimism and the census of 1801 and 1811 combined to reverse the common assumption that a growing population was an unmixed blessing.[9] The theory of Malthus, the

---

[7] *HT*, Bk. I, ch. ix, pp. 57–8; ch. xv, p. 100. Of this novel Dickens wrote, 'My satire is against those who see figures and averages, and nothing else . . . the addled heads who would take the average of cold in the Crimea during twelve months as a reason for clothing a soldier in nankeens on a night when he would be frozen to death in fur, and who would comfort the labourer in travelling twelve miles a day to and from his work, by telling him that the average distance of one inhabited place from another in the whole area of England, is not more than four miles' (to Charles Knight, 30 Jan. 1855, *Letters*, II, 620). The true force of the argument here is in the objection to bad mathematics.

[8] See Dickens's 1870 speech at Birmingham, *Speeches*, p. 411. Buckle believed that 'The most comprehensive inferences respecting the actions of men . . . rest on statistical evidence, and are expressed in mathematical language.' Typically, therefore, he may write, 'In a given state of society, a certain number of persons must put an end to their own life. This is the general law.' *History of Civilization in England*, 2 vols. (New York, 1858, 1861), I, 15–20. The index to the first volume (1850) of *Household Words* lists sixteen articles or portions of articles containing 'statistics'.

[9] G. Talbot Griffith, *Population Problems in the Age of Malthus* (Cambridge, 1926), p. 90; see also M. Dorothy George, *London Life in the Eighteenth Century* (London, 1925), ch. i.

manifest condition of the poor, and the expense of poor-relief, made it impossible to regard the growth of cities with complacency. But the city not only grows at an increased rate in the nineteenth century; it begins to exhibit the structural problems that we regard as peculiarly modern. The process known today as 'depopulation of the urban core' was under way in London by the first decades of the nineteenth century. Its effect on the City of London in particular is associated with 'deadness' by Dickens as early as *Martin Chuzzlewit*[10] and contributes to the atmosphere of many scenes in his later work. Moreover, the archaeological discoveries of the century made it possible to associate London with the lost cities of the ancient Near East. In *Little Dorrit*, when Arthur Clennam walks toward his mother's house in the City—the house that is shakily supported by great wooden crutches—he passes, 'now the mouldy hall of some obsolete Worshipful Company [i.e. one of the livery companies of London], now the illuminated windows of a Congregationless Church that seemed to be waiting for some adventurous Belzoni to dig it out and discover its history'.[11] The analogy, with its muted hint of the end of civilization, had some basis in fact in the depopulation of the most ancient part of London.

Still more disturbing are the unplanned structural changes in the city that take place as a direct result of well-meaning attempts to improve its design. The mixed social achievement and disaster of the 'redevelopment' of cities is only fitfully understood even today; yet, in the nineteenth century, it could already be seen that the clearing of slums, the cutting through of new streets, and the erection of railway termini within the city were creating nearly as many problems as they solved. For the result of wiping out an overcrowded district of the metropolis was a redoubling of the population in the adjacent slums. 'Thus, we make our New Oxford Streets, and our other new streets,' Dickens wrote in *Household Words*, 'never heeding, never asking, where the wretches whom we clear out, crowd.'[12] Destruction of open spaces within the city also worried Dickens, who

10 *MC*, ch. ix, p. 128.
11 *LD*, Bk. I, ch. iii, p. 31. Belzoni is the archaeologist Giovanni Battista Belzoni (1778–1823).
12 'On Duty with Inspector Field', *RP*, p. 518.

1. *Miseries of London*, by Thomas Rowlandson

STREET TRAFFIC.

TABLE SHOWING TOTALS OF EVERY DESCRIPTION OF VEHICLE PASSING PER HOUR AND PER DAY OF 12 HOURS THROUGH CERTAIN STREETS WITHIN THE CITY OF LONDON.

Date.	Situation.	Hours Ending												Total of 12 Hours	Average per Hour.
		9 A.M.	10 A.M.	11 A.M.	12 Noon	1 P.M.	2 P.M.	3 P.M.	4 P.M.	5 P.M.	6 P.M.	7 P.M.	8 P.M.		
1850.															
July 8	Temple Bar Gate	311	526	704	757	691	664	791	737	738	671	537	614	7741	645
,, 9	Holborn-hill, by St. And. Ch.	327	552	670	698	623	606	535	377	915	445	841	317	6906	575
,, 10	Ludgate-hill, by Pilgrim-st.	361	476	728	636	789	514	628	531	619	584	543	420	6829	569
,, 11	Newgate-st., by Old Bailey	320	528	628	509	555	537	564	738	572	563	467	394	6375	531
,, 12	Aldersgate-st., by Fann-st.	168	261	208	196	214	235	194	235	235	233	229	198	2590	215
,, 13	Cheapside, by Foster-lane	473	805	1124	1169	1020	1009	1007	1076	1106	964	808	492	11053	921
,, 15	Poultry, by Mansion House	414	762	1071	1080	1043	941	875	910	956	825	802	595	10274	856
,, 16	Finsbury-pave., by South-pl	262	385	475	387	364	345	293	347	483	475	400	244	4460	371
,, 17	Cornhill, by Roy. Exchange	161	364	479	461	487	441	493	451	468	430	354	327	4916	409
,, 18	Threadneedle-street	98	145	262	214	211	154	212	195	198	205	148	103	2150	179
,, 19	Gracech-st., by St.Pet.-alley	258	322	439	507	392	423	464	516	461	436	338	331	4887	407
,, 20	Lombard-st., by Birchin-la	137	117	156	183	169	232	237	304	243	209	130	106	2228	185
,, 22	Bishopsg.-st., by Gt St.Hel.	259	408	500	430	396	238	439	432	541	450	404	345	4842	403
,, 23	London Bridge	680	1128	1332	1124	1094	1048	1101	1180	1344	1308	962	798	13099	1091
,, 24	Bishp.-st. out, by Cy. Bound	203	329	447	286	307	342	390	335	430	439	323	279	4110	342
,, 25	Aldgate High-street, ditto	425	422	417	442	445	379	389	405	405	401	331	289	4754	396
,, 26	Leadenhall-st., E. I. House	251	429	595	495	594	563	525	569	466	588	437	418	5930	494
,, 27	Eastcheap, by Philpot-lane	335	346	398	372	378	343	368	393	398	349	294	128	4102	341
,, 29	Tower-street, by Mark-lane	169	222	262	271	292	324	290	262	282	238	164	114	2890	240
,, 30	L. Thames-st., by Botolph-la	88	130	175	105	105	103	118	147	168	121	69	46	1380	115
,, 31	Blackfriars Bridge	327	381	518	516	465	336	385	416	570	548	463	337	5292	438
Aug. 1	U.Thames-st., rear of Qn.-st	140	227	165	223	205	160	164	213	253	312	176	93	2331	194
,, 2	Smithfield Bars	203	230	202	277	276	255	334	267	328	289	288	159	3108	259
,, 3	Fenchurch-street	206	262	253	343	293	269	272	327	364	259	249	545	3642	303
		6576	9757	12208	11686	11498	10466	10968	11351	12543	11342	9757	7697	125859	10488

proposed to set aside parks and play areas.[13] And more pervasive in his work than this rational response to the problem, is the claustrophobic mood that it evokes—'the pressure of the town' that links the work of Dickens with that of Dostoevsky and Kafka.[14]

The growth of London also induced a new awareness of the tracts of land on the circumference of the city that were neither brick nor earth, neither town nor country, but rather what Dickens called in *Our Mutual Friend* a 'suburban Sahara, where tiles and bricks were burnt, bones were boiled, carpets were beat, rubbish was shot, dogs were fought, and dust was heaped by contractors'.[15] In this region the advance of the city is both active and highly disagreeable, for as it pushes out into the scar it has made in the countryside, it must push over and through the dubious waste of its earlier progress. Remaining near the centre of the city are only the abscessed lands that poor drainage has made least profitable to development. From the historical perspective of *David Copperfield* Dickens described one such area, Millbank, in the earlier part of the century:

There were neither wharves nor houses on the melancholy waste of road near the great blank Prison. A sluggish ditch deposited its mud at the prison walls. Coarse grass and rank weeds straggled over all the marshy land in the vicinity. In one part, carcases of houses, inauspiciously begun and never finished, rotted away. In another the ground was cumbered with rusty iron monsters of steam-boilers, wheels, cranks, pipes, furnaces, paddles, anchors, diving-bells, windmill-sails, and I know not what strange objects, accumulated by some speculator, and grovelling in the dust. . . . Slimy gaps and causeways, winding among old wooden piles, with a sickly substance clinging to the latter, like green hair, and the rags of last year's handbills offering rewards for drowned men fluttering above the high-water mark, led down through the ooze and slush to the ebb-tide. There was a story that one of the pits dug for the dead in the time of the Great Plague was hereabout; and a blighting influence seemed to have proceeded from it over the

---

[13] 2 May 1855, *Coutts Letters*, pp. 293–4; speech to the Playground and General Recreation Society, 1 June 1858, *Speeches*, pp. 272–4.

[14] The phrase occurs in *The Haunted Man*, *CB*, p. 318. Cf. Renato Poggioli, 'Mythology of Franz Kafka', in *The Spirit of the Letter* (Cambridge, Mass., 1965), pp. 254–63. For an important study of the interpretation of the city in Dickens, Balzac, and Dostoevsky, see Donald Fanger, *Dostoevsky and Romantic Realism* (Cambridge, Mass., 1965).

[15] *OMF*, Bk. I, ch. iv, p. 33.

whole place. Or else it looked as if it had gradually decomposed into that nightmare condition, out of the overflowings of the polluted stream.

It is here that David interviews Martha, the prostitute who appears 'as if she were a part of the refuse' of the polluted stream.[16]

If such waste-lands testify to the ambiguous progress of the city, their peculiar inhabitants and industries demonstrate very strangely the economic relations of urban life. *Our Mutual Friend* paradoxically insists that mysterious fortunes are made by dealers in 'dust'—a euphemism for ashes, bones, garbage, and excrement. In the same novel Mr. Venus, by name and temperament a man of love, is proprietor of a shop filled with anatomical specimens, human and otherwise; he is a dealer in that most intimate of all waste products, the dead body. The polluted Thames is 'meat and drink' to Gaffer Hexam and his daughter, specialists in still another trade. In *Bleak House* Mr. Krook, victim of spontaneous combustion (which certainly could have occurred in his shop), deals in paper and 'marine stores', a euphemism for bottles, metal, and other waste; and we share with Esther Summerson a glimpse of 'the extraordinary creatures in rags, secretly groping among the swept-out rubbish for pins and other refuse' of the street.[17] The same novels introduce street traders like Silas Wegg, vendor of fruit and sweets, and Jo, the crossing sweeper. Not before *Dombey and Son* does Dickens give much thought to the way the non-criminal poor of the streets—as opposed to servants and clerks—make their living. It has been argued that Dickens, vividly sensitive to class differences because of his own childhood, could not fully sympathize with the poor until he was sure that he could no longer be identified with them;[18] alternatively, that he only gradually perfected a technique of symbolic implication that enabled him to cope imaginatively with the entire city. The historical explanation is that the public consciousness of the city had changed, not only for Dickens but for other sensitive observers as well.

Henry Mayhew's *London Labour and the London Poor*, written

16 *DC*, ch. xlvii, pp. 679–80.
17 *BH*, ch. v, p. 48.
18 William O. Aydelotte, 'The England of Marx and Mill as Reflected in Fiction', *The Tasks of Economic History*, VIII (1948), 56.

in the 1840s and collected in book form in 1851 and 1861, remains a great monument to this changing attitude toward the city. Lately an attempt has been made to show that Dickens may actually have copied Betty Higden from Mayhew's pure-finder, or Gaffer Hexam from his dredgerman;[19] but the question of influence is surely much broader than this attempt supposes. Some features of Mayhew's work may readily be traced to the eighteenth century, in books that exhibited the street cries and costumes of London as oddities worth illustrating to the gentry. What distinguished his journalism was the infusion of statistics and his underlying grasp of the economic life of the urban poor. Mayhew undoubtedly appealed first to his reader's curiosity, but his effort to establish the number of rag-pickers and prostitutes in the metropolis and their earnings, to calculate the daily living expenses of countless barely-living persons, to describe the kinds of 'pure' found in the streets and its value in the wholesale market, was incurably scientific and businesslike.

Malthusian doctrine had already anticipated the possibility of a population greater than the available means of life; the data brought forth by Mayhew and others called in question the moralistic doctrine that employment was always available to those who honestly sought for it. Dickens called attention to the case of Plornish, a skilled and willing, but seldom employed plasterer, in *Little Dorrit*; and though he made some attempt to lay this situation at the door of the Barnacles, or the ruling classes, it is actually nearer to being 'Nobody's Fault'. Perhaps one reason that 'Nobody's Fault' did not prove a satisfactory title of *Little Dorrit*, was that it failed to be ironic after all. Satire cannot sustain the implication, now seemingly confirmed, that an evil is traceable to nothing more or less than an impersonal, amoral cause.

Next to the sheer size of London, and the strains and dislocations of its rapid growth, the foremost factor distinguishing mid-century attitudes toward the metropolis from those of earlier generations was the increasing conviction that the well-being or lack of well-being, and even the moral condition of the city-dweller, were being caused by forces beyond his individual control. Dickens's antipathy to Sabbatarians and temperance re-

19 Harland S. Nelson, 'Dickens's *Our Mutual Friend* and Henry Mayhew's *London Labour and London Poor*', *Nineteenth-Century Fiction*, XX (1965), 207–222.

formers moves him in this direction as early as *Sketches by Boz*:
'Gin-drinking is a great vice in England, but poverty is a
greater. . . . If Temperance Societies could suggest an antidote
against hunger and distress, or establish dispensaries for the
gratuitous distribution of Lethe-water, gin-palaces would be
numbered among the things that were.'[20] Dickens's position on
this issue never changed, but his later expression of it is notice-
ably different. When he replied to George Cruikshank, a recent
convert to teetotalism, in *The Examiner* in 1848, the lack of
irony and the stress on physical causation are very pronounced:
'Drunkenness, as a national horror, is the effect of many causes.
Foul smells, disgusting habitations, bad workshops and work-
shop customs, want of light, air, and water, the absence of all
easy means of decency and health, are commonest among its
common, everyday, physical causes.'[21]

Between these two expressions of Dickens's position on
drunkenness, the public health and sanitary movement of the
1840s has intervened. It is this movement that is chiefly responsible for a new awareness of the physical causes of the city's
ills. Dr. Southwood Smith, whom Dickens frequently con-
sulted during his own association with the sanitary movement,
stated the new attitude succinctly in a report on the conditions of
Bethnal Green and Whitechapel in 1839: 'in these pestilential
places the industrious poor are obliged to take up their abode;
they have no choice; they must live in what houses they can get
nearest the places where they find employment. By no prudence
or forethought on their part can they avoid the dreadful evils of
this class to which they are thus exposed.'[22] The public demand
for sanitary reform was created by the cholera epidemics, and
precisely because nobody knew what caused cholera, the whole
idea of causation of disease came rapidly forward. What the
General Board of Health had to go on in 1848 was the statistical
correlation between dirt and overcrowding and the disease. Ignorance of microbiology and germ-theory undoubtedly resulted

[20] 'Gin Shops', in *Sketches by Boz*, 2 vols. (London, 1836), I, 286–7. Even
Dickens's revision of the passage (*SB*, p. 187) shows his changing awareness.
'Poverty' becomes 'wretchedness and dirt'; 'until you can cure it' becomes 'until
you can improve the homes of the poor', etc.

[21] *Collected Papers*, I, 157. Cf. Forster (Bk. VI, ch. i), II, 12.

[22] Quoted by Sir John Simon, *English Sanitary Institutions* (London, 1890),
p. 183.

in some grievous mistakes—as when the Board of Health, with self-defeating energy, directed the flushing of sewers into the Thames, which in 1849 supplied most of the drinking water in London.[23] Yet the prevalence of the atmospheric theory made sanitary reform seem all the more urgent, since foul smells themselves might be responsible for illness and death. The gradual discovery of the microbe in the second half of the century was disturbing enough to the imagination, but it was accompanied by—even preceded by—the discovery of immunization and antisepsis. To walk through London at the mid-century and fancy that in certain districts and on certain days one could actually smell cholera, and to realize that the smell could not be eradicated without an almost superhuman task of cleansing and rebuilding, was much more disturbing.

You will have read in the papers that the Thames in London is most horrible. I have to cross Waterloo or London Bridge to get to the railroad when I come down here [to Gad's Hill], and I can certify that the offensive smells, even in that short whiff, have been of a most head-and-stomach distending nature. Nobody knows what is to be done; at least everybody knows a plan, and everybody else knows it won't do; in the meantime cartloads of chloride of lime are shot into the filthy stream, and do something I hope.[24]

The nineteenth century developed certain organic metaphors for the city. Wordsworth could contemplate the 'mighty heart' of London with satisfaction only while it lay asleep; and William Cobbett habitually referred to London as 'the Wen'. Dickens, in the description of the fog at the beginning of the third book of *Our Mutual Friend*, concluded that 'the whole metropolis was a heap of vapour charged with muffled sound of wheels, and enfolding a gigantic catarrh'.[25] Such metaphors connote an unpleasant or abnormal living thing, in which something has gone wrong with the system. They mark the beginning of an awareness of the city as a systemic problem, and therefore of a treatment or eventual cure for the city that is scientific rather than satiric. In writing to Angela Burdett-Coutts of Hickman's Folly—an area adjacent to Jacob's Island in London—as a possible site for new working-class housing, Dickens uses a

23 S. E. Finer, *The Life and Times of Sir Edwin Chadwick* (London, 1952), p. 347.
24 To W. F. de Cerjat, 7 July 1858, *Letters*, III, 30.
25 *OMF*, Bk. III, ch. i, p. 420.

variant of the same general metaphor, a metaphor that enhances his awareness of the recurrent problems of the city planner: 'It would be of no use to touch a limb of Hickman—his whole body is infected, and would spoil the mended part.'[26]

The historical forces that I have enumerated—the great size of the city, the pressure exerted by one part upon the others, the helplessness of the individual citizen, his dependence on the economy of the whole, and his reliance on physical conditions beyond his control—also fostered a view of the city as an organic system. The specific non-literary embodiment of this view can be found in plans dealing with sewage and water supply. Edwin Chadwick's 'venous and arterial system' of sanitary practice would combine a plentiful and constant water supply with adequate drains and sewers;[27] and the already mentioned report by Henry Austin on *The Means of Deodorizing and Utilizing the Sewage of Towns* surveyed the possibilities of returning water and sewage to the land as liquid fertilizer. Water supply was an acute problem in London at the mid-century, and the increased use of water itself requires better sewers. From Paris it was learned that the expense of emptying cesspools discouraged landlords from admitting piped water to their buildings; and from New York, that the opening of the Croton aqueduct had increased the drainage problems of Manhattan. The two functions were inextricably related, and the Board of Health studiously informed the Queen and Parliament in 1850 that it was 'necessary to consider works for the supply of water in connexion with works for the removal of soil and waste water . . . and to examine each as part of one system of works requisite for the improvement of the sanitary condition of a town population'.[28]

26 7 Jan. 1853, *Coutts Letters*, p. 220.

27 Finer, pp. 220–4.

28 *Report by the General Board of Health on the Supply of Water to the Metropolis, Parliamentary Papers*, 1850, xxii, 137–8; Appendix IV, p. 22; and p. 2. That the railway and telegraph helped contribute to the systemic idea is evident from the proposals of a doctor of the period: 'Our public roads,—the net-works of modern railways, indicate the appropriate lines [for a system of dealing with sewage],— and the electric telegraph will minister to its ubiquity, to govern and regulate valves for transmissive circulation. Should not the metropolis initiate a great "System", in union and co-operation with our sister towns, to "restore" to the land that which modern domestic adaptations has [sic] taken from our soil, in *violation* of the *Beneficent* law imposed on all human and animal existence, which ordained,—

It is a nice question to what degree this judgement was en-
forced by a moralistic prejudice against waste. When manure
had been heaped in unsanitary piles in yards and streets, it
could still be profitably carted away; but an efficient system of
drains and sewers threatened to wash it irrecoverably away.
Modern sanitation is an extravagant process, and some friction
was bound to develop between the ideals of cleanliness and
thrift. G. M. Young remarks that 'the mainspring of Chadwick's
career seems to have been a desire to wash the people of England
all over, every day, by administrative order'; whereas S. E.
Finer, Chadwick's biographer, believes that 'His motive was
neither religious nor benevolent—it was horror of waste.'[29]
Dickens gave 'Cleanliness and Decency' precedence over all
other social remedies; but he also observed, in admiring the
slaughtering methods of the Parisian *abattoirs*, that 'nothing in
Nature is intended to be wasted'.[30] The possible contradiction
of these ideals was obscured for the time being by the needs of an
army of hungry and shelterless urban scavengers, who were
recognized to be a vital part of the system. As Mayhew was able
to demonstrate, they scoured hundreds of miles of streets every
day; and their collective service to the city was as essential as
that of their mobilized and salaried counterparts today. In
Master Humphrey's Clock Dickens could remark, with superior
confidence in his own century, that kites and ravens were the
only scavengers that served the city in the time of James I; his
historical comparison is doubtful, but the implied value of
human scavengers is certain.[31] In *Our Mutual Friend* he again
compares the appearance of contemporary London unfavourably
with that of Paris, 'where nothing is wasted, costly and luxuri-
ous city though it be, but where wonderful human ants creep
out of holes and pick up every scrap'.[32]

---

that by the multiplication of living creatures *"the earth is to be replenished"* with the
elements of ever renewed and increasing fertility?' A. Sayer, M.D., *The Nature,
Value, and Disposal of Sewage, with Considerations on Drainage, Sewers, and Sewerage; Sketches of the Water Supply, and of the Legislation on Sewers, Ancient and
Modern*, 2nd ed. (London, 1858), p. 83.

[29] Young, p. 25; Finer, p. 3.

[30] Speech to the Metropolitan Sanitary Association, 10 May 1851, *Speeches*, p.
129; 'A Monument to French Folly', *RP*, p. 592. The title of the article is ironic.

[31] *MHC*, ch. iii, p. 71.

[32] *OMF*, Bk. I, ch. xii, p. 144.

Today we call the main vehicular routes of a city 'arteries', and traffic on the streets and rails, then as now, is another problem of the systemic city. The metaphor that aptly describes the flow of water and sewage, of supply and waste in the city is found appropriate in *Dombey and Son* to the traffic through and nearby the railway terminus that has supplanted Staggs's Gardens: 'To and from the heart of this great change, all day and night, throbbing currents rushed and returned incessantly like its life's blood.'[33] A long series of efforts to meet the internal transport problems of London, including the modern problem of commuting, were begun in the 1850s. The founding of the General Omnibus Company, and the crossing of the Thames by railways from the south, were followed by the construction of tramlines and more bridges. Above all, the Metropolitan Railway was authorized in 1853 and opened in 1863; London became the first city in which not only gas, water, and sewage, but streams of people began to flow underground in 'venous and arterial' style. A highly practical underground system (and deep tube construction) was not possible without the use of electric power; nevertheless, the London underground began operating eight years before Dicken's death, and had been conceived by engineers like Robert Stephenson and politicians like Charles Pearson as early as the 1830s.[34] The systemic problems of modern cities were sourly but unerringly linked together by Ruskin: 'cities in which the streets are not avenues for the passing and procession of a happy people, but the drains for the discharge of a tormented mob . . . in which existence becomes mere transition, and every creature is only one atom in a drift of human dust, and current of interchanging particles, circulating here by tunnels underground, and there by tubes in the air'.[35]

A metaphor related to that of a system is that of the city as a prison. In *Our Mutual Friend*, and indirectly in many places, Dickens compares the city to a prison and its citizens to prisoners. The subject, for example, would not seem very central to *Nicholas Nickleby*, yet, 'There, at the very core of London, in

[33] *D & S*, ch. xv, p. 218.

[34] T. C. Barker and Michael Robbins, *A History of London Transport*, I (London, 1963), pp. 100–1.

[35] 'The Study of Architecture in Our Schools' (1865), *The Works of John Ruskin*, 39 vols., ed. E. T. Cook and Alexander Wedderburn (London, 1903–12), XIX, 24.

the heart of its business and animation, in the midst of a whirl of noise and motion: stemming as it were the giant currents of life that flow ceaselessly on from different quarters and meet beneath its walls: stands Newgate.'[36] Another passage, in *The Old Curiosity Shop*, hovers between cheerfulness and dread because the writer apparently cannot make up his mind whether daylight frees the city from the prison of sleep or recalls the inmates to their habitual condition.[37] Mumford has noted the ambiguous history of the city as a citadel—a citadel ostensibly erected to protect the citizens from their enemies but in practice bringing them under forcible submission to a central authority.[38] He borrowed from *Hard Times* the name of Coketown to represent the nineteenth-century industrial city, and in Dickens's description of Coketown occurs the same dubious citadel. Stephen Blackpool lives 'in the innermost fortifications of that ugly citadel, where Nature was as strongly bricked out as killing airs and gases were bricked in; at the heart of the labyrinth of narrow courts upon courts, and close streets upon streets, which had come into existence piecemeal, every piece in a violent hurry for some one man's purpose, and the whole an unnatural family, shouldering, and trampling, and pressing one another to death'.[39] Still, the prison can be seen historically as an early model of the systemic city; and the prison reform movement that began in the late eighteenth century first acknowledged in miniature that at least one class of persons could not practically be held responsible for the sufficiency of their food, their living space, and sanitary procedures.   This lesson would be applied a century later to the city itself.[40]

The 'monster', as Dickens called London in *Dombey and Son*, or the 'machine' that is Coketown, may be taken for granted today, but were newly created in his lifetime. Discovering that the city was a systemic growth was in some ways encouraging; the monster or machine might be studied and somehow

[36] *NN*, ch. iv, p. 29. Cf. *OMF*, Bk. II, ch. xv, p. 393.

[37] *OCS*, ch. xv, pp. 113–14. For Dickens's compulsive need to walk the streets of London by night, see Forster (Bk. V, ch. v), I, 419–20; and Edgar Johnson, *Charles Dickens: His Tragedy and Triumph*, 2 vols. (London, 1953), I, 518–20.

[38] *The City in History* (New York, 1961), pp. 46–50.

[39] *HT*, Bk. I, ch. x, p. 63.

[40] For a detailed account of Dickens's views of prisons and systems of punishment, see Philip Collins, *Dickens and Crime*, Cambridge Studies in Criminology, XVII, 2nd ed. (London, 1964), chs. ii–iii, v–vii.

mastered. But the discovery was also frightening; the city seemed to exist for its own sake, obeying physical laws of its own and growing incessantly. In *Dombey and Son* and the later novels it becomes more and more difficult to judge whether Dickens is directing his satire at a morally responsible audience or at the city itself.

Those who study the physical sciences, and bring them to bear upon the health of Man, tell us that if the noxious particles that rise from vitiated air were palpable to the sight, we should see them lowering in a dense black cloud above such haunts, and rolling slowly on to corrupt the better portions of a town. But if the moral pestilence that rises with them, and in the eternal laws of outraged Nature, is inseparable from them, could be made discernible too, how terrible the revelation! Then should we see depravity, impiety, drunkenness, theft, murder, and a long train of nameless sins against the natural affections and re-pulsions of mankind, overhanging the devoted spots, and creeping on, to blight the innocent and spread contagion among the pure. Then should we see how the same poisoned fountains that flow into our hospitals and lazar-houses, inundate the jails, and make the convict-ships swim deep, and roll across the seas, and over-run vast continents with crime. Then should we stand appalled to know, that where we generate disease to strike our children down and entail itself on unborn generations, there also we breed, by the same certain process, infancy that knows no innocence, youth without modesty or shame, maturity that is mature in nothing but in suffering and guilt, blasted old age that is a scandal on the form we bear. Unnatural humanity! When we shall gather grapes from thorns, and figs from thistles; when fields of grain shall spring up from the offal in the bye-ways of our wicked cities, and roses bloom in the fat churchyards that they cherish; then we may look for natural humanity and find it growing from such seed.

Oh for a good spirit who would take the house-tops off, with a more potent and benignant hand than the lame demon in the tale, and show a Christian people what dark shapes issue from amidst their homes, to swell the retinue of the Destroying Angel as he moves forth among them! . . .[41]

In this well-known passage satire invokes the science of communicable disease; yet the scientific analogy diffuses the usual castigation of satire. Since the crimes that Dickens names are engendered 'by the same certain process' as disease, who is culpable? The context of the passage (only a part of which is

[41] *D & S*, ch. xlvii, pp. 647–8.

given here) is also perplexing. It is introduced in answer to the question, whether Mr. Dombey's pride, his 'master-vice', was an 'unnatural characteristic'? The problems of the city are so paramount in the novelist's mind as he writes *Dombey and Son*, that he tentatively applies the same relation of physical cause and moral ill to the character of his hero. The satire in *Bleak House* will employ the same impersonal analogy, insisting that the slum called Tom-all-Alone's is not only contiguous with the well-to-do districts of London but functionally related to the whole.

There is not a drop of Tom's corrupted blood but propagates infection and contagion somewhere. . . . There is not an atom of Tom's slime, not a cubic inch of any pestilential gas in which he lives, not one obscenity or degradation about him, not an ignorance, not a wickedness, not a brutality of his committing, but shall work its retribution, through every order of society, up to the proudest of the proud, and to the highest of the high.[42]

The city contains within itself a destructive growth, the pestilential gases from which can be measured both in moral retribution and in cubic inches.

In the nineteenth century the findings of science and statistics, of journalism and parliamentary reports, and the literature of the city in general, had one main tendency: the discovery of the city as a problem. Whereas 'in *Pickwick* a bad smell was a bad smell', Humphry House pointed out, 'in *Our Mutual Friend* it is a problem'.[43] Moreover, the discovery coincided with the rise of modern historicism, an outlook that regards the future as entirely open-ended, and therefore dreadful or hopeful according to the feeling of the moment. No one can say exactly when the metropolis underwent a subtle shift from the focus of satire to an object of investigation and anxiety for the future. Some such shifting of public attitude and private consciousness did take place; and because the city had always been a source of pride, a man-made thing, the new thought was discouraging and depressing. How science and engineering might contribute to solving the problem they had helped to define was dimly understood; but not less understood was the incalculable expense

42 *BH*, ch. xlvi, pp. 627–8.
43 *The Dickens World*, 2nd ed. (London, 1961), p. 135.

and exhausting detail of any solution. A heavier burden than in the past would be placed on the political organization of cities; but London at the mid-century had no metropolitan government. It was an age in which political remedies seemed even more remote and troublesome than they do today.

III

PUBLIC OPINION AND POLICEMEN

In his address to the Birmingham and Midland Institute in September 1869 Dickens offered to state his 'political creed'. 'My faith in the people governing, is, on the whole, infinitesimal,' he announced; 'my faith in The People governed, is, on the whole, illimitable.' The newspapers were quick to censure the apparent illiberalism of the statement, and Dickens offered to clarify his creed. The capitalization of 'People' has been established by his subsequent explanation to the same audience in January 1870:

When I was here last autumn I made, in reference to some remarks of your respected member, Mr. Dixon, a short confession of my political faith [*applause*], or perhaps I should better say, want of faith. [*Laughter.*] It imported that I have very little faith in the people who govern us—please to observe 'people' there will be with a small 'p' [*laughter*], but that I have great confidence in the People whom they govern: please to observe 'People' there with a large 'P'. [*Renewed laughter.*] This was shortly and elliptically stated; and was, with no evil intention I am absolutely sure, in some quarters inversely explained. Perhaps as the inventor of a certain extravagant fiction, but one which I do see rather frequently quoted as if there were grains of truth at the bottom of it, a fiction called 'The Circumlocution Office' [*laughter*], and perhaps also as the writer of an idle book or two, whose public opinions are not obscurely stated—perhaps in these respects I do not sufficiently bear in mind Hamlet's caution to speak by the card lest equivocation should undo me. [*Laughter and applause.*][1]

Notwithstanding Dickens's skill in extricating himself and his insertion of a capital 'P', he could hardly have hit upon a more ambiguous declaration of principle. The original statement is not merely unclear: it oscillates, like certain optical illusions of a drawing in perspective, between two mutually exclusive meanings. If 'the people' has the same denotation in each of

[1] 27 Sept. 1869, and 6 Jan. 1870, *Speeches*, pp. 407, 410–11.

the clauses—as we no doubt have a right to expect from the speaker—then the declaration is authoritarian: Dickens has little faith in democracy and illimitable faith in some other means of governing the people. Inserting the capital 'P' gives 'the people' a separate denotation in each clause and renders the declaration anti-authoritarian: Dickens has little faith in the government and illimitable faith in the people whom they govern.

Yet it can be argued that he meant both possible creeds.[2] Much evidence can be adduced to show that he had little faith in democracy, especially in the last two decades of his life. That he believed strongly in the necessity of the people being 'governed' in *some* fashion is less simply demonstrated, but emerges from his hatred of mobs, his conviction that criminals deserve to be severely punished or even eliminated, and his growing respect for soldiers and policemen. Moreover, the presumably correct interpretation commits Dickens to very little. The 'people governing' are simply not specified; in the September speech he went out of his way to caution that his creed 'has no reference to any party or persons'. His creed is apparently anti-authoritarian, but by no means democratic; he has faith in 'The People governed', but says nothing about their governing. The contradiction between the two interpretations, though it is felt by Dickens and his audience, becomes on closer inspection somewhat muddled. It reflects the puzzlement and self-contradiction of contemporaries who were better qualified to debate the necessity of government or the nature of democracy. Hatred or contempt of a vaguely specified 'people governing', praise of 'The People' coupled with open or hidden contempt of their ability to govern themselves, and trust in the efficacy of a strong police force, make up a political syndrome too familiar to be gainsaid, however fuzzy or irrational it may be in theory. Most pertinently, it summarizes the feelings of many persons, of mixed persuasions, toward the problem of governing cities: the seeming inevitability of wicked or weak government, the hopelessness of expecting the people of the city, much as one

---

[2] Cf. Forster (Bk. XI, ch. iii), II, 389: 'It may nevertheless be suspected . . . that the construction of his real meaning was not far wrong which assumed it as the condition precedent to his illimitable faith, that the people, even with the big P should be "governed".'

pretends to respect them, to govern themselves, and the de-
spairing trust in the police to put down crime in the streets.

In Victorian England the spirit of reform contended with the
doctrine of non-interference.[3] The conviction that the city was a
problem, the realization of its systemic nature, and the knowledge that many of its difficulties were impersonally caused did
not by any means point to a clear policy of government interference. For some authorities, that urban problems were caused,
was all the more reason for leaving them alone. The campaign
conducted for sanitary reform by Chadwick, Shaftesbury, and
others has to be weighed against the protest of Herbert Spencer,
the civil engineer, who saw that 'to divorce a cause and consequence which God has joined together' was to court disaster.
The chapter in *Social Statics* on the sanitary question contained
more caveats than concrete proposals; Spencer, too, was concerned with waste and drains, but if these matters could not be
profitably managed by private enterprise, then the sewers could
be stopped:

Houses might readily be drained on the same mercantile principle that
they are now supplied with water. It is highly possible that in the hands
of a private company the resulting manure would not only pay the cost
of collection, but would yield a considerable profit. But if not, the return on invested capital would be made up by charges to those whose
houses were drained: the alternative of having their connections with
the main sewer stopped, being as good security for payment as the
analogous ones possessed by water and gas companies.[4]

Similarly, that structural changes in the city might cause dis-
location and suffering could be admitted without conceding that
government should interfere with the process. Railway building
in London caused large areas of slum to be swept clear of dwellings and the means of livelihood for the poor, but *The Times* in
1861 argued that the government should do nothing to mend
the consequences. To do so would 'end in no good'—presumably
because the involvement of the government or railways in

[3] Cf. Young, *Victorian England*, p. 82: 'In all Dickens's work there is a confusion
of mind which reflects the perplexity of his time; equally ready to denounce on the
grounds of humanity all who left things alone, and on the grounds of liberty all who
tried to make them better.' The first half of Young's epigram fits Dickens more
closely than the second, though the perplexity was real enough. See also House, p.
201 n.

[4] *Social Statics* (London, 1851), pp. 379, 393–4.

housing the poor would merely injure the 'builders and specu-
lators ready to supply their wants'. Meanwhile London could
receive the simultaneous blessings of the railway and of slum-
clearance:

Government has nothing to do with providing dwellings for the poor,
and has no more right to impose an obligation of this sort on railways
than anybody else who pulls down a dwelling-house to build something else—a church, for example—in its place. The interference is
both idle and contrary to the usages of this country. It can end in no
good. We accept railways with their consequences, and we don't think
the worse of them for ventilating the City of London. . . . You can
never make these wretched alleys really habitable, do what you will;
but bring a railway to them, and the whole problem is solved.[5]

Dickens was never as sanguine as *The Times* in imagining that
'the whole problem is solved'; but neither does he unequivocally
suggest interference as a possible solution.

In two of his most graphic attacks on the slums of London,
Dickens blames neither government nor landlords, but rather
the lapse of private ownership. The description of Jacob's Island
in *Oliver Twist* notes that 'before losses and Chancery suits
came upon it, it was a thriving place'. At present, Dickens reports, 'The houses have no owners.'[6] The fault is not with the
landlords but with the poorly functioning legal system that has
diminished their responsibility. The description of Tom-all-
Alone's in *Bleak House* is even more disagreeable:

As, on the ruined human wretch, vermin parasites appear, so these
ruined shelters have bred a crowd of foul existence that crawls in and
out of gaps in walls and boards; and coils itself to sleep, in maggot
numbers, where the rain drips in; and comes and goes, fetching and
carrying fever, and sowing more evil in its every footprint than Lord
Coodle, and Sir Thomas Doodle, and the Duke of Foodle, and all the
fine gentlemen in office, down to Zoodle, shall set right in five hundred
years—though born expressly to do it.

Dickens sarcastically dismisses the capacity of the present regime
to do anything—the 'people governing', whoever they may be
—and again calls attention to the lapse in effective private

---

[5] *The Times*, 12 and 23 Mar. 1861, quoted by H. J. Dyos, 'Railways and Housing in Victorian London', *Journal of Transport History*, II (1955–6), 97.
[6] *OT*, ch. 1, pp. 381–2.

3. Entrance to the Clerkenwell Tunnel

LONDON'S NIGHTMARE.

4. *London's Nightmare*, by John Tenniel

ownership: 'This desirable property is in Chancery, of course.'[7]
Though Chancery and the law's delay are to blame in both
novels, the implication is that responsible private ownership
would be sufficient to correct the evil conditions. As a 'good,
practical, safe, and sound plan' for developing better housing in
London, Dickens urged Miss Coutts to demonstrate sanitary
improvements to 'any small proprietor' by constructing a model
house—'for the purpose of shewing him at how small an ex-
pence he can improve the houses he now lets—of giving him
friendly advice—and even of assisting him to do what is right,
if he will only do it'.[8] This cautious and practical advice, stripped
of the kindness and discretion characteristic of Dickens's philanthropy, is essentially the same as that of Spencer and the doctrine of non-interference: 'Let those who are anxious to improve
the health of the poor . . . prove to people of property that the
making of these reforms will pay.'[9]

On the other hand, Dickens favoured at least some degree of
centralization as a check against private interests in the city.
London consisted of independent boroughs; and even after 1855,
when the Metropolitan Board of Works was established, the
basic political unit was still the vestry, or parish government.
The Corporation of the City of London—which Mill called 'that
union of modern jobbing and antiquated foppery'[10]—was the
most powerful single body in the metropolis and the most
jealous of its prerogatives. Dickens shared the contempt of Mill
—and of a long satiric tradition—for the stuffy power of the
City. He defended the General Board of Health more tenaciously
than some of its friends, and in *All the Year Round* he directly

[7] *BH*, ch. xvi, p. 220.
[8] 1 Feb. 1853, *Coutts Letters*, p. 222.
[9] *Social Statics*, p. 385.
[10] John Stuart Mill, *Considerations on Representative Government* (London, 1861),
pp. 272–3: 'Paving, lighting, water supply, drainage, port and market regulations,
cannot without great waste and inconvenience be different for different quarters of
the same town. The sub-division of London into six or seven independent districts,
each with its separate arrangements for local business (several of them without
unity of administration even within themselves) prevents the possibility of con-
secutive or well regulated co-operation for common objects, precludes any uniform
discharge of local duties, compels the general government to take things upon itself
which would be best left to local authorities if there were any whose authority
extended to the entire metropolis; and answers no purpose but to keep up the fan-
tastical trappings of that union of modern jobbing and antiquated foppery, the
Corporation of the City of London.'

advocated equalization of the poor rates in London.[11] In a satire for *Household Words* he mocked the self-importance and righteousness of the vestries and belittled their right to free obstruction of sanitary reform:

[Our Vestry's] great watchword is Self-government. That is to say, supposing our Vestry to favour any little harmless disorder like Typhus Fever, and supposing the Government of the country to be, by any accident, in such ridiculous hands, as that any of its authorities should consider it a duty to object to Typhus Fever—obviously an unconstitutional objection—then, our Vestry cuts in with a terrible manifesto about Self-government, and claims its independent right to have as much Typhus Fever as pleases itself.

With cheerful irony he goes on to imagine the Vestry debating 'the question whether water could be regarded in the light of a necessary of life'.[12] At the first meeting of the Metropolitan Sanitary Association, in 1850, citing his familiar contention that disease was no respecter of social or political boundaries, Dickens went so far as to say that he would 'endeavour to force' the inhabitants of London 'to be pure and clean, and would place them under the control of a General Board for the general good'.[13] Here his support of centralization for the purpose of sanitary reform takes him very far in the direction of interference—but that, of course, is not inconsistent with his ambiguous political creed. He feels freer to recommend government action of one kind because he is contemning the power of another—the vestries. He is still expressing his contempt for the 'people governing' and the need for 'The People' to be governed.

An article in *Household Words* of the same period and on the same general topic of sanitation, which Dickens now denominates 'the most momentous of all earthly questions', is addressed explicitly 'To Working Men'. At first it seems to call, not merely for interference, but for outright governmental contributions to the welfare of the people: 'Neither Religion nor Education will make any way, in this nineteenth century of Christianity, until a Christian government shall have discharged its first obligation, and secured to the people Homes, instead of

11 'Wapping Workhouse', *UT*, p. 27.
12 'Our Vestry', *RP*, pp. 575, 578. Cf. 'On Duty with Inspector Field', *RP*, p. 518; and *Speeches*, p. 130.
13 6 Feb. 1850, *Speeches*, p. 107.

polluted dens.' But the proposal is very vague: 'secured' may
mean protected from interference of another kind rather than
purchased or constructed; Dickens writes 'Homes' rather than
houses; and the 'Christian government' is manifestly not the
one in power. The appeal of this document is not to government
but to 'The People':

Let *them* take the initiative, and call the middle-class to unite with
them: which they will do, heart and soul! Let the working people, in
the metropolis, in any one great town, but turn their intelligence, their
energy, their numbers, their power of union, their patience, their per-
severence, in this straight direction in earnest—and by Christmas
[i.e., in less than three months], they shall find a government in
Downing Street and a House of Commons within hail of it, possessing
not the faintest family resemblance to the Indifferents and Incapables
last heard of in that slumberous neighbourhood.

It is only through a government so acted upon and so forced to acquit
itself of its first responsibility, that the intolerable ills arising from the
present nature of the dwellings of the poor can be remedied. A Board
of Health can do much, but not near enough. Funds are wanted, and
great powers are wanted; powers to over-ride little interests for the
general good; powers to coerce the ignorant, obstinate, and slothful,
and to punish all who, by any infraction of necessary laws, imperil the
public health. The working people and the middle-class thoroughly
resolved to have such laws, there is no more choice left to all the Red
Tape in Britain as to the form in which it shall tie itself next, than there
is option in the barrel of a barrel-organ what tune it shall play.[14]

Does he mean to call out the mob? Dickens plans to topple the
government within three months, but mentions neither a revolution nor an election. In explaining his manifesto to Miss Coutts
he does not seem to have in mind an election and merely urges
that working people, who cannot vote in any case, influence
the election 'by every means in their power'.[15] The article
seems to have caused Miss Coutts to raise her eyebrows, but
was not widely offensive. It made very little stir, not because
Englishmen enjoy special liberties of speech, but because the
message could be readily understood as a call for a change in
public opinion, a process not thought to be revolutionary in anything but a wholesome way.

[14] 'To Working Men', 7 Oct. 1854, *Collected Papers*, I, 511, 512–13.
[15] 26 Oct. 1854, *Coutts Letters*, pp. 272–3.

The action of public opinion is at once democratic and authoritarian: by some unspecified process the people must 'force' the government to 'coerce' themselves (these are Dickens's terms) into being clean. The process does not require definition, since once the people have awakened to the point of forcing the government to action, only a few stragglers, 'the ignorant, obstinate, and slothful', will remain for government to coerce. The faith in the efficacy of public opinion minimizes the task of the 'people governing' and charges 'The People' with responsibility. It raises no tangled question of the franchise or of the precise method of political control. It allows the people to act without risking anything to their actions; it makes them responsible for progress while protecting them from possible self-injury.

The doctrine is the most common political creed of the Victorian age. Dickens's message 'To Working Men', while different in logic and style, is not very different in substance from Felix Holt's 'Address to Working Men', written by George Eliot just after the extension of the franchise in 1867.[16] 'I'll tell you what's the greatest power under heaven,' Holt declared in the novel, where he had opposed reform, 'and that is public opinion—the ruling belief in society about what is right and what is wrong, what is honourable and what is shameful. That's the steam that is to work the engines.'[17] The rejection of the ballot in Mill's *Representative Government*, the most sober and thoughtful treatise on democracy in this period, clearly implied that public opinion was a safer and more effective expression of the national will than the franchise. And as for Spencer, who endorsed extension of the franchise much more freely, or carelessly, he felt that the state was 'a mere dead mechanism worked by a nation's moral sense'.[18] Victorian workmen were indeed the most thoroughly lectured proletariat in history—at least until the establishment of the modern communist states. Lecturers of all shades of opinion took the position that the people are responsible, with or without the franchise, and that the successful management of the nation or lesser constituencies depends on their will. According to Mill the one condition of good govern-

[16] *Blackwood's Magazine*, CIII (Jan. 1868); in Pinney, *Essays of George Eliot*, pp. 415–30.

[17] *Felix Holt*, Bk. II, ch. xxx, p. 90. Passages in George Eliot's novels are quoted from the Cabinet Edition, 20 vols. (Edinburgh and London, 1878–80).

[18] *Social Statics*, p. 11.

ment that 'transcends all the others, is the qualities of the human beings composing the society over which the government is exercised'. Carlyle and Ruskin take essentially the same position.[19] Spencer preaches that 'misconduct among those in power is the correlative of misconduct among those over whom they exercise power',[20] and that is essentially the doctrine behind the private sentiments of Dickens:

As to the suffrage, I have lost hope even in the ballot. We appear to me to have proved the failure of representative institutions without an educated and advanced people to support them. . . . I do reluctantly believe that the English people are habitually consenting parties to the miserable imbecility into which we have fallen, *and never will help themselves out of it.* Who is to do it, if anybody is, God knows. But at present we are on the down-hill road to being conquered, and the people WILL be content to bear it, sing 'Rule Britannia,' and WILL NOT be saved.[21]

In his January 1870 speech Dickens further offered to 're-state' the meaning of his political creed by quoting a passage from Henry Thomas Buckle's *History of Civilization in England*: 'lawgivers are nearly always the obstructors of society, instead of its helpers'; they can help only when they obey 'the spirit of their time' and act as 'the mere servants of the people'.[22] According to Buckle, the very purpose of studying the history of England is that here progress has been 'so little interfered with'. The only happy use of legislation is in the repeal of earlier mistakes, 'not in doing something new, but in undoing something old'.[23] In this judgement Buckle echoes Spencer, who had written eight years earlier in *Social Statics* that 'Nearly every parliamentary proceeding is a tacit confession of incompetency. There is scarcely a bill introduced but is entitled "An Act to amend an Act".'[24]

[19] *Representative Government*, p. 28. Carlyle advises, '*Be* thyself a man abler to be governed': *Latter-Day Pamphlets*, No. III, in *Collected Works*, 30 vols. (London, 1870–1), XIX, 128. Cf. Ruskin, *Unto This Last:* 'all effectual advancement towards this true felicity of the human race must be by individual, not public effort', in *Works*, XVII, 111.

[20] *The Study of Sociology*, ed. Talcott Parsons (Ann Arbor, 1961), p. 363.

[21] To Macready, 4 Oct. 1855, *Letters*, II, 695. See also the letter to Austen Henry Layard, 10 Apr. 1855, II, 651–2.

[22] *Speeches*, p. 411. The passage is quoted from Buckle, II, 244.

[23] Buckle, *History of Civilization*, I, 183, 199–200.

[24] *Social Statics*, p. 11.

The logic and impatience of these observations are comparable to the mood of Dickens in this period. As House pointed out, the kinds of legislation that Dickens approved throughout his life were usually of this negative kind[25]—though not, of course, any less desirable or necessary for that reason. If Buckle and Spencer seem odd ideological companions for Dickens, the reason is that he was not deeply affected by their theory of social evolution: a theory, nevertheless, that is partly responsible for the idea of force that lurks behind the faith in public opinion. Buckle was an inveterate believer in public opinion; and public opinion always moves forward, not backward. 'To seek to change opinions by laws,' he writes, 'is worse than futile. It not only fails, but it causes a reaction, which leaves the opinions stronger than ever. First alter the opinion, and then you may alter the law.' The precedence of public opinion over law-making and the sequence of their relation go far to explain Dickens's direct appeal to working men to change the regulations governing conditions of life in the city. Buckle's analysis of society displays throughout a lack of faith in the people governing coupled with the more ambiguous, but compensating faith in the people governed. The means by which the people must take the initiative are left in doubt, just as it is not clear by what means Dickens would 'force' the government to conform to the people's will. If it were not for his saving belief that ultimately 'inconsistency is impossible' in the evolution of a nation, Buckle, too, might be thought to be consorting with revolution. At one point—rather inconsistently—he wonders what would happen if a government refused to respond to the force of opinion: 'Should the government remain firm, this is the cruel dilemma in which men are placed. If they submit, they injure their country; if they rebel, they may injure it still more.' In such an event, he cannot advise them; but no matter, the history of England has already demonstrated 'the great truth, that one main condition of the prosperity of a people is, that its rulers shall have very little power, that they shall exercise that power very sparingly,' etc.[26]

The belief that rulers should have little power invests power in public opinion instead. Felix Holt's comparison of public

[25] House, pp. 172–6.
[26] Buckle, II, 91, 255; I, 208.

opinion to the steam that drives an engine reflects this compen-
satory theory of power. The theory curiously justifies distrust
of representative government, the political institution that, as
it were, rivals public opinion in the attempt to attribute power
neither here nor there, neither to the ruling or the ruled, even
while it acknowledges that power must be exercised. Dickens's
attack on Parliament as an institution—as opposed to his ordinary human impatience with certain individual legislators—can be
dated from the well-known passage in *David Copperfield*, where
his fictional reminiscence of days as a parliamentary reporter is
coloured by a contemporary hatred of red tape: 'Night after
night, I record predictions that never come to pass, professions
that are never fulfilled, explanations that are only meant to
mystify. I wallow in words. Britannia, that unfortunate female,
is always before me, like a trussed fowl: skewered through and
through with office-pens, and bound hand and foot with red
tape.'[27] The novels of the next two decades are filled with satire
aimed at parliamentary government: the interchangeability of
Coodle and Doodle in *Bleak House*; the reference to parliament
as 'the national cinder heap' and to members of parliament as
'national dustmen' in *Hard Times*; the 'less distinguished
Parliamentary Barnacles' of *Little Dorrit*, who 'fetched and
carried, and toadied and jobbed, and corrupted, and ate heaps of
dirt, and were indefatigable in the public service'; and the challenge to 'my lords and gentlemen and honourable boards' in
Our Mutual Friend that invokes the lesson of Humpty Dumpty:
'when you in the course of your dust-shovelling and cinder-
raking have piled up a mountain of pretentious failure, you must
off with your honourable coats for the removal of it, and fall to
the work with the power of all the queen's horses and all the
queen's men, or it will come rushing down and bury us alive.'[28]

The climax of Dickens's disgust with government undoubtedly came, as it came for many of his countrymen, in the winter
of 1854–5, after the revelations of the government's mishandling
of the Crimean War had been published in *The Times*. Address-
ing the Administrative Reform Association in June 1855,

[27] *DC*, ch. xliii, p. 626.

[28] *BH*, ch. xl, pp. 562–3; *HT*, Bk, II, ch. xi, p. 206; ch. xii, p. 215; *LD*, Bk. I,
ch. xxxiv, pp. 406–7; *OMF*, Bk. III, ch. viii, p. 503. See also 'Mr. Bull's Somnam-
bulist', *Collected Papers*, I, 317–22; 'Medicine Men of Civilization', *UT*, 280–8;
Forster (Bk. XI, ch. iii), II, 386–7; Johnson, I, 317.

Dickens delivered his most sustained nonsatiric attack on the people governing, both political and administrative. The speech reflects that strange vision—strange in view of the actual strength and world position of England in 1855—of the imminent collapse of the nation:

When the *Times* newspaper proved its then almost incredible case, in reference to the ghastly absurdity of that vast labyrinth of misplaced men and misdirected things, which made England unable to find on the face of the earth, an enemy one-twentieth part so potent for the misery and ruin of her noble defenders as she has been herself, I believed that the gloomy silence into which the country fell, was by far the darkest aspect in which a great people had been exhibited for very many years. [*Cheers.*] With shame and indignation lowering among all classes of society, and this new element of discord piled on the heaving basis of ignorance, poverty and crime, which is always below us—with little adequate expression of the general mind, or apparent understanding of the general mind, in Parliament—with the machinery of the Government and legislation going round and round, and people fallen from it and standing aloof, as if they had left it to its last remaining function of destroying itself, when it had achieved the destruction of so much that was dear to them—I did believe, and I do believe, that the only wholesome turn affairs so menacing could take, was, the awakening of the people, the outspeaking of the people, the uniting of the people in all patriotism and loyalty to effect a great peaceful constitutional change in the administration of their own affairs. [*Cheers.*][29]

The 'gloomy silence' and 'shame and indignation' that Dickens invokes help explain the exaggerated feeling of being on the brink of national disaster: the Crimean débâcle was offensive to the degree that one believed, vocally or otherwise, in the superior advance of civilization in England. The newspaper that exposed this administrative scandal, after all, was the same that gazed with such complacency on the progress of railway building in London.

The stress on administrative reform was anticipated by Carlyle in 'Downing Street' (1850). There he had set forth the principle that political reform without administrative reform 'is naught and a mere mockery'. 'Who made [Colonial Offices,

---

[29] 27 June 1855, *Speeches*, p. 201. For the relation of the administrative reform movement to *Little Dorrit*, see John Butt and Kathleen Tillotson, *Dickens at Work* (London, 1957), ch. ix; and John Butt, 'The Topicality of *Little Dorrit*', *University of Toronto Quarterly*, XXIX (1959–60), 1–10.

Foreign, Home, and other Offices], ask me not. Made they clearly were; for we see them there in a concrete condition, writing dispatches, and drawing salary with a view to buying pudding.'[30] Dickens assumed a similar stance in *Little Dorrit*, in which Carlyle's several offices are lumped together in the mysterious Circumlocution Office. The famous chapter 'Containing the Whole Science of Government' is not directed against bureaucracy as such. The office procedures merely serve as a cloak for indifference and privilege; the toadies who run the Circumlocution Office are chiefly responsible for the science of 'How not to do it'. The satire of *Little Dorrit* as a whole is directed against the monopoly of administrative power in the hands of a few, the injustice of this monopoly and its impracticality for a modern nation. Barnacles, as the name suggests, are merely parasites.[31] Yet Dickens does not advocate a more bureaucratic organization, since he is well aware of the Office's capacity for extinguishing action in a blanket of minutes, memoranda, and letters of instruction. As Bagehot complained, 'Mr. Dickens never ceases to hint that these evils are removable, though he does not say by what means.'[32] The impasse is one that is inherent in the jealous relation of radicalism to the bureaucracy that it seeks to create. Radicalism may strengthen public administration by breaking the monopoly of office-holding, but it also strives to minimize administrative authority in the name of public opinion.[33]

By 1871 Huxley was pointing out the contradiction between Spencer's conception of government as the 'cerebrum' of the state, which implied a strong central administrative system, and his doctrine of non-interference, which implied that most public

---

[30] *Latter-Day Pamphlets*, No. III, in *Works*, XIX, 113, 124.

[31] The same general point was well worked over by Dickens in satires for *Household Words* such as 'The Story of Scarli Tapa and the Forty Thieves' and 'The Toady Tree' (*Collected Papers*, I, 580–7, 594–9). A third such satire, 'Prince Bull, a Fairy Tale', almost certainly echoes Carlyle's 'Downing Street'. Prince Bull directs a Roebuck (alluding to the Roebuck Committee of 1855) to get rid of the bad servants of the crown, but is informed that there are only twenty-five servants to choose from in a nation of twenty-seven millions (*RP*, pp. 544–9). Carlyle similarly demands, 'The most Herculean Ten Men that could be found among the English Twenty-seven Millions, are these?' (*Works*, XIX, 133).

[32] 'Charles Dickens', in *Works*, III, 101.

[33] See Max Weber, *Wirtschaft und Gesellschaft*, Pt. III, ch. vi, trans. and ed. by H. H. Gerth and C. Wright Mills, *From Max Weber: Essays in Sociology* (New York, 1958), p. 226.

administration was harmful or unnecessary.[34] The contradictory attitude toward administration and bureaucracy reflects the ambivalence with which the faith in public opinion fluctuates between democratic and authoritarian attitudes. It is a corollary of the belief that the people can 'force' the government to 'coerce' themselves into being good. Margaret Hale, the intelligent heroine of Mrs. Gaskell's *North and South* once says to Mr. Thornton, a Manchester-school manufacturer who admires Cromwell, 'I am trying to reconcile your admiration of despotism with your respect for other men's independence of character.'[35] Whether Margaret's Christianity and her marriage to Mr. Thornton can bring about this reconciliation is doubtful; but the intellectual inconsistency of the captain of industry has been momentarily exposed.

The important result of this wavering between advocacy of more government and of less, is the increased respect for the role of the military and of the police. Though Dickens worried that 'the old cannon-smoke and blood-mists' of war with Russia would distract the English people from needed reforms at home, he concurred in the popular feeling 'that Russia MUST BE stopped, and that the future peace of the world renders the war imperative upon us'.[36] In this period his public speeches begin to be embroidered with toasts to the army and navy;[37] and in one letter he writes of the union between 'Defence' and 'Home, love, children, mother', as 'one of the most natural, significant, and plain in the world'.[38] His sentiments about military courage and simplicity are displayed in the Christmas story for 1857, 'The Perils of Certain English Prisoners', in which the good faith and decision of the soldiers, and the beauty and heroism of their womenfolk, are laboriously contrasted with the fumbling and indirection of civil authority. When the cargo of a sinking sloop, threatened by pirates, has been hastily unloaded on the beach by orders of Captain Maryon, Commissioner Pordage protests, 'No docu-

---

[34] T. H. Huxley, 'Administrative Nihilism', in *Collected Essays*, 9 vols. (New York, 1894), I, 269–72.

[35] *North and South*, Knutsford Edition (London, 1906), ch. xv, p. 145. The novel appeared in *Household Words* in 1854–5.

[36] To Mrs. Richard Watson, 1 Nov. 1854, *Letters*, II, 603; to W. F. de Cerjat, 3 Jan. 1858, II, 615.

[37] See especially his addresses to the Commercial Travellers' Schools, 30 Dec. 1854 and 22 Dec. 1859, *Speeches*, pp. 170–1, 288–9.

[38] To W. H. Wills, 4 July 1853, *Letters*, II, 474.

ments have passed, no memoranda have been made, no entries and counter-entries appear in the official muniments. This is indecent.' More significantly, though the pirates 'have despoiled our countrymen of their property, burnt their homes, barbarously murdered them and their little children, and worse than murdered their wives and daughters', Commissioner Pordage seems to believe that no violence should be used in retaliation: 'Captain Carton, I give you notice. Government requires you to treat the enemy with great delicacy, consideration, clemency, and forbearance.'[39] 'Government' emerges as not only incompetent and obstructive but perversely criminal in its reluctance to extirpate the pirates.

The contrast between Commissioner Pordage and the honest soldiers is the same that is implicit in Dickens's admiration for the Metropolitan Police. For, as Orwell and House have both argued, Dickens's respect for the police becomes most significant when compared with his contempt for every other kind of official.[40] He exaggerated the ingenuity and efficiency of the police—in the portraits of Inspector Bucket in *Bleak House* and the Night-Inspector in *Our Mutual Friend*, but also in his reporting on the police in *Household Words*.[41] Where the usefulness of the police is called in doubt, it is only because there are not enough of them on the job, or because they are not empowered to punish offenders swiftly and directly. By 1868 Dickens was arguing in *All the Year Round* that, because of the merely 'contemplative' attitude of the Police System, 'the Ruffian becomes one of the established orders of the body politic'.

It is to the saving up of the Ruffian class by the Magistracy and Police —to the conventional preserving of them, as if they were Partridges— that their number and audacity must be in great part referred. Why is a notorious Thief and a Ruffian ever left at large? He never turns his liberty to any account but violence and plunder, he never did a day's work out of gaol, he never will do a day's work out of gaol. As a proved notorious Thief he is always consignable to prison for three months. When he comes out, he is surely as notorious a Thief as he was when he went in. Then send him back again. 'Just Heaven!' cries the Society

[39] *CS*, pp. 172–3, 179.
[40] George Orwell, 'Charles Dickens', *A Collection of Essays* (New York, 1954), p. 74; House, pp. 201–3.
[41] See 'The Detective Police', 'Three "Detective" Anecdotes', 'On Duty with Inspector Field', and 'Down with the Tide', *RP*, pp. 485–536.

for the protection of remonstrant Ruffians. 'This is equivalent to a sentence of perpetual imprisonment!' Precisely for that reason it has my advocacy. I demand to have the Ruffian kept out of my way, and out of the way of all decent people. I demand to have the Ruffian employed, perforce, in hewing wood and drawing water somewhere for the general service, instead of hewing at her Majesty's subjects and drawing their watches out of their pockets. If this be termed an unreasonable demand, then the tax-gatherer's demand on me must be far more unreasonable, and cannot be otherwise than extortionate and unjust.[42]

The added fillip against taxation at the end of this paragraph tells us immediately where to look for the theoretic ground of Dickens's authoritarian indignation: namely, in the doctrine of non-interference. The argument that minimizes the role of the state ironically stresses the role of the police. Since liberty should be interfered with only when it imposes on the liberty of another individual, it seems, even in theory, that all the state need consist of are some policemen to keep the ruffians 'out of my way, and out of the way of all decent people'. In his indictment of legislation Buckle writes, 'with the exception of certain necessary enactments respecting the preservation of order, and the punishment of crime, nearly everything that has been done, has been done amiss.'[43] The exceptions are significant.

Dickens's earlier concern with prison reform, which weighed one kind of punishment against another, and genuinely pondered the aims of punishment, dwindles to a sense of outrage that criminals have a better time of it than honest men. The ironic exhibition of Uriah Heep and Littimer as 'Model Prisoners' at the end of *David Copperfield* is a sign of this change.[44] 'We have come to this absurd, this dangerous, this monstrous pass,' Dickens now exclaims, 'that the dishonest felon is, in respect of cleanliness, order, diet, and accommodation, better provided for, and taken care of, than the honest pauper.'[45] But this protest reflects the wider logic of his political position. A faith in public

[42] 'The Ruffian', UT, pp. 304, 301–2.

[43] Buckle, I, 201.

[44] The fate of Heep and Littimer was undoubtedly influenced by Carlyle's attack on prison reform in the spring of 1850: see 'Model Prisons', *Latter-Day Pamphlets*, No. II, in *Works*, XIX, 61–103. Dickens's article in *Household Words*, 'Pet Prisoners', 27 Apr. 1850 (*Collected Papers*, I, 278–91) was presumably also inspired by Carlyle.

[45] 'A Walk in a Workhouse', RP, p. 539.

opinion as the moving force for good in society places a heavy burden on men as individuals—their intelligence, their good will, their patience, and self-restraint. Faith in 'The People' is therefore a faith that is morally hypersensitive. Since the burden of wisdom and restraint may simply be refused by ignorant or ill-intentioned persons, it must be shouldered by those who are morally most deserving. Moreover, though the doctrine of public opinion may be preached without condescension and often is, it is usually preached by those who believe themselves to be sincerely engaged in the practice of restraint that it imposes. No wonder that, to the degree that people do voluntarily obey the dictates of public opinion, the individual who is deaf to its moral appeal is likely to be execrated. Those who defy opinion take advantage of those who submit to it; those who litter the streets with rubbish seem to be mocking those who restrain themselves. Towards the end of his life Freud rather poignantly observed that one who chooses to obey the command of civilization to love his neighbour as himself, merely 'puts himself at a disadvantage beside all those who set it at naught'.[46] Dickens expressed this frustration very succinctly: 'we are all of us powerless against the Ruffian, because we submit to the law, and it is his only trade, by superior force and violence, to defy it.'[47]

Viewed critically, policemen are an admission that public opinion is neither uniform nor omnipotent. Spencer and Buckle did not worry very much on this account; for them public opinion was an approximate statement of the very complex condition of society at any given time. The violations of this opinion were only wrinkles, to be ironed out in the process of slow but inevitable adaptation. 'Evil perpetually tends to disappear,' Spencer assured the readers of *Social Statics*. 'Always toward perfection is the mighty movement—towards a complete development and a more unmixed good; subordinating in its universality all petty irregularities and fallings back, as the curvature of the earth subordinates mountains and valleys.'[48] Though this argument overlooks how mountains must appear to a man standing in the valley, it has a millennial appeal. Science will reveal history, and history, whatever we may imagine to the contrary, contains no contradictions. The last words of Buckle's

[46] *Civilization and its Discontents*, trans. Joan Rivière (London, 1957), p. 140.
[47] 'The Ruffian', *UT*, p. 308.   [48] *Social Statics*, pp. 59, 293.

History of Civilization in England are a paean to this faith: 'it shall be clearly seen, that, from the beginning there has been no discrepancy, no incongruity, no disorder, no interruption, no interference; but that all the events which surround us, even to the furthest limits of the material creation, are but different parts of a single scheme, which is permeated by one glorious principle of universal and undeviating regularity.'[49]

The evidence that Dickens, too, believed in progress seems incontrovertible. In each of his fictions that are deliberately 'historical' the past is compared unfavourably with the present. 'Mr. Pickwick's Tale' records that in the time of James I 'nothing was abroad but cruelty, violence, and disorder'; and *A Tale of Two Cities* portrays pre-revolutionary France as priest-ridden, England beset with criminals, and both nations foolishly ruled.[50] Dickens's main idea of earlier periods seems to have been that they suffered from inferior law enforcement—the idea that he turns round at the end of his life to apply to the present. His supposed nostalgia for stage-coaching days has to be set against his explicit scorn for the 'good old times': 'If ever I destroy myself,' he wrote to Douglas Jerrold in 1843, 'it will be in the bitterness of hearing those infernal and damnably good old times extolled.'[51] He took a normal pride in industrial advances, and in the Birmingham speech in which he announced his political creed he defended technological progress in general, and repudiated the pejorative use of 'material age' to characterize the nineteenth century.[52] For all this, however, Dickens was not able to submerge his political uncertainty in the evolutionary stream of natural history, in the manner of Spencer and Buckle. The developmental thesis shows up only indirectly in his work, and he was temperamentally unable to appreciate the doctrine of survival of the fittest. Dickens, who could muster a personal and self-righteous cruelty, had only antipathy for a Malthusian or Spencerian cruelty inherent in the nature of things. His idea of progress was just coherent enough to sharpen his sense of frustration, and to blunt the edge of his satire.

[49] Buckle, II, 472. With a slight shift of focus, Buckle's determined negation of discrepancy, incongruity, disorder, etc. may seem anxious or frightened rather than triumphant.

[50] *MHC*, ch. iii, p. 72; *TTC*, Bk. I, ch. i.

[51] 3 May 1843, *Letters*, I, 517.

[52] *Speeches*, p. 404.

Dickens's inability to define a political creed finally comes
down to the doubly ironic proposition that whatever is wrong is
'Nobody's Fault'. 'Nobody' is ironic because it stands for some-
body, and doubly ironic because Dickens finally does not know
who that somebody may be: it may as well be nobody after all.
The impasse that he has reached is evident when he writes in
Household Words that Nobody is 'the great irresponsible, guilty,
wicked, blind giant of this time'. If Nobody were the satiric
name of an identifiable target, the irony would make sense. But
Nobody is nobody, the vaguely defined 'people governing', the
Establishment, as it is called today, and sometimes 'The
People', who are responsible for public opinion. 'Nobody has
done more harm in this single generation than Everybody can
mend in ten generations. Come, responsible Somebody; ac-
countable Blockhead, come!'[53] The irony seems to have been
borrowed by Samuel Smiles:

When typhus or cholera breaks out, they tell us that Nobody is to
blame.
     That terrible Nobody! How much he has to answer for. More mis-
chief is done by Nobody than by all the world besides. Nobody adul-
terates our food. Nobody poisons us with bad drink. Nobody supplies
us with foul water. Nobody spreads fever in blind alleys and unswept
lanes. Nobody leaves towns undrained. Nobody fills jails, peniten-
tiaries and convict stations. Nobody makes poachers, thieves, and
drunkards.[54]

Since Smiles goes on to identify Nobody's theoretical justification as that of *laissez-faire*, he is apparently making a much less
ambiguous charge than Dickens. The ambiguity is restored
when one recalls that Smiles is the Victorian prophet of self-help,
not of state interference.

     As Stephen Blackpool concludes, in *Hard Times*, it's 'A mud-
dle! Aw a muddle!' Science and journalism—and the faith in

---

[53] 'Nobody, Somebody, and Everybody', 30 Aug. 1856, *Collected Papers*, I,
659–60.
[54] *Thrift* (London, 1880), p. 337. Another apparent borrowing from Dickens
is the extended conceit that, just as surely as knowledge is power, 'Ignorance is
Power'. Cf. *Thrift*, pp. 57–8 with Dickens, *Speeches*, p. 82. The issue of precedence
here is somewhat mysterious: Dickens spoke to the Mechanics' Institution at Leeds
on 1 Dec. 1847, but Smiles also lectured working men at Leeds in the 1840s. The
preface (1875) to *Thrift* claims that 'Much of this book was written, and some of it
published, years ago.' See also Asa Briggs, *Victorian People* (Chicago, 1955), ch. v.

progress—have conspired against satire as a way of responding
to the evils of the nineteenth century. The alienation of urban
life, the unrelatedness of people and the interrelatedness of the
city as a functional system, the sense that the problems are too
many and too complex, that they grow at a rate with which it is
impossible to keep up, throw a heavy burden on political organization. But in the metropolis there is no political organization
to receive the burden; and still less of confidence in politics.
What is yearned for is a confidence that will transcend uncertainty and pain, that will heal even the city-dweller's ulcerous
hatred of politics, that will make politics unnecessary now, without waiting for the Spencerian millennium. Everything points
to some religious solution, in fact: perhaps the star that has
brought hope to Stephen Blackpool at the bottom of the mine-
shaft. 'Often as I coom to myseln, and found it shinin on me
down there in my trouble, I thowt it were the star as guided to
Our Saviour's home. I awmust think it be the very star!' But at
that point Stephen dies.[55]

In a late article for *All the Year Round* that touches on 'lazy
tacit police connivance with professional crime', Dickens recorded another of his extraordinary encounters with the people
of London. He stumbles over a wretched child and gives it a coin,
only to be surrounded in an instant by fifty more, of both sexes.
'The piece of money I had put into the claw of the child I had
overturned was clawed out of it, and was again clawed out of
that wolfish gripe, and again out of that, and soon I had no
notion in what part of the obscene scuffle in the mud, of rags and
legs and arms and dirt, the money might be.' A policeman comes
to his rescue—'a genuine police constable', Dickens sarcastically
writes—and the children scatter in all directions. There follows
this speculation on the history of the earth:

I looked at him, and I looked about at the disorderly traces in the mud,
and I thought of the drops of rain and the footprints of an extinct
creature, hoary ages upon ages old, that geologists have identified on
the face of a clift; and this speculation overcame me: If this mud could
petrify at this moment, and could lie concealed here for ten thousand
years, I wonder whether the race of men then to be our successors on
the earth could, from these or any marks, by the utmost force of the

---

[55] *HT*, Bk. III, ch. vi, pp. 272–3, 274.

human intellect, unassisted by tradition, deduce such an astounding inference as the existence of a polished state of society that bore with the
public savagery of neglected children in the streets of its capital city,
and was proud of its power by sea and land, and never used its power
to seize and save them!

The 'claws' of the children and their 'obscene scuffle' in the mud
are obviously related to the evolution of society and the struggle
for survival. That they are encountered thus in the stream of
geological time is not a happy discovery for Dickens; his vision
is all the more dismal in comparison with Buckle's worship of the
'glorious principle . . . of regularity'. Significantly enough, yet
oddly for Dickens, the state power to which he appeals is symbolized in the next paragraph by Newgate Prison:

After this, when I came to the Old Bailey and glanced up it towards
Newgate, I found that the prison had an inconsistent look. There
seemed to be some unlucky inconsistency in the atmosphere that day;
for though the proportions of St. Paul's Cathedral are very beautiful,
it had an air of being somewhat out of drawing, in my eyes. I felt as
though the cross were too high up, and perched upon the intervening
golden ball too far away.[56]

And the inconsistency extends to St. Paul's; the failure to ad-
minister London effectively is associated with a failure of religion. The cross of institutional Christianity is too remote, and
there is an 'intervening golden ball'. Dickens borrowed the
symbolism and part of the innuendo from his own more memorable vision of the crossing sweeper in *Bleak House*: 'And there
he sits, munching and gnawing, and looking up at the great
Cross on the summit of St. Paul's Cathedral, glittering above a
red and violet-tinted cloud of smoke. From the boy's face one
might suppose that sacred emblem to be, in his eyes, the crowning confusion of the great, confused city; so golden, so high up,
so far out of his reach.'[57]

[56] 'On an Amateur Beat', *UT*, pp. 346–7.
[57] *BH*, ch. xix, p. 271.

Part Two

THE EARTHLY CITY

Of these two first parents of the human race, then, Cain was the first-born, and he belonged to the city of men; after him was born Abel, who belonged to the city of God. . . . When these two cities began to run their course by a series of deaths and births, the citizen of this world was the first-born, and after him the stranger in this world, the citizen of the city of God, predestined by grace, elected by grace, by grace a stranger below, and by grace a citizen above. . . . Accordingly, it is recorded of Cain that he built a city, but Abel, being a sojourner, built none.

—St. Augustine, *The City of God*

IV

DEATH AND MONEY

THE city of satire, the city of medicine and engineering, of compassionate journalism and political despair, coincided in the nineteenth-century imagination with still another city. Dickens and his contemporaries were steeped in the Christian tradition—Pauline, Augustinian, and Puritan—of two cities: the earthly city of men and the city of God. The first confirmed their view of the contemporary historical city; the second could be no more than a promise.

> Now faith is the substance of things hoped for, the evidence of things not seen. . . . By faith Abel offered unto God a more excellent sacrifice than Cain, by which he obtained witness that he was righteous. . . . By faith Abraham, when he was called to go out into a place which he should after receive for an inheritance, obeyed; and he went out, not knowing where he went, not knowing whither he went. By faith he sojourned in the land of promise, as in a strange country, dwelling in tabernacles with Isaac and Jacob, the heirs of him of the same promise: For he looked for a city which hath foundations, whose builder and maker is God.

As the early church moved from the rural setting of the gospels to urban enclaves within the Roman world, the myth of two cities proved an attractive one. The conclusion in the Epistle to the Hebrews that 'here have we no continuing city, but we seek one to come',[1] geographically symbolized the path of hoped-for salvation. And condemnation of the earthly city may have been linked with satire as early as the fourth century: 'Jerome can rarely mention the contemporary world without adding the portrayal of silken garments, gluttonous banquets, and marble-encrusted buildings.'[2]

The hold of this symbolism was still strong in the nineteenth century, though it was often ironically invoked. Matthew

---

[1] Hebrews 11:1–10; 13:14.
[2] David Wiesen, *St. Jerome as a Satirist* (Ithaca, 1964), p. 61.

Arnold writes of the metropolis: 'And the work which we collective children of God do, our grand centre of life, our *city* which we have builded for us to dwell in, is London! London, with its unutterable external hideousness, and with its internal canker of *publicè egestas, privatim opulentia,*—to use the words which Sallust puts into Cato's mouth about Rome,—unequalled in the world!'[3] Here one may say that Arnold's Hellenism is balanced by his Hebraism, the classical allusion introduced by Biblical phrasing, by the emphasis on '*city*', and by the ironic 'collective children of God'. The persistence of religious terminology in more casual contexts is probably more significant. It was, for example, perfectly common to refer to London as Babylon. When Arthur Pendennis, Thackeray's hero, moves to London, the chapter is entitled 'Babylon'; and about the same time Mr. Micawber is introducing young David Copperfield to 'the arcana of the Modern Babylon'. If one stops to think of them, a whole range of casual expressions reflects the tradition of the two cities: the sunlight and shadow striking 'bars of the prison of this lower world' at the end of *Little Dorrit*; or the remark in *Barnaby Rudge* that London is 'visible in the darkness by its own faint light, and not by that of Heaven'.[4]

The Pilgrim's Progress was by far the most popular exposition of this tradition for English Protestantism, and the epitome of the wayfaring metaphor in Puritan literature.[5] The influence of this work is hard to pin down, but at least one Victorian novel, *The Old Curiosity Shop*, is visibly modelled on Bunyan's allegory. 'The two pilgrims,' Dickens writes of Little Nell and her grandfather, 'often pressing each other's hands, or exchanging a smile or cheerful look, pursued their way in silence'—almost as if he were writing of Christian and Faithful on their journey from the City of Destruction to the Celestial City.

This quarter passed, they came upon the haunts of commerce and great traffic, where many people were resorting, and business was already rife. The old man looked about him with a startled and bewildered gaze, for these were places that he hoped to shun. He pressed his finger on his lip, and drew the child along by narrow courts and winding ways, nor did he seem at ease until they had left it far behind,

---

[3] *Culture and Anarchy*, ed. J. Dover Wilson (Cambridge, 1963), p. 59.
[4] *DC*, ch. xi, p. 156; *LD*, Bk. II, ch. xxx, p. 763; *BR*, ch. iii, p. 26.
[5] See William Haller, *The Rise of Puritanism* (New York, 1957), pp. 146–50.

often casting a backward look towards it, murmuring that ruin and
self-murder were crouching in every street, and would follow if they
scented them; and that they could not fly too fast. . . .

This was a wide, wide track—for the humble followers of the camp
of wealth pitch tents round about it for many a mile. . . .[6]

Bunyan's repudiation of the earthly city is based on the saying
of Paul that 'the end of those things is death', and indirectly on
Calvin's interpolation that 'death is owing to men's deserts but
life rests solely upon God's mercy'.[7] From the moment Christian
flees from his home crying 'Life! life! eternal life!' to the river
of death that flows before the gates of the celestial city, we
understand that this is an allegory of death. He cannot be saved
until he dies; but the life that he has fled is another form of
death. The hurry and activity, the commerce, even the emotional
ties of the city of destruction are so many signs of death, which
will soon bring all to a stop. Similarly, Nell and her grandfather
are travelling toward death, but away from destructive death
(and wealth) in the city. The earthly city primarily signifies
death.[8]

Countless passages in Dickens associate death with the city.
In *Martin Chuzzlewit* 'the house was quiet as a sepulchre; the
dead of night was coffined in the silent city'; in Tom-all-alone's
of *Bleak House* 'every door might be Death's Door'; on the
Sabbath in *Little Dorrit* the bells toll 'as if the Plague were in
the city and the deadcarts were going round'.[9] There is, for
Dickens, a felt personal dimension to this association. In
Nicholas Nickleby, with morbid irony, Tim Linkinwater defends
London against the country in terms of a few hyacinths growing
in an attic window opposite him. 'Are there any country flowers
that could interest me like these, do you think?' The hyacinths
are grown in old blacking bottles by a sickly hump-backed boy
who is dying. Dickens seems to be perversely indulging himself
here, not only because the blacking bottles call to mind the early
experience that fretted him so long and so intensely, but because

[6] *OCS*, ch. xv, pp. 114–15.
[7] Romans 6:21; Calvin, *Institutes of the Christian Religion*, ed. John T. McNeill,
trans. Ford Lewis Battles, 2 vols. (Philadelphia, 1960), Bk. III, ch. xiv, sec. 21.
[8] In 'A December Vision', *Collected Papers*, I, 335–9, Dickens writes a short
dream-vision of his own in which Death sweeps over the city.
[9] *MC*, ch. xxv, p. 413; *BH*, ch. viii, pp. 96–7; *LD*, Bk. I, ch. iii, p. 28.

sometimes his heroes imagine themselves as dead or dying in childhood.[10] Yet this degree of morbidity the novelist was ready to share with his public; the inspiration may have been private, but its expression was sanctioned by the folklore of the city and its association with death. How else could the beginning writer presume to conclude a story: 'The boy raised himself by a violent effort, and folded his hands together—"Mother! dear, dear mother, bury me in the open fields—anywhere but in these dreadful streets. I should like to be where you can see my grave, but not in these close crowded streets; they have killed me; kiss me again, mother; put your arm round my neck——"'?[11] The association appealed to by the apprentice Dickens is essentially the same as that to which Henry James appeals seventy years later near the end of his career. In *The Wings of the Dove* the 'grey immensity of London' symbolizes the 'grey immensity' of death for Milly Theale, as she leaves the offices of Sir Luke Strett and walks alone in the city. At this juncture James even compares his fabulously wealthy heroine, the 'heiress of all the ages', to a girl with her rent to pay, as if she were spiritually related in the city of destruction to humble virgins of all classes.[12]

The association of death with the city was reinforced in the nineteenth century by specific data neither religious nor literary in origin. The death-rate in large towns was known to be measurably higher than in the country; and the urban death-rate leaped dramatically in the 1840s—whether because of worsening conditions or because of civil registration of deaths.[13] Dickens takes such data for granted when he writes, in *Bleak House*, 'It is a fine steaming night to turn the slaughter-houses, the

[10] *NN*, ch. xl, pp. 514–15. Some of the dead children in the novels are patently representations of the hero, most notably the dead child of Murdstone and the hero's mother in *DC* who 'was myself' (ch. ix, p. 133). Sydney Carton entertains a similar fancy: 'I am like one who died young. All my life might have been' (*TTC*, Bk. II, ch. xiii, p. 143). The infant Esther Summerson was actually left for stillborn: 'I had never, to my own mother's knowledge, breathed—had been buried—had never been endowed with life—had never borne a name' (*BH*, ch. xxxvi, p. 513).

[11] 'Our Next-Door Neighbour', *SB*, p. 46.

[12] *The Wings of the Dove*, Bk. V, ch. iv, pp. 247, 253. All quotations from James are from the New York Edition (New York, 1907–9).

[13] See Griffith, *Population Problems*, pp. 185–8; and Barbara Hammond, 'Urban Death Rates in the Early Nineteenth Century', *Economic History*, I (Jan. 1928), 419–28.

unwholesome trades, the sewerage, bad water, and burial-grounds to account, and give the Registrar of Deaths some extra business.'[14] Like many anxious observers of welfare practices then and now, he was also under the misapprehension that the city attracted the old and destitute in numbers disproportionate to the young and ambitious. The city becomes a huge 'receiver', as he calls it in *Hard Times*,[15] for bodies dead or alive. From her house on the great north road in *Dombey and Son* Harriet Carker watches the poor trudging toward London:

Day after day, such travellers crept past, but always, as she thought, in one direction—always towards the town. Swallowed up in one phase or other of its immensity, towards which they seemed impelled by a desperate fascination, they never returned. Food for the hospitals, the churchyards, the prisons, the river, fever, madness, vice, and death,—they passed on to the monster, roaring in the distance, and were lost.[16]

Here the 'monster' serves as a figure for both the city and death, and 'lost' means both lost to sight and not saved.

The rapid growth of London contributed a special luridness to the association of the city with death. Sheer numbers, as it were, confirmed the surprise of Dante that death could undo so many. One observer of early nineteenth-century London, for example, imagines a man looking from the dome of St. Paul's and thinking 'that in those houses and streets there are no fewer than two millions of his fellow-beings, and yet of this vast number, though now as bustling as if this world were to be their eternal home, there will not, in all probability, ere the lapse of a century, be one solitary individual whose body is not moldering in the dust'.[17] The young Tennyson's melancholy was similarly affected by the city: 'He remembered how, when in London almost for the first time, one of these moods came over him, as he realized that "in a few years all its inhabitants would be lying horizontal, stark and stiff in their coffins".'[18] No wonder that Little Nell, glancing from her window in the curiosity shop, 'would perhaps see a man passing with a coffin on his

[14] *BH*, ch. xxxii, p. 444.
[15] *HT*, Bk. I, ch. x, p. 63.
[16] *D & S*, ch. xxxiii, p. 480.
[17] [James Grant], *The Great Metropolis*, 2 vols. (New York, 1837), I, 19.
[18] Hallam Tennyson, *Alfred Lord Tennyson: A Memoir*, 2 vols. (New York and London, 1898), I, 40.

back, and two or three others silently following him to a house
where somebody lay dead', and then begin to dream of her
grandfather's blood creeping, creeping beneath her bedroom
door.[19] The larger the city, in point of fact, the more persons
are dying around one, in the near vicinity, every day. But if one
compresses time and thinks strictly in terms of space in the city,
the number of dead has long ago outnumbered that of the living.
This thought, too, occurs to Dickens:

it was a solemn consideration what enormous hosts of dead belong to
one old great city, and how, if they were raised while the living slept,
there would not be the space of a pin's point in all the streets and ways
for the living to come out into. Not only that, but the vast armies of
dead would overflow the hills and valleys beyond the city, and would
stretch away all round it, God knows how far.[20]

Nor is the population of the dead in cities an altogether fanci-
ful question. One does not have to believe in ghosts, but merely
in the law of the conservation of matter, to come up against a
very different aspect of the problem. No tampering with time
and no dualistic belief of any kind is necessary to realize the
problem of where the mortal bodies of the dead must go. The
problem of where bodies went in London became acute by the
middle of the century. Interment was historically a responsibility
of parishes, but parish churchyards in the metropolis had finite
dimensions. The burial ground near Tom-all-alone's in *Bleak
House*, where Jo saw Nemo's corpse being stomped on to get
it under ground, had its original in a burial ground near Drury
Lane that was by no means unique.[21] The sanitarians of Dickens's
day understandably called for the prohibition of burial in the
most crowded districts of London; but sextons and undertakers
and some preachers jealously defended the right of every man,
woman, and child to be buried in his own churchyard. 'No
General Interments. Carrion for ever!' Dickens mocked in
Household Words, and his sarcasm can still be felt in *Our Mutual
Friend* when he writes of the churchyard where Bradley Headstone forces himself on Lizzie Hexam: 'Here, conveniently and

19 *OCS*, ch. ix, p. 69.
20 'Night Walks', *UT*, p. 133.
21 *BH*, ch. xi, pp. 151–2; ch. xvi, p. 225; see *Letters*, III, 642 (to Miss Palfrey,
4 Apr. 1868) and Trevour Blount, 'The Graveyard Satire in *Bleak House* in the
Context of 1850', *Review of English Studies*, XIV (1963), 370–8.

healthfully elevated above the level of the living, were the dead, and the tombstones.'[22]

To meet this real problem a Necropolis Company was founded in 1851, for the purpose of opening a cemetery outside London. The company went bankrupt three years later.[23] What the controversy over intramural interments ultimately established was that the city was already a kind of necropolis.

A solemn consideration, when I enter a great city by night, that every one of those darkly clustered houses encloses its own secret; that every room in every one of them encloses its own secret; that every beating heart in the hundreds of thousands of breasts there, is, in some of its imaginings, a secret to the heart nearest it! Something of the awfulness, even of Death itself, is referable to this. No more can I turn the leaves of this dear book that I loved, and vainly hope in time to read it all. No more can I look into the depths of this unfathomable water, wherein, as momentary lights glanced into it, I have had glimpses of buried treasure and other things submerged. It was appointed that the book should shut with a spring, for ever and for ever, when I had read but a page. It was appointed that the water should be locked in an eternal frost, when the light was playing on its surface, and I stood in ignorance on the shore. My friend is dead, my neighbour is dead, my love, the darling of my soul, is dead; it is the inexorable consolation and perpetuation of the secret that was always in that individuality, and which I shall carry in mine to my life's end. In

[22] 8 June 1850, *Collected Papers*, I, 251; *OMF*, Bk. II, ch. xv, p. 394. At a meeting in 1850 at which Dickens was also a speaker, Lord Ashley remarked, 'Under a surface of ground not amounting to 250 acres there had been interred within thirty years in the metropolis far more than 1,500,000 human beings. What must be the condition of the atmosphere affected by the exhalations from that surface?' (quoted by Jephson, *Sanitary Evolution*, p. 63). The argument echoed Chadwick: 'In the metropolis, on spaces of ground which do not exceed 203 acres, closely surrounded by the abodes of the living, layer upon layer, each consisting of a population numerically equivalent to a large army of 20,000 adults, and nearly 30,000 youths and children, is every year imperfectly interred. Within the period of the existence of the present generation, upwards of a million dead must have been interred in those same spaces.' Chadwick's respect for the temporal dimension of the problem is correctly scientific; his equal respect for the gaseous state of matter brings him to a vision as graphic as that of Dickens, in which the souls of the dead overflow into the hills and valleys beyond the city: 'A layer of bodies is stated to be about seven years in decaying in the metropolis; to the extent that this is so, the decay must be by the conversion of the remains into a gas, and its escape, as a miasma, of many times the bulk of the body that has disappeared.' *A Supplementary Report on the Results of a Special Inquiry into the Practice of Interment in Towns* (London, 1843), p. 27.

[23] Finer, *Edwin Chadwick*, pp. 413, 420.

any of the burial-places of this city through which I pass, is there a
sleeper more inscrutable than its busy inhabitants are, in their innermost personality, to me, or than I am to them?[24]

In this meditation from *A Tale of Two Cities* Dickens stresses his
conviction of the final 'secret' or separateness of human beings,
intensified by their isolation in the great city. But it is note-
worthy how rapidly this separateness is referred to the separateness of death, and how death is regarded in this context with
finality, as destruction or the stopping of time for each person.

Along with the thought that the living of the city are already
dead is the possibility that the dead are painfully alive—or not
dead enough, like Palinurus. Both ideas are morbidly struck off
in the opening pages of *The Old Curiosity Shop*. Master Humphrey's thoughts are weighed down with 'crowds for ever
passing and repassing on the bridges', with the Thames winding
slowly to sea, and dreams of 'loung[ing] away one's life . . . in a
dull, slow, sluggish barge', with drowning and suicide—all
images of life equivalent to death. At the same time his thoughts
turn to the horrors of a death that is conscious:

That constant pacing to and fro, that never-ending restlessness, that
incessant tread of feet wearing the rough stones smooth and glossy—
is it not a wonder how the dwellers in narrow ways can bear to hear it!
Think of a sick man, in such a place as Saint Martin's Court, listening
to the footsteps . . . think of the hum and noise being always present to
his senses, and of the stream of life that will not stop, pouring on, on, on,
through all his restless dreams, as if he were condemned to lie, dead
but conscious, in a noisy churchyard, and had no hope of rest for centuries to come![25]

The sick man in St. Martin's Court is in the same state as the
madman of Tennyson's *Maud*, who fancies himself 'only a yard
beneath the street', subject to an endless beating of hoofs and
passing feet.[26]

Footsteps on the stair in *Dombey and Son* symbolize death;
and Rosa Bud's impression of London in *The Mystery of Edwin
Drood* is that of a 'miserably monotonous noise of shuffling of

[24] *TTC*, Bk. I, ch. iii, p. 10.
[25] *OCS*, ch. i, pp. 1–2.
[26] *Maud*, Pt. II, V, i. In *The Poems of Tennyson* (London, 1969) Christopher
Ricks notes the same parallel and credits J. C. Maxwell. All quotations from Tennyson are from this edition.

feet on hot paving-stones'.[27] Shallow graves and incessant footsteps give Dickens's London something like an image of classical hell. Perhaps it was the sanitary movement, again, that compelled attention to what was happening underground in London, and the exhalations therefrom; but there was, after all, a more ancient tradition of an underground city from which even the sanitary movement did not free itself entirely. As *The Times* reported in 1847, 'To investigate the source of a malaria or stench Mr. Chadwick would swim through the stagnant pools of Avernus and enter the pestiferous jaws of Orcus itself: *per loca foeda situ* he would track the secrets of the nether world, to rescue his Eurydice from the reign of Black Dis.'[28] In the 1850s official reports described the Rotherhithe open sewers as 'Stygian pools', and even Engels permits himself to call the Old Town of Manchester a 'Hell upon Earth'.[29]

Besides its association with death, and its figurative reduction to hell, the earthly city is properly associated with greed and selfishness, and hence with money. According to Augustine, 'two cities have been formed by two loves: the earthly by the love of self, even to the contempt of God; the heavenly by the love of God, even to the contempt of self'. Therefore the earthly city 'has its good in this world, and rejoices in it with such joy as such things can afford'.[30] Whether or not this ancient conclusion was based on objective examination of the Roman world, it would be hard to say; it has never ceased to be prophetic of the accumulation of wealth and power in cities of the modern world. Poor Barnaby Rudge would dearly like to discover some gold to give to his mother, and has looked for gold in the sky, and among the grass and moss of wooded places: he is advised by Stagg, 'It's in the world, bold Barnaby, the merry world; not in solitary places like those you pass your time in, but in crowds, and where there's noise and rattle.'[31] Satire joins in the indictment of cities for wealth and luxury, but stops short of attacking wealth that is venerable and possessed with dignity.

---

[27] *D & S*, ch. lix, pp. 840–1; ch. lxi, pp. 860–1; *MED*, ch. xx, p. 227.

[28] Quoted by Finer, p. 315.

[29] Jephson, p. 101; Engels, *Condition of the Working Class*, p. 53.

[30] *The City of God*, trans. Marcus Dods, 2 vols. (New York, 1948), Bk. XIV, ch. 28; Bk. XV, ch. 4.

[31] *BR*, ch. xlvi, pp. 349–50.

In the Christian view no sort of wealth or worldliness is wholly out of danger, and not even those Protestants whom Max Weber credited with the rise of capitalism ever imagined that they were pursuing money for its own sake.

The underlying religious basis of Dickens's attack on moneyed society is suggested by the satire on worldliness in *Little Dorrit*. Before his fall Merdle, the non-entity who will soon become 'the body of a heavily-made man, with an obtuse head, and coarse, mean, common features', is described as a kind of anti-Christ—or anti-Paul:

> Merdle! O ye sun, moon, and stars, the great man! The rich man, who had in a manner revised the New Testament, and already entered into the kingdom of Heaven. The man who could have any one he chose to dine with him, and who had made the money! As he went up the stairs, people were already posted on the lower stairs, that his shadow might fall upon them when he came down. So were the sick brought out and laid in the track of the Apostle—who had *not* got into the good society, and had *not* made the money.[32]

The rise and fall of Merdle are counterpointed by the fall and rise of William Dorrit. The latter, who begs as self-consciously as he spends ostentatiously, is finally saved; but the point of both story-lines is the final irrelevance of worldly fortune. *Our Mutual Friend* teaches a similarly comprehensive lesson on the deception of riches. The single most prominent relation among the characters of *Our Mutual Friend*, good and bad alike, is that of deception. Money, either to be gained (by adherents of the earthly city) or in some way to be repudiated (by those who hope to be saved) is the motive of deception in each case, and perhaps no other novel of Dickens has so many characters concerned with money and with death.[33] The same novel recalls a fairy-tale in which children, oppressed by adults, must endure until they can free themselves or be set free. Since the older generation—including 'Society' as well as the two fathers, old Harmon and Gaffer Hexam—has devoted itself to money, the young must labour to be free of it. The association of this strug-

[32] *LD*, Bk. II, ch. xxv, p. 705; ch. xvi, p. 614. 'O ye sun, moon, and stars' is a travesty of Psalm 148:3 and the *Benedicite, omnia opera Domini* canticle of *The Book of Common Prayer*.

[33] Cf. J. Hillis Miller, *Charles Dickens: The World of His Novels* (Cambridge, Mass., 1958), p. 316.

gle within the city (through such diverse characters as Hexam
and Fledgeby) is accentuated by the historical coincidence that
the financial centre of the kingdom was, and is, the City of
London proper, hence 'the City'.

Because most English novels of the late eighteenth and nineteenth centuries are novels of courtship, repudiation of money or
worldliness characteristically demands the rejection of marriage
for money and position: a theme that has been traced in the
novels of Dickens by Ross H. Dabney.[34] Sometimes, as in *Little
Dorrit*, even the confession of disinterested love by both parties
is not sufficient assurance against mercenary marriage. After
Arthur Clennam realizes that he loves Little Dorrit and that she
loves him, he still refuses her hand. If he had realized his love
when she was poor, he says, marriage might have been possible
for them—'But, as it is, I must never touch [your fortune],
never!'[35] Earlier Nicholas Nickleby and his sister congratulated
themselves on rejecting their respective lovers, though to do so
was patently to deny their own love as well as any putative ambition. The chapter is entitled, 'Wherein Nicholas and his Sister
forfeit the good Opinion of all worldly and prudent People'.
Such scruples are imperative on the part of the male, who is empowered to 'raise' the female, but not to live on her income.[36]
They give pause to the naïve assumption that romantic love
between the sexes is the highest value celebrated by the English
novel.

English novelists often constructed plots by which love and
property could be celebrated simultaneously, or even synony-
mously (Scott, Jane Austen, and Trollope, for example).
Nicholas Nickleby follows this conventional solution: Nicholas
and his sister deny not only money but romantic love itself, and
once this ritual has been enacted, the Cheeryble brothers see to
it that love and fortune are theirs forever. *Martin Chuzzlewit*
and *Our Mutual Friend* essentially adhere to the same convention.
In such novels the characters who have grace, as it were, leave
the earthly city behind them; then the novelist decrees that the
rewards of heaven are temporal after all. But this typical procedure does not sit comfortably with Dickens. His endings,

[34] *Love and Property in the Novels of Dickens* (London, 1967).
[35] LD, Bk. II, ch. xxix, p. 760.
[36] Cf. Orwell 'Charles Dickens', pp. 83–5.

taken as a whole, are much more subdued than those of courtship novels generally. And whereas the selflessness of heroes and heroines in Scott, Jane Austen, and Trollope is partly due to certain aristocratic and political motives, the antipathy to money in Dickens is essentially Christian. The plight of Arthur Clennam, who loves Little Dorrit and is loved by her, is also resolved happily, but not through any joint celebration of love and property. The heroine loses her fortune—through the false speculation in which Clennam himself has participated—and returns to the Marshalsea. The words with which Little Dorrit announces her return, the climax of their love, deserve emphasis: 'I have nothing in the world. I am as poor as when I lived here.'[37] Not only *Little Dorrit*, but *Dombey and Son*, *David Copperfield*, *Bleak House*, and *Great Expectations* (either conclusion) are novels notable for their subdued endings as far as money is concerned; *The Old Curiosity Shop* carries unworldliness to its logical extreme. In each of these novels the modest disposal of worldly affairs is prepared for by an experience of loss, humiliation, or suffering among the main characters.

The dust heaps of *Our Mutual Friend*, their supposed value in pounds, shillings, and pence, and the fact that 'dust' is a euphemism for several varieties of human waste, tempt the psychoanalytic critic to relate money in the novels of Dickens to excrement, along the lines indicated by Freud and Ferenczi and publicized by Norman O. Brown.[38] There are not only the ambiguous dust heaps of that novel but 'paper currency which circulates in London when the wind blows' and other casual associations between waste and money. The mud in *Bleak House* 'accumulat[es] at compound interest'; and in Tellson's bank in *A Tale of Two Cities*, 'Your bank-notes had a musty odour, as if they were fast decomposing into rags again. Your plate was stowed away among the neighbouring cesspools, and evil communications corrupted its good polish in a day or two.'[39] Nevertheless, the primary association of money in these novels is with death. The mounds in *Our Mutual Friend* are the legacy of the dead Harmon and his means of manipulating the living. The underground vaults at Tellson's are linked in Jarvis Lorry's

---

[37] *LD*, Bk. II, ch. xxxiv, p. 817.
[38] See Norman O. Brown, *Life against Death* (London, 1959), Pt. V.
[39] *OMF*, Bk. I, ch. xii, p. 144; *BH*, ch. i, p. 1; *TTC*, Bk. II, ch. i, p. 50.

5. *Ludgate Hill*, by Gustave Doré

6. *The Spirit of Love and Truth,* by Joseph Edwards

7. *Time Unveiling Truth,* by George Frederick Watts

half-conscious thoughts with the grave from which Dr. Manette
has been called back to life, and Jerry Cruncher, the unofficial
porter at Tellson's, works evenings as a 'Resurrection-Man', or
trader in corpses. So that if late Dickens novels present a series
of scattered associations between money and excrement, they
continue to play with an earlier association of money and
death.

The common ground of waste, money, and death may well be
the decomposition of the human body. 'Mr. Mould' is the name
chosen for the undertaker in *Martin Chuzzlewit*: 'Deep in the
City, and within the ward of Cheap, stood Mr. Mould's establishment.'[40] Mr. Mould's object, like that of other men of business in the City, is to convert life (that is to say, death) into
money.

At length the day of [Anthony Chuzzlewit's] funeral, pious and
truthful ceremony that it was, arrived. Mr. Mould, with a glass of
generous port between his eye and the light, leaned against the desk
in the little glass office with his gold watch in his unoccupied hand, and
conversed with Mrs. Gamp; two mutes were at the house-door, looking as mournful as could be reasonably expected of men with such a
thriving job in hand; the whole of Mr. Mould's establishment were on
duty within the house or without; feathers waved, horses snorted, silk
and velvets fluttered; in a word, as Mr. Mould emphatically said,
'everything that money could do was done.'

'And what can do more, Mrs. Gamp?' exclaimed the undertaker, as
he emptied his glass and smacked his lips.

'Nothing in the world, sir.'

'Nothing in the world,' repeated Mr. Mould. 'You are right, Mrs.
Gamp. Why do people spend more money:' here he filled his glass
again: 'upon a death, Mrs. Gamp, than upon a birth? Come, that's
in your way; you ought to know. How do you account for that now?'

'Perhaps it is because an undertaker's charges comes dearer than a
nurse's charges, sir,' said Mrs. Gamp, tittering, and smoothing down
her new black dress with her hands. . . .

'So be it,' replied Mr. Mould, 'please Providence. No, Mrs. Gamp;
I'll tell you why it is. It's because the laying out of money with a well-
conducted establishment, where the thing is performed upon the very
best scale, binds the broken heart, and sheds balm upon the wounded
spirit. Hearts want binding, and spirits want balming when people

[40] *MC*, ch. xxv, p. 401.

die: not when people are born. Look at this gentleman to-day [Jonas Chuzzlewit]; look at him.'

'An open-handed gentleman?' cried Mrs. Gamp, with enthusiasm.

'No, no,' said the undertaker; 'not an open-handed gentleman in general, by any means. There you mistake him: but an afflicted gentleman, an affectionate gentleman, who knows what it is in the power of money to do, in giving him relief, and in testifying his love and veneration for the departed. It can give him,' said Mr. Mould, waving his watch-chain slowly round and round, so that he described one circle after every item; 'it can give him four horses to each vehicle; it can give him velvet trappings; it can give him drivers in cloth cloaks and top-boots; it can give him the plumage of the ostrich, dyed black; it can give him any number of walking attendants, dressed in the first style of funeral fashion, and carrying batons tipped with brass; it can give him a handsome tomb; it can give him a place in Westminster Abbey itself, if he choose to invest it in such a purchase. Oh! do not let us say that gold is dross, when it can buy such things as these, Mrs. Gamp.'

The novelist allows us to judge for ourselves what gold can do for the bereaved Jonas—a judgement lightened, to be sure, by this informative dialogue of the nurse and the undertaker. But as for what gold can do for the deceased, we are informed directly: 'Plunge him to the throat in golden pieces now, and his heavy fingers shall not close on one!'[41]

The most ironic (happily ironic) of Dickens's novels, *Martin Chuzzlewit*, portrays the builders of the earthly city in all their glory. The earthly city, according to the tradition, was founded on the love of self, and selfishness, according to Forster, was the theme deliberately chosen by Dickens for this novel.[42] The several incarnations of selfishness in *Martin Chuzzlewit* glibly imagine, like the characters Hold-the-world, Money-love, and Save-all in *The Pilgrim's Progress*, that they are children of Providence and will be saved. The devout Pecksniff, for example, believes that 'Providence, perhaps I may be permitted to say a special Providence', has blessed his efforts to make money, just as Mr. Mould replies 'please Providence' to Mrs. Gamp's perceptive analysis of his higher fees. The satire on the Anglo-Bengalee Disinterested Loan and Life Assurance Company is

---

[41] *MC*, ch. xix, pp. 320–1; ch. xviii, p. 309.
[42] Forster (Bk. VI, ch. ii), II, 19.

apposite in this novel because life insurance is the modern institutional means of anticipating the acts of Providence with money. Jonas Chuzzlewit (who has tried to murder his father) decides to insure his wife with the Company:

'. . . one never knows what may happen to these women, so I'm thinking of insuring her life. It is but fair, you know, that a man should secure some consolation in case of meeting with such a loss.'

'If anything *can* console him under such heart-breaking circumstances,' murmured Tigg [Chairman of the Board at the Anglo-Bengalee], with his eyes shut up as before.

Dickens's satire on the relation of life insurance, money, and death rests on the disparity between the pious tone of the salesman and the worldliness of the proffered consolation. Dr. Jobling, medical examiner for the Company, subtly underlines the point by applying still another interpretation of 'providence' to his dinner: '"Ha!" said the doctor, jocularly, as he rubbed his hands, and drew his chair nearer to the table. "The true Life Assurance, Mr. Montague. The best Policy in the world, my dear sir. We should be provident, and eat and drink whenever we can. Eh, Mr. Crimple?"'[43]

'Money, Paul, can do anything,' in the opinion of the senior partner of Dombey and Son. 'Why didn't money save me my Mama?' replies the son, and Mr. Dombey is sharply taken aback. 'Mr. Dombey . . . expounded to him how that money, though a very potent spirit, never to be disparaged on any account whatever, could not keep people alive whose time was come to die; and how that we must all die, unfortunately, even in the City, though we were never so rich.' For reasons that are not explained, little Paul turns out to be a very different person from his father. Later at Brighton he tells Mrs. Pipchin what he plans to do when he grows up: 'I mean . . . to put my money all together in one Bank, never to try to get any more, go away into the country with my darling Florence, have a beautiful garden, fields, and woods, and live there with her all my life! . . . That's what I mean to do, when I— . . . If I grow up.'[44]

Little Paul is one of the sojourners in the city. He journeys toward death, but away from destructive death, or life that is

[43] *MC*, ch. xx, p. 328; ch. xxvii, pp. 442–3; 436–7.
[44] *D & S*, ch. viii, pp. 92–3; ch. xiv, p. 190.

defined by death. All his money he will invest in one Bank, which is not one of the banks in the City. Ironic in relation to traditional Christianity and veiled in its denotation, the code word 'Bank' typifies Victorian indirection in matters of religious faith.

V

WORK

To compile an exhaustive account of the religious influences on Dickens's life and work would be as nearly impossible as it is unnecessary. The influence of Christianity in the nineteenth century ranges from private feelings to the broadest spirit of public reform, and has been shown by Elie Halévy and others to be a steady force in English history. But where religious influence apparently raises a contradiction between accepted doctrine and fictional theme, it is worth pursuing. Stated values are often transformed or applied selectively when they are expressed by action and the outcome of actions in a novel. If heroes and heroines are sometimes exempt from the standards of judgement that are applied to the generality of characters, it is evidently because who they are and what becomes of them are more important than what they do. The reader of traditional English novels is usually asked to wait and see if his expectation of happiness for a few characters is not confirmed. The suspense of the action is directed toward and resolved by the ending, and the permanent condition of the principal characters commences beyond the ending, as if they belonged to a different city from the one we have been contemplating. Comparison of doctrine and theme is therefore not only of deep interest to the social historian, but an introduction to the way in which such novels mirror the idea of providential design.

Evangelical influence contributed in many ways to make Victorian Christianity a revival of Puritanism: a circumstance that renders Dickens's position doubly confusing. For Dickens is about as fond of Puritanism and Dissent as any English satirist. One has only to recall his hilarious preachers, the Reverends Stiggins and Chadband, the treatment of Little Bethel Chapel in *The Old Curiosity Shop*, or the forbidding picture of Mrs. Clennam in *Little Dorrit*.[1] But satire need not conceal the underlying

[1] See Arthur H. Adrian, 'Dickens and the Brick-and-Mortar Sects,' *Nineteenth-Century Fiction*, X (1955), 188–201.

religious thrust of so much of Dickens's writing—any more than
the hilarious mothers in his novels belie his official respect for
motherhood. David Masson could write in 1859 that 'the philosophy of Dickens may be defined as Anti-Puritanism, whereas
that of Thackeray may be defined as Anti-Snobbism';[2] but the
evidence will show that Dickens was also very much a Puritan,
just as Thackeray's *The Book of Snobs*, by his own admission,
was written 'By One of Themselves'. Humphry House observed that 'Dickens's deep and bitter hatred of evangelicalism
in its most malignant forms was not usually directed against any
of its typical Christian doctrines', and there is no understatement by this critic that needs to be taken more seriously.[3]

The complexity of Dickens's position is immediately evident
in his attitude toward work. For one thing, as a writer, he is
wary of restricting work to production as it is usually understood. A two-fold classification of work, as either deeds or
thought, indirectly emerges in *Little Dorrit*, when he charges
that Merdle has never 'done any good to any one, alive or dead,
or to any earthly thing', *nor* has he thrown any 'ray of light on
any path of duty or diversion, pain or pleasure, toil or rest, fact
or fancy'.[4] This suggests a division of work into useful production
and art—but Dickens is doing more than carving out a niche for
his own profession. The juxtaposition of 'duty' with 'diversion',
and so forth, is anti-Puritan in spirit. Samuel Smiles was the
complete secular translator of Puritan literature, for whom the
lives of the saints became *Lives of the Engineers*; Smiles accepts
the idea that artists may work hard and even introduces a few in
his calendar of successful men, but he squirms uncomfortably
when the question of amusement arises. Dickens was the life-
long champion of amusement. Many of the issues on which his
voice is clearest, his opposition to teetotalism and Sabbath laws,
for example, became clear to him precisely because of his Sleary
philosophy: 'People must be amuthed, Thquire, thomehow . . .
they can't be alwayth a working, nor yet they can't be alwayth a
learning.' And though *Hard Times* argues that unless the poor
are trained in 'the utmost graces of the fancies and affections'

---

[2] 'Dickens and Thackeray', in *British Novelists and Their Styles*, reprinted in
The Dickens Critics, ed. George H. Ford and Lauriat Lane, Jr. (Ithaca, 1961), pp.
32–3.

[3] House, *The Dickens World*, p. 121.

[4] *LD*, Bk. II, ch. xii, p. 556.

there is likely to be a 'wolfish' revolution some day, Dickens's main position here is one of basic kindness, riled by Puritanism.[5]

But with this important qualification, he endorses a Puritan doctrine of work, renewed by Evangelicalism and by *laissez-faire* for the nineteenth century. The Victorians tirelessly preached the necessity of work and of 'earnestness'—the term that conveys their sense of the importance of work to character. One of the few virtues within reach of the lower classes, work can be safely recommended to all classes. As Smiles urged, even peers of the realm might earn distinction through work—indeed, one might rise to the peerage by hard work. 'Energy enables a man to force his way through irksome drudgery and dry details, and carries him onward and upward in every station of life,' reads the gospel of *Self-Help*. 'It accomplishes more than genius, with not one half the disappointment and peril. It is not eminent talent that is required to insure success in any purpose,—not merely the power to achieve, but the will to labour energetically and perseveringly. Hence energy of will may be defined to be the very central power of character in a man,—in a word, it is the Man himself.'[6] Edgar Johnson's biography has shown how much of Dickens's own career can be reduced to 'energy of will'. At Birmingham in 1869 Dickens held up that career as an illustration of the value of work, arguing, with Smiles, the predominance of work over talent as well as class: 'My own invention and imagination, such as it is, I can most truthfully assure you, would never have served me as it has, but for the habit of commonplace, humble, patient, daily, toiling, drudging attention. [*Applause.*] Genius, vivacity, quickness of penetration, brilliancy in association of ideas . . . will not be commanded; but attention, after due term of submissive service, always will.'[7] He was essentially repeating the autobiographical sentiment of *David Copperfield*, where the writer speaks of his determination to learn shorthand: 'I never could have done what I have done, without the habits of punctuality, order, and diligence, without the determination to concentrate myself on one object at a time . . . I have always been thoroughly in earnest . . . there is no substitute for thorough-going, ardent, and sincere earnestness.'[8]

---

[5] *HT*, Bk. I, ch. vi, p. 41; Bk. II, ch. vi, pp. 162–3.

[6] *Self-Help* (Boston, 1861), p. 203.

[7] *Speeches*, p. 406.   [8] *DC*, ch. xlii, p. 606.

This typical Victorian sentiment, derived from Puritanism and seconded by business enterprise, was ironically intensified by religious doubt.[9] The Puritans had always recognized that hard work might assuage the still harder doubt of salvation. The generations of the eighteenth century and after were exposed to more and more public doubt, not merely of salvation, but of the continuance of life after death in any form. Hence the assuagement of work in the nineteenth century is typically urged, even by transcendentalists like Carlyle, on the grounds that death awaits each one of us. The climax of *Sartor Resartus*, a study of philosophical idealism, is preached on that favourite Victorian text, 'Whatsoever thy hand findeth to do, do it with thy might; for there is no work, nor device, nor knowledge, nor wisdom, in the grave, whither thou goest.'[10] If there is no purpose beyond life, or doubtful purpose, then work can serve as a purpose here and now. Dickens lifts his voice in harmony with a large chorus, when he preaches to a young lady correspondent:

Be earnest—earnest—in life's reality and do not let your life, which has a purpose in it—every life upon the earth has—fly by while you are brooding over mysteries.
The mystery is not here, but far beyond the sky. The preparation for it, is doing duty. Our Saviour did not sit down in this world and muse, but labored and did good. In your small domestic sphere, you may do as much good as an Emperor can do in his.[11]

The doctrine enters into his fiction, up to a point, much as we should expect. George H. Ford is certainly correct in saying that *Bleak House*, for example, has more consistently to do with earnestness or the lack of it than with the satire of Chancery.[12] Whereas Mr. Jarndyce, Esther Summerson, and Ada Clare are able to detach themselves from Jarndyce v. Jarndyce, Richard Carstone is ensnared by the lawsuit. For Carstone the celebrated Chancery case is an exaggerated instance of the 'expectations' that may destroy a weak young man's ambition. He is pointedly contrasted with the physician Allan Woodcourt, just as Henry

9 See Walter Houghton, *The Victorian Frame of Mind* (New Haven, 1957), ch. x.
10 Ecclesiastes, 9:10; cf. Carlyle, *Sartor Resartus*, ed. C. F. Harrold (New York, 1937), Bk. II, ch. ix; and Ruskin, *Works*, XVIII, 175, 395; XXVIII, 419.
11 To Miss Emmely Gotschalk, 1 Feb. 1850, *Letters*, II, 203.
12 'Self-Help and the Helpless in *Bleak House*', in *From Jane Austen to Joseph Conrad*, ed. Robert C. Rathburn and Martin Steinman, Jr. (Minneapolis, 1958), pp. 92–105.

Gowan, whom Little Dorrit characterizes as 'not earnest enough',[13] is contrasted with Clennam, or Steerforth with Copperfield. In *Hard Times* Dickens goes so far as to argue that those who are not earnest, like James Harthouse, are worse than wicked: 'Publicly and privately, it were much better for the age in which he lived, that he and the legion of whom he was one were designedly bad, than indifferent and purposeless. It is the drifting icebergs setting with any current anywhere, that wreck the ships.'[14] In the 1850s Dickens associates this type and class with administrative failure in the nation. The Barnacles 'abhorred and dreaded' earnestness, 'since in a country suffering under the affliction of a great amount of earnestness, there might, in an exceeding short space of time, be not a single Barnacle left sticking to a post'.[15] It is only in the 1860s that Dickens could regard a Eugene Wrayburn sympathetically, probably because by then he had grown sons who were not easily settling down to a profession.

In such instances the ideal of work is defined negatively, however. If we search for some positive embodiment of the ideal in the novels, Dickens will disappoint us. Daniel Doyce 'soberly worked on for work's sake', in spite of his treatment by the Barnacles.[16] But Daniel Doyce is a rare character in Dickens; in fact workers for the sake of the work, like Caleb Garth in *Middlemarch* or Thackeray's J. J. Ridley, are rare altogether in memorable Victorian fiction. Nor are they the protagonists of their respective novels. Protagonists—Arthur Clennam, Will Ladislaw, Clive Newcome—are often the least workmanlike of all characters. At the end of *Great Expectations* the hero who has learned the folly of false expectations devotes a single paragraph of his narrative to the true expectations of a business career. Amid puritanic self-congratulation ('I . . . lived frugally, and paid my debts, and maintained a constant correspondence with Biddy and Joe') and flattering revelations (Clarriker one day reveals that Pip has charitably purchased Herbert Pocket's place in the firm) a single sentence characterizes the business itself: 'We were not in a grand way of business, but we had a good name, and worked for our profits, and did very well.'[17] And in

[13] *LD*, Bk. II, ch. iv, p. 468. [14] *HT*, Bk. II, ch. viii, p. 179.
[15] *LD*, Bk. II, ch. viii, p. 514. [16] *LD*, ibid.
[17] *GE*, ch. lviii, pp. 455–6.

that sentence, whatever talent and effort went into the modest, unspecified business hang on the verb 'worked'. But 'worked for our profits', note: it would be unnecessary to mention work at all except to distinguish the right way of making profits from the wrong; the work is recalled not as an experience but as a moral score.

One would suppose that *David Copperfield* would be an exception here, since novel-writing is work that Dickens should be able to represent as an experience as well as a duty. Yet David does not tell us what it feels like to be a writer beyond the inference that it is hard work. After he meets Aunt Trotwood, the problems of his education and career become those of a young gentleman. She not only writes her will in David's favour but is prepared to article him as a law proctor at the cost of a thousand pounds. To be sure, when Aunt Trotwood is 'ruined', David resolves to master shorthand and become a reporter, and this on his own initiative, like the young Dickens. But much later it turns out that Aunt Trotwood has kept, in addition to the five thousand pounds stolen by Heap and now restored, two thousand pounds 'secretly for a rainy day'; and she comments, 'I wanted to see how you would come out of the trial, Trot.'[18] All along David needed only to work *as if* he were on his own. The purely moral nature of this exercise is as evident as it is in the trial of Bella Wilfer by Boffin and Rokesmith-Harmon, or of young Martin Chuzzlewit under the aegis of old Martin.

The doctrine of work turns out to be moralistic, since the novels (and Dickens is not alone in this respect) espouse work as a value but not as an experience. This contradiction accounts for the apparent disagreement of two such astute readers as House and Orwell. House claims that 'Nearly everybody in Dickens has a job: there is a passionate interest in what people do for a living and how they make do. . . . The typical rootless, baffled person is one who, like Richard Carstone, cannot settle to a profession and make good.' Orwell, on the other hand, says flatly that Dickens 'has no ideal of *work*'.[19] Among the countless characters in the novels many occupations are certainly identified, but none is really described. House is speaking of work as

[18] *DC*, ch. xxiii, p. 346; ch. liv, p. 776.

[19] House, p. 55; Orwell, 'Charles Dickens', pp. 93–4. Cf. Robert Garis, *The Dickens Theatre: a Reassessment of the Novels* (Oxford, 1965), pp. 130–1.

a moral category—of 'making do' and 'making good'—of work
as it is understood by the Victorian doctrine. Orwell's complaint
is that work is nowhere depicted as a concrete experience.
Orwell may have in mind chiefly the protagonists, as opposed to
the host of minor characters. The thematic orientation of his remark becomes clear when he goes on to cite the spirit of 'radiant
idleness' at the end of the novels, and attributes this spirit to the
historical period: 'Home life is always enough. And, after all,
it was the general assumption of [Dickens's] age. The "genteel
sufficiency," the "competence," the "gentleman of independent
means" (or "in easy circumstances")—the very phrases tell one
all about the strange, empty dream of the eighteenth- and nineteenth-century middle bourgeoisie. It was a dream of *complete
idleness*.' If Orwell is right, the dream seems at strange odds
with the doctrine of work.

Part of the difficulty can be traced to the general rule for
English novels that heroes should be gentlemen. For though
gentlemen may engage in certain professions, they do not ideally
work for a living—a principle that is bound to conflict with the
preaching of earnestness. In his early novels, possibly because
he was writing then in the shade of the Waverley Novels,
Dickens enlists a couple of gentlemen heroes who suffer very
typical anguish, not just over love, but because of the stigma
attached to work. When Nicholas Nickleby is forced to seek
work at an employment agency, he shudders just as a Scott hero
would in this extremity: 'I have undergone too much . . . to feel
pride or squeamishness now. Except . . . such squeamishness as
is common honesty, and so much pride as constitutes self-respect.' Since he feels it would be a 'greater degradation' to
borrow money from Newman Noggs, he obviously feels it a
degradation to teach French for five shillings a week; to conceal
his shame he teaches under the pseudonym 'Mr. Johnson'. The
vocation at which he is most successful, acting with the Crummles
company, Nicholas simply won't take seriously—'Oh! that I
should have been fooling here!' In the end his financial troubles
are taken care of by the Cheeryble brothers, and the hero reverts
to the status of a landed gentleman: 'The first act of Nicholas,
when he became a rich and prosperous merchant, was to buy his
father's old house.'[20] The other young hero who has difficulties

20 *NN*, ch. xvi, pp. 201–2; ch. xxx, pp. 398; ch. lxv, p. 830.

with work, Martin Chuzzlewit, carefully avoids any course that would be 'ungentlemanly and indecent' and, with Dickens's approval, lectures Americans for not being gentlemen. It is certainly hard to believe that Martin as architect has tossed off in a week's time the design for a grammar school that Pecksniff finds worth stealing. After his conversion from selfishness in Eden, he simply borrows money from Mr. Bevan in order to return to England. But the enterprising Mark Tapley takes a job on the *Screw* as cook—'"And my wages, sir," said Mark in high glee, "pays your passage"'—thus re-enacting from romance the eagerness of retainers to rise to the financial occasions of their masters. Since the intention of the plot is to ransom him from work by means of his grandfather's fortune, young Martin never does find a suitable occupation. He does say to old Martin near the end, 'Help me to get honest work to do, and I would do it,' but the mood of the verb gives away his thought that he does not deserve such a fate and will not suffer it.[21] Nicholas Nickleby and Martin Chuzzlewit are the stiffest young gentlemen heroes of Dickens, but none is wholly free of the inhibitions of that code with respect to work. Arthur Clennam, for example, makes a very awkward businessman—and not merely in his carelessness with Doyce's funds. In hiring Pancks to trace the history of the Dorrits' fortunes Arthur confesses, 'It may not give you a very flattering idea of my business habits, that I failed to make my terms beforehand . . . but I prefer to make them a point of honour.'[22]

At a reading of *A Christmas Carol* in 1853, at Birmingham, Dickens spoke of 'the fusion of different classes, without confusion'; he said that this ideal was particularly well served by a Mechanics' Institution.[23] Scott argued a quarter of a century earlier—a quarter of a century that measures a great distance in British history—that the same ideal was served by the Yeomanry: it was 'improper' and 'impossible' that the proprietors and the cultivators of land should mix freely, but 'the drilling field and a well regulated mess' afforded a healthful meeting ground of the two classes.[24] No two institutions could differ more than a

[21] *MC*, ch. xxxiv, p. 546; ch. xliii, p. 668.

[22] *LD*, Bk. I, ch. xxiii, p. 277.

[23] *Speeches*, p. 167.

[24] To J. B. S. Morritt, 14 Dec. 1827, in *The Letters of Sir Walter Scott*, ed. H. J. C. Grierson, 12 vols. (London, 1932–7), X, 337.

volunteer cavalry and a mechanics' institute, one harking back
to the feudal past and the other marching steadfastly toward
universal education; yet both are defended on the same principle
of separate but co-operating classes. The great difficulty with
Dickens is in determining where he believes the line between
gentlemen and others should be drawn. The older criterion of
property in land is far too exclusive. Possession of an 'independence' comes closer, but this status is not limited, as in Scott or
Jane Austen (and ideally for Thackeray and Trollope), to an
unearned income, and is therefore incalculably vague. Maintenance of some household servants is perhaps the closest economic
test of the gentleman. No genteel woman, at any rate, can live
without at least one female servant. Whether one serves or is
served by others is clearly of importance, and Ford speculates
that Dickens's inability to sympathize with unionized workmen
'is attributable to their not quite belonging to either the dependent status or the independent one'.[25]

In Victorian novels a member of the lower classes may have
the manners of a gentleman without being regarded as a gentleman in status. Manners alone, or morals alone, do not make a
gentleman, in spite of many official sentiments to that effect. If
we attend carefully the bright chapter of *The Old Curiosity Shop*
in which Kit Nubbles and his mother, and Barbara and her
mother, visit Astley's, we find Dickens assuming that happiness
for the lower classes consists of the pleasure of being called 'sir'
by a waiter, of spending a whole evening in innocent imitation
of the middle class. 'And didn't she look genteel, standing there
with her gloves on,' he writes of Barbara's mother; and
'wouldn't anybody have supposed [Kit's mother] had come of a
good stock and been a lady all her life!'[26] The pleasantries here
depend on these two good women *not* being ladies, and no degree of goodness or sensitivity can make them ladies. Little
Dorrit, who was born in a debtor's prison, is a lady; but John
Chivery, who so willingly serves the Dorrits out of love, is not
a gentleman. Little Dorrit's firmness and courtesy in refusing
his suit, therefore, can make Chivery's heart swell 'to the size
of the heart of a gentleman'! 'As she held out her hand to him
with these words, the heart that was under the waistcoat of

25 'Self-Help and the Helpless in *Bleak House*', p. 94.
26 *OCS*, ch. xxxix, p. 291.

sprigs—mere slop-work, if the truth must be known—swelled
to the size of the heart of a gentleman; and the poor common
little fellow, having no room to hold it, burst into tears.'[27] The
references to dress in these passages suggest still another serious
test of gentility.

The code of the gentleman, however, cannot by itself explain
the ambiguity of work, the contradiction between doctrine and
theme, in the novels of Dickens. Dickens does not rule out, as
Scott rules out, a business career for his heroes. Nor was he
personally confused, as Thackeray was confused, by the conflicting pieties of gentlemanliness and work. He simply renders
the specific career of the hero irrelevant when he constructs his
plot; and though he believes in the pieties, he subordinates them
to the interest of fortune. Dickens is in this sense a more 'primitive' story-teller. He and his readers relish the account of what
befalls a hero through no fault of his own. Hence he is much
more willing than other major novelists to rely on such fairy-
tale figures of benevolence as Mr. Brownlow, the Cheeryble
brothers, the Single Gentleman, Mr. Chuzzlewit, Betsey Trotwood, and their late mutations, the 'Golden Dustman' and the
ambiguous trio of Magwitch, Miss Havisham, and Jaggers. The
novel, and before novels the romance, and the daydream, have
always favoured good fortune over hard work. Even the rags-
to-riches novels of Horatio Alger in America are not stories of
the rewards of hard work, but stories that inevitably turn on
strokes of good fortune.[28] There are world enough and time for
work in real life, and too little good fortune. Dickens picks up
the theme of fortune inherent in most story-telling and uses it
unabashedly as a source of pleasure. Even those novels that
challenge the pleasurability of fortune, of which *Great Expectations* is the most notable, do not deny fortune's role in shaping
events.

The gentlemanly disparagement of work might be said to be
classical; the traditional education of the English upper class
kept it in touch with the classical preference of *otium* to *negotium*

[27] *LD*, Bk. I, ch. xviii, p. 219. Cf. Private Gill in 'The Perils of Certain English
Prisoners', who remarks of the heroine (*CS*, p. 207), 'I well know what an immense and hopeless distance there was between me and Miss Maryon . . . and yet I
loved her . . . the suffering to me was just as great as if I had been a gentleman.'

[28] John Tebbel, *From Rags to Riches: Horatio Alger, Jr., and the American Dream*
(New York, 1963), pp. 14–17.

—the former a philosophical ideal and the latter its necessary interruption.[29] On the other hand, the doctrine of work, coupled to a thematic preference for fortune, is a configuration peculiarly Calvinistic and middle-class. It is worth noting that when Dickens preaches the doctrine of work, he is likely to link it to the idea of Providence. In 'Tom Tiddler's Ground', his fictional tract against ascetic retirement, Mr. Traveller defines 'the healthy tenure on which we hold our existence' as, 'according to Eternal Providence, that we must arise and wash our faces and do our gregarious work and act and re-act on one another'.[30] In *Bleak House* Jarndyce lectures Richard Carstone in similar terms:

> Trust in nothing but in Providence and your own efforts. . . . Constancy in love is a good thing; but it means nothing, and is nothing, without constancy in every kind of effort. If you had the abilities of all the great men, past and present, you could do nothing well, without sincerely meaning it, and setting about it. If you entertain the supposition that any real success, in great things or in small, ever was or could be, ever will or can be, wrested from Fortune by fits and starts, leave that wrong idea here, or leave your cousin Ada here.[31]

The casual linking of Providence with the incitement to work, with the parallel between Providence and Fortune, brings to mind the so-called Protestant ethic; and regularity, persistence, 'constancy in every kind of effort' are the very qualities preached by Calvinism, in particular.

Calvinism, even while it drummed away on work as duty, theoretically denied that work contributed to one's salvation: work might be a sign of salvation, but no more. The contradiction between doctrine and theme in Dickens's fiction corresponds to Calvin's notorious difficulty in wedding his ethic to his theology. House states that Dickens's religion 'is emphatically one of works, not faith'—which is the opposite of Calvin's position.[32] And if one asked Dickens his opinion on the relative efficacy of works and faith, he would undoubtedly reply 'works', because, in his words, 'the mystery is not here, but far beyond the sky'. To reply 'faith' would seem complacent to his lay mind.

---

[29] See Sebastian de Grazia, *Of Time, Work, and Leisure* (New York, 1964), ch. i.
[30] *CS*, p. 300.
[31] *BH*, ch. xiii, p. 180.
[32] House, p. 111.

If one wisely declines to ask Dickens a question of theology point blank, however, and looks instead for the secular equivalent of salvation in his fiction, examining the turns of what he alternately calls Providence and Fortune, the answer is something like faith. For the protagonists of the novels depend not at all on work, and only sporadically on good works, to make their way through the world. They usually seem appointed to their destined end from the beginning. When House continues that in Dickens 'there is no dwelling on any religious merit works may win', he shifts from a doctrinal to a thematic view, and in so doing brings the novelist in harmony with Calvin's position. When he adds that for Dickens 'Heaven is more a compensation than a prize', he nearly repeats one of Calvin's defences of justification by faith: if heaven were a prize, that would imply that a man could be saved for his own merit.[33]

Calvin had good reasons for justification by faith. If God is omnipotent, how can a man in any sense 'earn' his salvation by being good? He based his argument on St. Paul's Epistle to the Romans. According to Paul, he argues, 'faith excludes all boasting', and it is a form of boasting to assume that man's puny works can influence God. Moreover, a reward made for good works would imply that God owes us the reward until it is paid. And God cannot be in our debt.[34] When Calvin thinks in terms of actions and outcome, when he conceives of human life thematically, in short, he is forced by his theology to stress fortune rather than achievement. 'As the Psalmist shows, it is in vain to rise up early in the morning, and go to bed late, and drink water and eat only half enough bread; that will advance one not at all unless God extends His hand and bounty. On the contrary, goods sometimes come to his children as they sleep. And this shows that men err if they think they enrich themselves by their own merit.'[35] This is Calvin's story of men's fate, his story of men awaiting the outcome of their lives. The ethic derived from this story is paradoxical. The ethic becomes that of unrelenting effort in one's 'calling'. One could do nothing about one's salvation except to work, in deep humility, as if one were

[33] Cf. *Institutes*, Bk. III, ch. xviii, sec. 4.
[34] *Institutes*, Bk. III, ch. xi, sec. 13; cf. Romans 4.
[35] Quoted by Georgia Harkness, *John Calvin: the Man and His Ethics* (New York, 1931), p. 169.

saved. Logic could not affirm that the industrious were saved, but it was logical to assume that those who did not work, nor behave well in other respects, had received no true intimation of their salvation.[36] Since not to work evidenced the loss of hope, to work was hopeful evidence of salvation. As Erich Fromm has argued, the paradox of Calvinism makes sense psychologically, by making neurotics out of Calvinists; it signifies a compulsion to work in order to overcome a sense of utter powerlessness, and an irrational attempt to control the outcome of an event by manipulating the evidence for the event.[37]

The Victorian doctrine of work is a muffled echo of the same paradox. For Calvin's logical denial of the final efficacy of work it merely substitutes a polite agnosticism. The preachment of work is intensified, but its end is obscure. The paradox invades the novels of Dickens. The humble, would-be member of the elect discovers in his belief a powerful energizing principle, neurotic or not; the ambitious, scheming rascal aspires to a station in life that Victorian novels define very selectively: Uriah Heep is the grotesque embodiment of both these unfortunate types. The most 'umble' man in Dickens, he works hard to get ahead. But energy and humility are not what finally count, for heroes thrive in the same fiction that drives a Heep to a frenzy of the damned. The heroes are thoroughly in earnest, but what they do also has little bearing on the outcome. The reader pays less attention to their works than to the events that befall them and the denouement. The empty dream of idleness at the end, which Orwell protests against, is the reward of a devotion to work that is equally empty. But Dickens shares these patterns with many story-tellers, and the whole question arises as to whether Calvin himself might have fixed upon his particular theory of salvation because of the tension and excitement it engenders. Puritan theology and the code of the gentleman agree on the existence of a few persons who differ from the rest of the population. Each viewpoint overlooks the necessity of work that it officially approves, and imagines that some live happily ever after while others do not.

[36] Cf. Edmund S. Morgan, *The Puritan Family* (New York, 1966), pp. 4–5.
[37] *Escape from Freedom* (New York, 1941), pp. 90–3.

VI

CHARITY

THE Victorian attitude toward charity is the logical correlative of the doctrine of work. The attitude is chiefly distinguished by its emphasis on the character of the recipient of charity, an emphasis that inverts the long tradition of Christian charity as a practice contributing to the salvation of the charitable. The elevating influence of the gift on the giver is never denied, but the giver is asked to subordinate this (almost selfish) consideration to a concern for the effect of his gift on the recipient's character—an effect that is regarded as dubious at best. 'Who will be frugal and provident, when charity offers all that frugality and providence can confer?' asks Smiles. 'Is not the circumstance that poverty is the only requisite qualification on the part of the applicant for charity, calculated to tempt people to self-indulgence, to dissipation, and to those courses of life which keep them poor?'[1] Puritanism gave a powerful impetus to charitable practices in England, comparable to its influence on the doctrine of work. Yet Puritanism was also peculiarly responsible for this precautionary attitude. In Calvin's theology, charity must follow from grace and cannot directly contribute to the giver's salvation; and begging and other forms of dependence were severely discouraged.[2]

[1] *Thrift*, p. 303.

[2] According to R. H. Tawney, the Swiss reformers regarded pauperism 'not . . . as a problem of police, nor . . . as a problem of social organization, but as a question of character. Calvin quoted with approval the words of St. Paul, "If a man will not work, neither shall he eat," condemned indiscriminate alms-giving as vehemently as any Utilitarian, and urged that the ecclesiastical authorities should regularly visit every family to ascertain whether its members were idle, drunken, or otherwise undesirable.' *Religion and the Rise of Capitalism* (New York, 1926), p. 114; cf. Max Weber, *The Protestant Ethic and the Spirit of Capitalism*, trans. Talcott Parsons (New York, 1958), pp. 163, 177–8, 268 n. 45. Sidney and Beatrice Webb concur in attributing to religious influences the broad shift in opinion that began in the seventeenth century in England and culminated in the new Poor Law of 1834. In *English Local Government*, 11 vols. (Hamden, Conn., 1963), VII, 409, they paraphrase Tawney nearly word for word, except that for 'any Utilitarian' they prudently substitute the Charity Organization Society. See also VIII, 456. These volumes were originally published as *English Poor Law History* in 1927-9.

The attitude toward charity that dwells on the character of the recipient can be reduced to the worry that, despite our eloquence, ordinary men will not work unless they are forced to. This worry, which sometimes amounts to a conviction, is the back-handed acknowledgement of the emptiness of the doctrine of work itself—its purely moral emphasis and the Puritan logic that makes work ultimately unrelated to the end of life.

The deep distrust of charity in the nineteenth century was related to the growth of population in cities and extended to private as well as public measures for relieving the poor. By the end of Dickens's lifetime the popular impression was that charity had failed to do anyone, except charitable persons themselves, any good. 'If charity could help or elevate the poor,' Smiles speculates, without citing the source of his figures, 'London would now be the happiest city in the world; for about three millions of money are spent on charity, and about one in every three of the London population are relieved by charitable institutions.'[3] This impression may have derived from a rough comparison of the sheer number of charitable institutions, sometimes satirized by Dickens himself, and the manifest condition of the poor. But it was also accepted theory that a little charity could be a dangerous thing. Beatrice Webb recalled from her own childhood the obsession of the 1860s 'that the mass-misery of great cities arose mainly, if not entirely, from spasmodic, indiscriminate, and unconditional doles, whether in the form of alms or in that of Poor Law relief'.[4] Charity was actually thought to worsen the condition of the poor, by undermining their character and increasing their numbers. The combined moral and economic effect of charity—usually qualified as 'indiscriminate' charity—was the process known as 'pauperization'.

Malthus was the first widely-read exponent of this theory. In the second edition of his *Essay on Population* he parlayed the obvious implications of his laws of population into a direct attack on poor relief, which, he charged, created 'tyranny, dependence, indolence, and unhappiness'.[5] 'Parson Malthus' was not merely an economist but a clergyman of the Church of England, and in

---

[3] *Thrift*, p. 302.

[4] Quoted by David Owen, *English Philanthropy, 1660–1960* (Cambridge, Mass. 1964), p. 217.

[5] *An Essay on the Principle of Population*, 2nd ed. (1803), Bk. IV, ch. viii, in *On Population*, ed. Gertrude Himmelfarb (New York, 1960), p. 529.

fact the agitation against the old poor law at the close of the eighteenth century and after was often dominated by clerical and Evangelical voices.[6] The marriage of piety and political economy in this respect lasted throughout the nineteenth century, and is well illustrated by the moral tales of Harriet Martineau. Such writers had polite words for the virtue of charity but became serious when the dire consequences were taken into account. Roughly speaking, the public or private relief of sudden accidents or innate disabilities, over which the sufferer has no possible control, affords a safe way to accomodate the generous impulses of mankind; but if conditions are such that relief may be anticipated by a potential recipient, character will be destroyed and more and more men will become deliberately poor.

The small unproductive consumption [a Malthusian concept] occasioned by the relief of sudden accidents and rare infirmities is necessary, and may be justifiably provided for by charity, since such charity does not tend to increase of numbers; but, with this exception, all arbitrary distribution of the necessaries of life is injurious to society, whether in the form of private almsgiving, public charitable institutions, or a legal pauper-system.[7]

To this way of thinking careless charity is a form of 'interference' that will play havoc with the smooth operation of *laissez-faire*.

Transformed by rationalism and science, the marriage of piety and economics became a marriage of natural selection and economics. Spencer epitomizes the age's grudging tolerance of small acts of charitable indulgence that will not have important or lasting effect. Go ahead and give a little, he seems to say, if you are so weak that you cannot control yourself; but you are most likely to do harm, commit a 'breach of equity', bring about 'pure evil', 'positive misery', 'the multiplication of those worst fitted for existence', and inhibit those 'most fitted for existence'.[8] The tone of *Social Statics* is such that Spencer often seems either hypocritical or self-contradictory; nevertheless, it would be hard to overestimate the hold of this fundamental attitude toward charity over the minds of the Victorians. In *Physics and Politics*,

[6] See *English Local Government*, VIII, 15–18.

[7] Harriet Martineau, 'Cousin Marshall', in *Illustrations of Political Economy*, 11 vols. (London, 1832–4), IV, 130.

[8] *Social Statics*, pp. 380–1.

a work intended to refute some applications of evolutionary
theory, Bagehot took essentially the same position as Spencer:
'Great good, no doubt, philanthropy does, but then it also does
great evil. It augments so much vice, it multiplies so much suffering, it brings to life such great populations to suffer and to be
vicious. . . .'[9] And according to Mill, one of the unfortunate results
of women's inferior education was that they persisted in adding
to the 'great and continually increasing mass of shortsighted
benevolence, which, taking the care of people's lives out of their
own hands, and relieving them from the disagreeable consequences
of their own acts, saps the very foundations of the self-respect,
self-help, and self-control which are the essential conditions both
of individual prosperity and of social virtue'.[10] Nor should the
harshness or outspokenness of these writers obscure the real problem of 'pauperization' that confronts the social worker in practice
both then and now.

Dickens's best known sallies into the field of charity do not
tell us as much as we would like of his true attitude. His management, for a brief period, of the home for fallen women established
by Miss Coutts in Shepherd's Bush, was not an original under-
taking. The Magdalen Hospital for the rehabilitation of prostitutes had been founded a hundred years earlier, and in 1850
there were between twenty-five and thirty homes for former
prostitutes in London. The historian of modern British philanthropy, David Owen, concluded—perhaps somewhat mischiev-
ously—that at least this 'category of metropolitan needy, whose
claims always exerted a singular pull on Victorian sensibilities,
was adequately, if not redundantly, provided for'.[11] Dickens's
early satires of foreign charities, culminating in the memorable
antics of Mrs. Jellyby and Mrs. Pardiggle, with their consorts
Quale and Gusher, were originally directed against 'those who
pamper their compassion and need high stimulants to rouse it'.
And he spells out this motive in *Nicholas Nickleby*: 'There are
not a few among the disciples of charity who require, in their
vocation, scarcely less excitement than the votaries of pleasure

[9] *Works*, VIII, 122.
[10] *The Subjection of Women* (London, 1869), p. 163.
[11] Owen, pp. 163–4. For Dickens's account of the home in Shepherd's Bush in
Household Words, 23 Apr. 1853, see *Collected Papers*, I, 425–39; also Philip
Collins, *Dickens and Crime*, ch. iv.

in theirs . . . charity must have its romance.'[12] As Dickens grew famous and successful, he was exposed to more and more charitable requests, both honest and dishonest. Increasingly he came to resent such demands, though usually with good humour. He writes to Edmund Yates in 1858:

Benevolent men get behind the piers of the gates, lying in wait for my going out; and when I peep shrinkingly from my study-windows, I see their pot-bellied shadows projected on the gravel. Benevolent bullies drive up in hansom cabs (with engraved portraits of their benevolent institutions hanging over the aprons, like banners on their outward walls), and stay long at the door. Benevolent area-sneaks get lost in the kitchens and are found to impede the circulation of the knife-cleaning machine.[13]

His late novels make sly allusions to the very kind of societies that he was asked repeatedly to speak for—a 'Combined Additional Endowed Dignitaries Committee' in *Little Dorrit*, the 'Annual Dinner of the Family Party Fund' and 'Society for Granting Annuities to Unassuming Members of the Middle Classes' in *Our Mutual Friend*. That a more pointed satire of charities was forthcoming we know from the presence of Mr. Honeythunder and the Haven of Philanthropy in *Edwin Drood*, in which Philanthropists are compared unfavourably to Pugilists.[14] If Dickens had confined himself to working for charitable organizations on the one hand, or satirizing them on the other, the task of sifting his views would be simpler.

The serious issues of Victorian charity leave Dickens very uncertain. It is as hard for him as for any kindly man to believe that his gift must 'pauperize' someone. '"It's pauperizing a man, sir, I have been shown, to let him into a hospital?" said Pancks,' in *Little Dorrit*. '"I have been shown so too," said Clennam, coldly.'[15] This interchange clearly implies Dickens's scorn for the theory of 'pauperization'—or at least a conviction that the theory applies only to the able-bodied pauper. But he does not repudiate that theory, either. The purpose of sanitary institutions, he writes Miss Coutts, is 'to assist the poor to help themselves,

[12] *NN*, ch. xviii, p. 215. Cf. 'The Niger Expedition', *The Examiner*, 19 Aug. 1848, in *Collected Papers*, I, 160–78.

[13] 28 Apr. 1858, *Letters*, III, 19.

[14] *LD*, Bk. I, ch. xxi, p. 252; *OMF*, Bk. I, ch. xvii, pp. 210–13; *MED*, ch. xvii, pp. 189–90.

[15] *LD*, Bk. I, ch. xxiii, p. 278.

and not to pauperize them'.[16] He is unexcelled at exposing the inhumane administration of charity or in suggesting the unpleasant sensations of individuals whose lives are governed by the laws of population. The rhetoric of Sir Joseph Bowley, M.P. in *The Chimes* is almost too splendid for Dickens's serious purpose, making the reader grateful that poor Trotty Veck exists to be patronized; and Mr. Filer's Benthamite reasonings are handled no less exuberantly:

> 'Who eats tripe?' said Mr. Filer, warmly. 'Who eats tripe?'
> Trotty made a miserable bow.
> 'You do, do you?' said Mr. Filer. 'Then I'll tell you something. You snatch your tripe, my friend, out of the mouths of widows and orphans.'[17]

Yet Dickens admires as much as any Benthamite certain well-intentioned, orderly experiments in coping with the destitute of London. Notable, for example, is his visit in 1852 to a Ragged School dormitory in Farringdon Street, where he was favourably impressed by the lay-out of the sleeping cribs on the floor, the filing-in of the paupers 'quietly and in good order', the uniform ration of one six-ounce loaf, the way in which the dormitory was hosed out with water every morning, and the cheapness of the whole operation.[18] In one expression of sober indignation, also in *Household Words*, he seems to argue that the theories of charity current in his day may be 'reasonable' but cannot be invoked as an excuse for inaction. During a night-time walk he encounters five persons—'five bundles of rags'—who have been shut out of the casual ward of the Whitechapel workhouse:

> I know that the unreasonable disciples of a reasonable school, demented disciples who push arithmetic and political economy beyond all bounds of sense (not to speak of such a weakness as humanity), and hold them to be all-sufficient for every case, can easily prove that such things ought to be, and that no man has any business to mind them. Without disparaging those indispensable sciences in their sanity, I utterly renounce and abominate them in their insanity; and I address people with a respect for the spirit of the New Testament, who do mind such things, and who think them infamous in our streets.[19]

16 2 Sept. 1852, *Coutts Letters*, p. 205.
17 *CB*, pp. 105–6, 95.
18 'A Sleep to Startle Us', *Collected Papers*, I, 394–7.
19 'A Nightly Scene in London', *Collected Papers*, I, 634.

The famous novelist is able to hand each of the shivering paupers a shilling, without patronizing them and, one trusts, without pauperizing—but also without resolving their plight.

Dickens put much greater stock in education and sanitary reform than in charity as a solution for social destitution. But these are remedies affecting the future. The absence of a remedy affecting present conditions makes his complaint of the malfunctioning of poor relief too shrill. 'There was old people, after working all their lives, going and being shut up in the workhouse, much worse fed and lodged and treated altogether, than —Mr. Plornish said manufacturers, but appeared to mean malefactors.' The truth in Plornish's complaint is sapped by Dickens's refusal to say who is responsible, let alone how the situation can be righted. He cannot seriously mean that the Circumlocution Office should undertake 'that line of business'. When he adds Plornish's opinion 'that if you couldn't do nothing for him, you had better take nothing from him for doing of it,' he seems to be cantankerously attacking the poor rates.[20] The conversation on the same subject between the 'meek man' and Podsnap in *Our Mutual Friend*, conducted also in indirect discourse, is similarly inconclusive. Podsnap raises the cry of 'centralization', on which the meek man has no opinion, except that he is against 'dying of destitution and neglect'.[21] When the question of what should be done comes around to asking for donations of money, as it inevitably does, an amused but somewhat petulant note enters Dickens's voice. As Mr. Chops the dwarf says to Magsman the showman, 'Everywheres, the sarser was a goin round. Magsman, the sarser is the uniwersal Institution.'[22]

Though Dickens is of mixed minds about the economic laws that make charity inadvisable, and not nearly so concerned as some Victorians with its debilitating influence on weak characters, he thoroughly agrees that to receive charity is not respectable. However he may differ on the subject with his contemporaries, he joins them in the assumption that those who accept charity, whether in consequence of their own acts or not, are a race apart. This lesson was beaten into the Victorian mind, not by stories of able-bodied men who had been pauperized by charity, but by stories of good persons, preferably children, women, or unable

[20] *LD*, Bk. I, ch. xii, p. 143.   [21] *OMF*, Bk. I, ch. xi, pp. 140–1.
[22] 'Going into Society', *CS*, p. 219.

men, who had refused charity in order to remain morally respectable. In his Birmingham speech of 1869 Dickens tells the story of an industrial student who, 'through illness in his family, had . . . been obliged to part with his best clothes' and was unwilling to attend classes in his work clothes lest he attract attention. When offered a loan 'to enable him to rehabilitate his appearance', he refused, 'on the ground that he came to the Institution to learn, and to know better how to help himself [*applause*]: not otherwise to ask help, or to receive help, from any man. [*Loud applause.*]'23 Dickens does not report at what point the student was able to dress himself well enough to resume his studies; it is enough that the student has saved himself from falling to the class who receive help. His most elaborate story of this kind is the tale of Betty Higden in *Our Mutual Friend*.

The reader can readily sympathize with Betty Higden's fear of forcible confinement in a workhouse, but she is also the creature of Victorian propaganda in a much broader issue, and a thoroughly fictitious creature. Dickens needed to invent a representative of the 'decent poor' whose experiences with poor-law abuses would speak for itself. He was working from such a distance, or in such a hurry, that he invented instead a witness whose knowledge of these abuses is derived from reading newspapers and whose testimony is phobic.

Kill me sooner than take me there. Throw this pretty child under cart-horses' feet and a loaded waggon, sooner than take him there. Come to us and find us all a-dying, and set a light to us all where we lie, and let us all blaze away with the house into a heap of cinders, sooner than move a corpse of us there! . . .

Do I never read in the newspapers . . . God help me and the like of me!—how the worn-out people that do come down to that, get driven from post to pillar, and pillar to post, a-purpose to tire them out! Do I never read how they are put off, put off, put off—how they are grudged, grudged, grudged the shelter, or the doctor, or the drop of physic, or the bit of bread? Do I never read how they grow heartsick of it and give it up, after having let themselves drop so low, and how they after all die out for want of help? Then I say, I hope I can die as well as another, and I'll die without that disgrace. . . .

Johnny, my pretty . . . your old Granny Betty is nigher fourscore

23 *Speeches*, p. 402.

year than threescore and ten. She never begged nor had a penny of the Union money in all her life. She paid scot and she paid lot when she had money to pay; she worked when she could, and she starved when she must. You pray that your Granny may have strength enough left her at the last (she's strong for an old one, Johnny), to get up from her bed and run and hide herself, and swown to death in a hole, sooner than fall into the hands of those Cruel Jacks we read of, that dodge and drive, and worry and weary, and scorn and shame, the decent poor.

Betty's indictment of the administration of relief, even if it is based on hearsay, seems irrefutable. Why should the poor be 'grudged, grudged, grudged' even that disagreeable form of relief which is their due by law? But the last paragraph of her tirade sounds the theme of her part in the novel: her absolutely clean record of never accepting charity and her successful determination to preserve this record by dying on her feet. From Betty's story emerges the ideal figure of the decent poor, a creature so independent that she cannot even accept a kindness. 'I never did take anything from any one,' she insists, and then, to escape one awkward implication of extreme independence, she defends herself by the doctrine of work: 'It ain't that I'm not grateful, but I love to earn it better.' When she encounters the charitable Boffins again, she is just as firm: 'I've never took charity yet, nor yet has anyone belonging to me.' Dickens is so charmed by this ideal that it does not occur to him that, if Betty had been a little less independent, Johnny's illness need not have been fatal. He regards Betty Higden as an effective protest against the operation of the poor laws:

For when we have got things to the pass that with an enormous treasure at disposal to relieve the poor, the best of the poor detest our mercies, hide their heads from us, and shame us by starving to death in the midst of us, it is a pass impossible of prosperity, impossible of continuance. . . . This boastful handiwork of ours, which fails in its terrors for the professional pauper, the sturdy breaker of windows and the rampant tearer of clothes, strikes with a cruel and a wicked stab at the stricken sufferer, and is a horror to the deserving and unfortunate.[24]

Betty's story is too broadly conceived to support this charge. She will not accept charity in any form, public or private. She will not even accept a position as housekeeper to the friendly Boffins.

[24] *OMF*, Bk. I, ch. xvi, pp. 199–200, 203; Bk. II, ch. xiv, p. 383; Bk. III, ch. viii, p. 503.

What possible system of poor relief could benefit the Betty Higdens of this Victorian, and Puritan world? None at all, surely. And that was the broad intention of the Poor Law Amendment Act of 1834, which construed poor relief as relief that no decent person would accept, and therefore legislated only for the indecent poor. With the intention of the Act of 1834, Dickens was in essential sympathy. In the postscript to *Our Mutual Friend*—he composed such non-apologies for his work with care—Dickens not only restricted his criticism to abuse of the poor law but deliberately broadened his position to include the old law that the new amended: 'I believe there has been in England, since the days of the STUARTS, no law so often infamously administered, no law so often openly violated, no law habitually so ill-supervised.'[25] He had joined his countrymen in scathing attacks on the most notorious of such abuses, like that exposed by the cholera epidemic at Drouet's farm in 1849.[26] But the intention of the new poor law was one with which Dickens and his countrymen instinctively agreed. In fact, enough influential Victorians continued to believe in that intention that the General Report that preceded the law was reprinted by the Stationery Office three times at the very end of the century.[27] The new poor law was aimed primarily at the 'able-bodied' pauper, and it sought to eliminate what Dickens calls the 'professional pauper' by administering a workhouse test: that is, if an able-bodied pauper wanted relief, he would have to receive it within the confines of a workhouse under conditions less attractive than those prevailing on the outside. This test would assure that only those who were truly helpless would apply. As the Webbs noted, with characteristic understatement, there was 'a certain weakness in the intellectual defence of the new system': namely, that not much thought was given to the welfare of those so genuinely helpless that they passed this test and accepted relief on these terms. The workhouse was to serve as both a deterrent and a refuge.[28] Indoor relief never did become the dominant form of poor relief in Victorian England, either in

[25] *OMF*, p. 822.
[26] See Dickens's three articles in *The Examiner*, 20 Jan., 27 Jan., and 21 Apr. 1849, *Collected Papers*, I, 193–205.
[27] *English Local Government*, VIII, 92 n. 1.
[28] *Ibid.*, VIII, 156–8.

terms of cost or in numbers of persons relieved, but the survival of the general mixed workhouse assured that this anomaly in the law wrought individual havoc on the aged, the infirm, and the children. Why did the Commissioners of 1832–4 not foresee this anomaly? Unquestionably they were mindful, like Dickens later, of the 'enormous treasure' being expended from the poor rates, which had tripled in the first decades of the century. They wished to remove as many able-bodied paupers from the rolls as possible. To do this they had to postulate a certain level of subsistence that was both tolerable and intolerable. Only the premise of the existence of good and bad poor, decent and indecent, makes their intention logical; the workhouse test makes sense as a test of character, not of means. The decent poor would not tolerate the workhouse, and their resistance to it would be self-rewarding, since they would somehow find jobs. Those of weak enough character to accept relief, cannot really be saved. In the later, Spencerian translation of this Puritan conviction, those who fail to adapt are almost a different species from the healthy generality of mankind.

Dickens is receptive from the first to the idea of physical causation of moral ills, and this receptivity enables him to support heartily the causes of sanitary reform and education. But he cannot readily conceive of any self-respecting person accepting charity. 'Old Betty Higden, however tired, however footsore, would start up and be driven away by her awakened horror of falling into the hands of Charity.' The word 'Charity' is pronounced with bitter irony: 'It is a remarkable Christian improvement, to have made a pursuing Fury of the Good Samaritan,' Dickens continues.[29] But his illustration is overdrawn. Betty refuses private charity, gentle and considerate charity, with equal fortitude. Far more than fear of the workhouse is implied. From the potential recipient's point of view any charity is to be avoided at all costs. In a context devoid of all irony, at a dinner for the General Theatrical Fund, Dickens urged, 'If you help this Fund you will not be performing an act of charity, but you will be helping those who help themselves.' He goes out of his way to show that the fund is a 'Provident Institution', that the recipients of benefits will feel no 'disgrace' because they have contributed to the fund themselves. 'If you help this Fund you will

[29] *OMF*, Bk. III, ch. viii, p. 506.

not be performing an act of charity, but you will do an act of
Christian kindness, benevolence, encouragement. . . . I will not
so wrong a body of men struggling so manfully for independence,
as to solicit you to perform, in their behalf, an act of charity.'[30]
'Charity' could be a dirty word in the nineteenth century. In
one vehement assault on begging-letters Dickens goes so far as
to call misdirected charity 'the offals of our duty'.[31]

The dread aspect of charity finally lies not in the evil social
consequences preached by Malthus and Spencer, but in the
thought that to receive charity is somehow to lose something,
to break irreparably some hidden law, to cross some dividing
line. Observe how Little Dorrit implores Clennam not to understand her father if he asks for money, and not to give it him:
'Save him and spare him that, and you will be able to think
better of him!' Much of the emotional purchase of *Little Dorrit*
turns on this repeated embarrassment—and more than embarrassment, too, for it is 'Save him' as well as 'think better of
him'. In the dialogue of the novel Dickens ingeniously allows
William Dorrit to betray his own embarrassment—or the beg-
gar's sensitivity to the donor's embarrassment: 'sometimes—
hem—it takes one shape and sometimes another; but it is generally—ha—Money.'[32] It often seems as if the nineteenth century
simply took literally the dictum of Christ that it is better to give
than to receive—so literally that no allowance is made for a class
of people who may happily receive what Christians give.

Harold Skimpole in *Bleak House* is at once the dread incarnation of the eleventh commandment, 'Thou shalt not receive',
and the irrepressible attorney for the position that, if anyone is
to give, then *someone* must receive. 'I don't feel any vulgar
gratitude to you. I almost feel as if *you* ought to be grateful to
me, for giving you the opportunity of enjoying the luxury of
generosity. I know you like it. For anything I can tell, I may
have come into the world expressly for the purpose of increasing
your stock of happiness.' And Skimpole is incapable of work; he
is the mirror opposite of Betty Higden. Dickens, the creator of
this run-away logician and stealer of scenes, takes every opportunity to throw him morally to the ground and prove him a

[30] 14 Apr. 1851, *Speeches*, pp. 121–2.
[31] 'The Begging-Letter Writer', *RP*, p. 386.
[32] *LD*, Bk. I, ch. xiv, pp. 171–2; ch. viii, p. 84.

hypocrite. So that the reader may see what a knave he is, Dickens makes Skimpole neglect his family, tolerate slavery in America, toady to Sir Leicester, and betray Jo for a five-pound note. He seems to construe Skimpole's role in the novel as merely a foil to the naïve goodness of Jarndyce and the shrewd goodness of Esther Summerson. And in the end, at the expense of consistency of character, Dickens delivers his parting thrust by having Skimpole indite in his diary, 'Jarndyce, in common with most other men I have known, is the Incarnation of Selfishness.' His readers, and perhaps Dickens also on some less moral plane, are likely to protest, in Harold's own words, 'let Harold Skimpole live!'[33]

Skimpole's astonishing logic bypasses the logic of debt and payment, bewilders the Puritan mind, and appeals to the Christianity of the Gospels. His parables are unfortunately related of himself by himself, but are memorable for other reasons than their conceitedness. In the parable of the butcher's bill and the spring lamb, for example, the butcher is dumbfounded when Skimpole reduces their relative economic positions to this essential point: the butcher has something to eat and Skimpole is hungry. The story is recalled (or invented) by Skimpole when Jarndyce challenges his theory that 'meaning' to pay a bill is as good as paying it: what if the butcher merely 'meant' the meat instead of providing it?

My dear Jarndyce . . . you surprise me. You take the butcher's position. A butcher I once dealt with, occupied that very ground. Says he, 'Sir, why did you eat spring lamb at eighteen-pence a pound?' 'Why did I eat spring lamb at eighteen-pence a pound, my honest friend?' said I, naturally amazed by the question. 'I like spring lamb!' This was so far convincing. 'Well, sir,' says he, 'I wish I had meant the lamb as you mean the money!' 'My good fellow,' said I, 'pray let us reason like intellectual beings. How could that be? It was impossible. You *had* got the lamb, and I have *not* got the money. You couldn't really mean the lamb without sending it in, whereas I can, and do, really mean the money without paying it.' He had not a word. There was an end of the subject.[34]

The comedy, or even the hypocrisy, of this repartee must not be allowed to conceal Skimpole's grasp of an elemental truth

[33] *BH*, ch. vi, p. 71; ch. lxi, p. 831; ch. vi, p. 70.
[34] *BH*, ch. xv, p. 205.

about charity. Charity is an act in which something is given for nothing; it is a violation of the morality of debt and payment; it is an act of injustice. While Dickens hounds Skimpole for his selfishness, he forgets—what Jarndyce does not forget—that charity is not just. To the Puritan imagination, only God is big enough to do something for nothing; or if a generous man like Mr. Jarndyce is permitted to commit charitable acts of injustice, no one has a right to benefit from injustice.

Skimpole's appeal resides in his 'drone philosophy', his laziness and his logic, his freedom from time and money, his Bohemian apartment and lackadaisical daughters, his breakfast of coffee, claret, and a peach. But what makes us almost envious is his freedom from guilt. Recall how embarrassed are Richard and Esther when Skimpole is arrested by Neckett, and how they offer 'delicately' to pay his debt. Esther is astonished at his freedom, and 'Richard and I seemed to retain the transferred impression of having been arrested since dinner.'[35] Harold Skimpole does not work, and accepts charity without feeling any guilt. His considerable power over Dickens's imagination and that of his readers is a measure of the degree to which work and avoidance of charity (i.e., receiving charity) are irrational and compulsively imposed values.

'Rokesmith', the disguised hero of *Our Mutual Friend*, gives it as his opinion that Betty Higden's independence ought to be respected. But his reverence for Betty's independence is not thought to conflict in any way with the prospect that he and Bella Wilfer will live happily ever after on unearned income. Nor in the meanwhile does Dickens suggest that it is wrong for Bella to accept the charity of the Boffins, however wrong it is for her to be greedy about money. He regards Betty as 'this brave old heroine', but in nowise argues that Betty's refusal to accept help from others makes her better than his young heroine, for all the latter's faults. On the contrary, Betty 'put her old withered arms round Bella's young and blooming neck, and said, repeating Johnny's words: "A kiss for the boofer lady"'.[36] If Betty Higden, who refuses gifts not because she is ungrateful but because she would rather earn her meagre living, is an idealized character, why should she pay obeisance to one who accepts gifts ungratefully and will never have to work at anything more

[35] *BH*, ch. vi, p. 77.   [36] *OMF*, Bk. II, ch. xiv, pp. 384–5; 391.

arduous than keeping her doll's house for the hero? Why, for that matter, has the dying Johnny (named for the hero) singled out Bella as someone special? One can answer that Betty and her grandson instinctively appreciate either Bella's higher social class, or her state of grace. For all its satire of 'Society', *Our Mutual Friend* willingly confuses these two possible sources of Bella's distinction, and of her exemption from the very attitudes toward work and charity that Dickens apparently approves.

VII

FORGIVENESS

DICKENS formulated a special doctrine of the function of memory in moral life. Its most deliberate articulation is the fifth Christmas book, *The Haunted Man*, a poor story with inconsistencies and a few unintelligible sentences, but of importance to Dickens personally. The haunted man of the story is Redlaw, a professor of chemistry; he is haunted by the 'sorrow, wrong, and trouble' he has known, and by a ghost, who is his double. The ghost offers Redlaw an insidious gift of forgetfulness, and Redlaw accepts this gift, along with the involuntary power of destroying other people's memories of *their* wrongs. In the course of the story Dickens's doctrine of memory is proved and demonstrated to the hero: memories of past wrongs and sorrows are not emotionally destructive, but morally constructive; without such memories human beings will harden and become friendless, because they will have no continuing need to practise forgiveness.

The specific sorrow and wrong in Redlaw's past, which have tormented him so that he would like to forget, are the death of his sister and the elopement of his friend Longford—who was engaged to his sister—with Redlaw's own girl. In this Christmas season Longford has returned to the scene, and Redlaw learns that if he cherishes the past instead of trying to escape it, he can forgive the friend who has wronged him. He is gradually freed from his temptation to forget by the influence of the good angel of the story, his housekeeper, Milly Swidger:

'I have no learning, and you have much,' said Milly; 'I am not used to think, and you are always thinking. May I tell you why it seems to me a good thing for us to remember wrong that has been done us?'

'Yes.'

'That we may forgive it.'

'Pardon me, great Heaven!' said Redlaw, lifting up his eyes, 'for having thrown away thine own high attribute!'[1]

[1] *CB*, p. 393.

Milly's is the simplest expression of the doctrine Dickens is promulgating: it is good (necessary, we might add) to remember wrong that has been done to us, in order to forgive it.

The autobiographical content of this story is remarkable for its indirection. *The Haunted Man* reflects not so much the facts of Dickens's life as certain recognizable distortions of self-pity. The individual represented by Redlaw and his ghost experienced in childhood 'No mother's self-denying love . . . no father's counsel'. As in *David Copperfield*, which was shortly to appear, 'A stranger came into my father's place when I was but a child, and I was easily an alien from my mother's heart. My parents, at the best, were of that sort whose care soon ends. . . .' These complaints, it is true, are put in the mouth of the ghost alone, as if Dickens acknowledged their slight impropriety. Redlaw's dead sister apparently recalls Mary Hogarth, Dickens's dead sister-in-law: 'Such glimpses of the light of home as I had ever known, had streamed from her. How young she was, how fair, how loving! I took her to the first poor roof that I was master of, and made it rich. She came into the darkness of my life, and made it bright.'[2] Though this autobiographical content helps us understand *The Haunted Man*, however, it does not resolve all the difficulties in the fiction—any more than Dickens's parents or Mary Hogarth resolved the difficulties they contributed to the novelist's life.[3]

In the story Redlaw's ghost is his double—'an awful likeness of himself', 'the animated image of himself dead', and the 'Evil spirit of myself'.[4] Thus a part of himself, at first, longs to forget the sorrow and wrong of the past. The feeling that he has been cheated and betrayed is, after all, not a pleasant feeling to live with. The better half of the hero yields to this temptation only to learn, under the tutelage of the same ghost, the necessity of preserving the memory of his wrongs. But does he finally preserve this memory in order to overcome his sorrow, or to indulge it? to forgive the wrong, or to nurse a hatred? Dickens refuses to state, even at the beginning of the story, that Redlaw has been overwhelmed by his sister's death or that he hates

[2] *CB*, p. 332.
[3] For an introduction to the role of Mary Hogarth in Dickens's imagination, see Johnson, I, 191–204.
[4] *CB*, pp. 330, 331, 334.

Longford—only that he is obsessed by the memory of the past. The emotions of the hero are handled so coyly that they falsify the argument. The story skirts the possibility of memory fostering resentment or vengeance; the writer's silence on this point conceals the unspoken possibility of grief and unforgiving hatred. Conversely, the story treats forgetfulness as morally neutral or worse, and ignores its more hopeful implications. Surely forgetfulness may often imply forgiveness—in common saying, complete forgiveness. *The Haunted Man* denies this possibility, too, and contends that one must forgive but never forget.[5]

The process of memory operates only selectively, then. It occurs to us at once that other characters in Dickens, Miss Havisham in *Great Expectations* and Mrs. Clennam in *Little Dorrit*, remember the past so as never to forgive. The latter has as her motto, 'Do not forget', and practises a Calvinist vengefulness that Dickens condemns,[6] yet these two have as powerful memories and as great awareness of their wrongs as Redlaw. The difference is that the hero has a special gift of translating memory into forgiveness. Dickens's attempt to include a social message in *The Haunted Man*, by means of the 'savage' boy of the streets who has taken shelter in Redlaw's college, merely aggravates the selective nature of these assumptions. The savage boy is pointedly the only character (besides the angelic Milly) who is immune to the infection of Redlaw's temporary forgetfulness, and the ghost later expounds the significance of the boy's immunity:

This . . . is the last, completest illustration of a human creature, utterly bereft of such remembrances as you [Redlaw] have yielded up. No softening memory of sorrow, wrong, or trouble enters here, because this wretched mortal from his birth has been abandoned to a worse condition than the beasts, and has, within his knowledge, no one contrast,

---

[5] In a letter of 21 Nov. 1848 Dickens states the moral of the story misleadingly: 'Of course my point is that bad and good are inextricably linked in remembrance, and that you could not choose the enjoyment of recollecting only the good. To have all the best of it you must remember the worst also.' Forster somewhat more accurately expounds the theme in his own words: 'The old proverb does not tell you to forget that you may forgive, but to forgive that you may forget' (Forster [Bk. VI, ch. iv], II, 61). But the story itself does not admit any forgetting.

[6] *LD*, Bk. II, ch. xxx, p. 777.

no humanizing touch, to make a grain of such a memory spring up in his hardened breast. All within this desolate creature is barren wilderness. All within the man bereft of what you have resigned [i.e., the memory of sorrow, wrong, or trouble], is the same barren wilderness. Woe to such a man! Woe, tenfold, to the nation that shall count its monsters such as this [the boy of the streets], lying here, by hundreds, and by thousands![7]

Memory has here become the product instead of the cause of the 'humanizing touch', but the analogy between Redlaw and the boy—if it survives this inconsistency—implies that the poor and destitute of the nation could be, like Redlaw, morally improved by the steady recollection of the wrongs and sorrows they have suffered—an implication that contravenes Dickens's own analysis of revolutionary passions in *A Tale of Two Cities* and elsewhere. Either the analogy is false, and the hero is able to translate the memory of wrongs into forgiveness because of a special grace, or the doctrine of memory is a false cover for the spirit of vengeance and revolution in heroes, too.

Why this long story enshrines a truism (that one must remember in order to forgive) and elevates it to the level of moral doctrine seems clear. To stress the virtue of forgiveness is not enough. By stressing memory the doctrine endorses forgiveness while permitting concealed satisfaction in being wronged; it makes the wrong permanent by fixing it in memory even as one forgives it. The process by which a hero passes surely from recollection to forgiveness is not explained, though in *The Haunted Man* Milly Swidger contributes to this process. But the novelist providentially renders forgiveness easy by punishing beforehand the person to be forgiven. Thus Longford is destitute and near death by the time of the action. And Dickens has Longford confess outright that his betrayal of Redlaw has led directly to his own material and moral collapse: 'from the day on which I made my first step downward, in dealing falsely by you, I have gone down with a certain, steady, doomed progression.'[8] The low state at which he has arrived is ultimately proved by his receiving charity from the hero.

The wronged hero is no stranger to Dickens's fiction. In the stories for *Household Words* and *All the Year Round* that replaced the separately published Christmas books the theme of

[7] *CB*, p. 378.   [8] *CB*, p. 394.

wrong and forgiveness is carried on in the same uncompromising terms. Christmas is a season of forgiveness, but it is the other man who has done the injury. 'In yonder shadow, do we see obtruding furtively upon the blaze, an enemy's face? By Christmas Day we do forgive him! If the injury he has done us may admit of such companionship, let him come here and take his place.'[9] Two such stories reproduce even the rough character relationships of *The Haunted Man*. The gist of the whimsical 'Poor Relation's Story' is simply: I pretend that Christiana and my partner behaved well toward me; they did not behave well at all, but this little pretence enables me to forgive them. The scheme is repeated in 'Mugby Junction': years ago Beatrice broke her engagement to the hero and married one Tresham; even though she and Tresham have lost the first five out of six children, and though Tresham is dying of an incurable disease, the point of 'Mugby Junction' is that Jackson, the hero, must learn to forgive them, or rather, erase the impression that he (not the author or Providence) has put a curse upon them. Jackson, to be sure, once refers to himself as 'a blind and sinful man', but not before Beatrice has gone down on her knees and passionately confessed her fault: 'You generous man! You good man! So to raise me up and make nothing of my crime against you!'[10]

Of the novels of Dickens only *Pickwick* is an exception to the pattern of personal wrongs to the hero. Even there, as Chesterton reminds us, the hero rescues from the Fleet prison 'the man and the woman who have wronged him most'.[11] But Mr. Pickwick is primarily, in his own expression, the victim of circumstances. It is easy to feel that this was the first and last novel in which Dickens did not in a significant degree project himself as the protagonist.[12] After *Pickwick* the reader seems always to be asked, however subtly or indirectly, to join in the hero's or heroine's sense of personal wrong. *David Copperfield*, to choose the best example, magnificently recreates the sufferings of childhood, and the divulging of Dickens's own extraordinary reaction to his days in the blacking warehouse is too well known

9 'What Christmas Is As We Grow Older', *CS*, p. 23.

10 *CS*, pp. 514, 510.

11 G. K. Chesterton, *Charles Dickens* (New York, 1965), p. 98.

12 See my essay, 'Waverley, Pickwick, and Don Quixote', *Nineteenth-Century Fiction*, XXII (1967), 19–30.

to require comment. But the trail of wrongs winds on through the later, less compelling pages of that novel as well. The narrator-hero makes a few of these wrongs explicit, but they are unerringly revealed by the machinery of poetic justice powered by the narrator-novelist. The hero holds no grudges except the famous ones of his childhood, but he proves a dangerous young man to cross in love just the same. Each death in the novel answers in some respect to an injury to the hero: the two Mrs. Copperfields, child-mother and child-bride, who do not love David capably enough; Mr. Spenlow, who disapproves David's marriage with his daughter; Steerforth and Ham, unknowing rivals with David for the love of Little Em'ly.

Barkis's death seems almost an exception in *David Copperfield* —unrelated to any wrong suffered by the hero. Yet Barkis's death is curiously superimposed with 'A Greater Loss', the departure of Little Em'ly to a fate worse than death, which occurs the same night. Before her flight Emily's anxiety is attributed by the others to a 'dread of death', and afterward her letter is read by the mourners 'in the midst of the silence of death'.[13] Except for an early hint, the 'indescribably sensitive pleasure, that a very little would have changed to pain', with which David reacts to the news of Emily's engagement to Ham, the reader would hardly be able to guess that she has somehow injured the hero by her behaviour. Yet in the extraordinary discovery of Emily's return, scrupling 'that it was for Mr. Peggotty alone to see her and recover her', the hero remains concealed while Rosa Dartle delivers a brutal verbal lashing to the girl who has been ruined by his own friend. 'Would he never, never come? How long was I to bear this? How long could I bear it?' David asks, retrospectively. How long did he suppose Emily could bear it? Then Mr. Peggotty rushes in at last; as Emily faints, he kisses her and draws a handkerchief over her face, as if she were dead; and they pass David on the way out. The hero never does meet Emily face to face after the elopement, explaining to Ham that 'It would be too painful to her, perhaps'.[14] The gist of the whole relation is that Emily's behaviour has affronted the hero in another sense.

13 *DC*, ch. xxx, p. 444; ch. xxxi, p. 452.
14 *DC*, ch. xxi, p. 315; ch. l, pp. 718, 722; ch. li, p. 737. For the discovery scene, see Butt and Tillotson, *Dickens at Work*, pp. 164-5.

That his heroes are so persistently wronged must qualify our interpretation of Dickens as a novelist of guilt. As early as *Oliver Twist* his heroes experience dramatic feelings of guilt. Yet in so far as these feelings are consciously portrayed by Dickens, it is to expel them. Charges of guilt, and accompanying anxieties, are levelled against heroes so that their innocence can be proved. This is manifestly so in the case of a child like Oliver. The same holds for the later, more problematic attributions of guilt in *Little Dorrit* and *Great Expectations*. Lionel Trilling's introduction to the former called attention to the hero's sudden intuition that his mother or father might be responsible for the imprisonment of the Dorrits: 'What if his mother had an old reason she well knew for softening to this poor girl! . . . What if any act of hers, and of his father's, should have even remotely brought the grey heads of those two brothers so low!' But the issue is raised, after all, in order to prove Clennam's well-meaning innocence, his generous sense of responsibility for deeds not his own. He voluntarily tries to uncover the past so that he can make reparation for whatever his parents, whom he distrusts so, may have done. The most elaborate expression of the hero's guilt feelings in *Little Dorrit* is this:

As though a criminal should be chained in a stationary boat on a deep clear river, condemned, whatever countless leagues of water flowed past him, always to see the body of the fellow-creature he had drowned lying at the bottom, immovable, and unchangeable, except as the eddies made it broad or long, now expanding, now contracting its terrible lineaments; so Arthur, below the shifting current of transparent thoughts and fancies which were gone and succeeded by others as soon as come, saw, steady and dark, and not to be stirred from its place, the one subject that he endeavoured with all his might to rid himself of, and that he could not fly from.[15]

But in spite of the astonishing simile, the 'one subject' referred to is merely the possible relationship of Mrs. Clennam and Rigaud. A similar procedure is followed in *Little Dorrit* with respect to the Circumlocution Office's talent for making its clients, including the hero, feel like criminals: the point is that they are not criminals and should not be expected to feel like criminals.

Great Expectations is the novelist's most concerted effort to

---

[15] *LD*, Bk. I, ch. viii, p. 89; Bk. II, ch. xxiii, p. 679. See Trilling, Introduction, pp. v–xvi; reprinted in *The Opposing Self* (New York, 1959), pp. 50–65.

create a hero who wrongs others. With respect to Pip's relation to Joe and Biddy, this effort is at least partially successful; his injury to these two is of the nature of an insult, and, when he finds they are married, he rightly asks forgiveness for his presumption.[16] But the plot of the novel is still such that the hero is more sinned against than sinning. He is persecuted or misled by Mrs. Gargery, Pumblechook, Miss Havisham, Estella, Jaggers, and Magwitch, and all except Jaggers are punished for their trouble. Pip may say to Miss Havisham, 'I want forgiveness and direction far too much, to be bitter with you', but Miss Havisham kneels to Pip in an attitude of prayer, exclaiming, 'What have I done! What have I done!' Pip's complex reaction to the return of Magwitch is not easily unravelled; but only after Magwitch is condemned to death is Pip at ease once again. Magwitch notices this himself in his cell: 'you've been more comfortable alonger me, since I was under a dark cloud, than when the sun shone.' In that final scene Dickens blunders, by reversing Christ's parable of the publican and the Pharisee. 'Mindful, then, of what we [Pip and Magwitch] had read together, I thought of the two men who went up into the Temple to pray, and I knew there were no better words that I could say beside his bed, than "O Lord, be merciful to him a sinner!"' Christ's preference was 'Be merciful to *me* a sinner,' and the difference reflects the assumption that heroes may be wronged but do not wrong others.[17]

Yet Dickens's position is essentially Christian. The righteousness of his heroes may be suggestive of the Old Testament and occasionally pharisaical, but the stress on forgiveness was consciously derived from the Gospels. The teaching of Jesus on the subject is active: to forgive, not to ask for forgiveness of others. 'If ye forgive men their trespasses, your heavenly Father will also forgive you: but if ye forgive not men their trespasses, neither will your Father forgive your trespasses.'[18] The Lord's

[16] Garis, *The Dickens Theatre*, pp. 200–3, discusses whether Pip's snobbishness is convincingly rendered.

[17] *GE*, ch. xlix, p. 377; ch. lvi, p. 436; cf. Luke, 18:13. Julian Moynahan, in 'The Hero's Guilt: The Case of *Great Expectations*', *Essays in Criticism*, X (Jan. 1960), 60–79, was the first to call attention to this slip, which has since become widely remarked. Joseph E. Baker, in 'Thackeray's Recantation', *PMLA*, LXXVII (1962), 588, has pointed out, in *The Adventures of Philip*, a similar distortion of the story of the woman taken in adultery.

[18] Matthew 6:14–15.

Prayer is not strictly a prayer for reciprocal acts of forbearance in the affairs of men, but for divine forgiveness in exchange for a symbolic act that brings one closer to God. 'Forgive us our debts as we forgive our debtors' does not imply the moral equivalence of the human agents involved; nor are the two 'debts' equivalent, since the debts of the creditor whom Jesus appeals to are between himself and God, and the debts that the creditor forgives between himself and other human beings. The two different levels of relationship are reflected in the version of the Gospels that Dickens wrote for his own children: 'We learn from [Jesus's forgiveness of Mary Magdalene] that we must always forgive those who have done us any harm, when they come to us and say they are truly sorry for it. Even if they do not come and say so, we must still forgive them, and never hate them or be unkind to them, if we would hope that God will forgive us.'[19] The infinite difference between the relationship of man with God and that of man with man is deeply ingrained in the Puritan tradition in which Dickens shares. For Calvin, citing Augustine, 'The righteousness of the saints in this world consists more in the forgiveness of sins than in perfection of virtues.'[20] What allows the stress on forgiveness, in Dickens's period, to become so nearly self-righteous, and the absence of reciprocity on the human level so apparent, is the weakening of faith in a personal God—the very premise of the original idea.

In a sense Jesus invites the believer to become like God, and this invitation the heroes of Dickens may accept. Thus Redlaw, at the conclusion of *The Haunted Man*, offers a prayer of thanksgiving that construes himself as an imitator of Christ and Christian martyrs: 'Oh Thou . . . who through the teaching of pure love, has graciously restored me to the memory which was the memory of Christ upon the cross, and of all the good who perished in His cause, receive my thanks, and bless [Milly Swidger].'[21] Indeed, Christ is the type of all heroes who have been wronged, and it is certainly open to Christians to associate with the Christ who was crucified as well as the sinners for whom the sacrifice was made. *A Tale of Two Cities*, with its two heroes,

19   *Life of Our Lord* (New York, 1934), ch. v, p. 49.
?   .stitutes, Bk. III, ch. xi, sec. 22; cf. *The City of God*, Bk. XIX, ch. xxvii.
      ⌐B, p. 396.

affords both opportunities; Charles Darnay is beloved by and married to Lucie Manette, but needs the help of the wronged man, Sydney Carton. As Carton walks through Paris brooding on his scheme to sacrifice his life for Darnay, 'solemn words, which had been read at his father's grave', force themselves upon his thoughts: 'I am the resurrection and the life, saith the Lord; he that believeth in me, though he were dead, yet shall he live; and whosoever liveth and believeth in me, shall never die.'[22] These words, which recur to Carton three or four times before his execution by the guillotine, are not incanted by the hero in order to overcome a fear of death. His last thoughts indicate fairly clearly that he merely hopes to survive in the memory of those he loves. Rather, Carton is playing the role of Christ in the lives of those who have, however innocently, wronged him. It is Darnay who, apparently marked for dead, will yet live and who, married to Lucie, cannot die.

It would be easy to put down Dickens's fondness for the hero who has been wronged to his own temperament as a person. We know, for example, that *A Tale of Two Cities* owes a good deal to the emotional thrill that he experienced in performing the part of Wardour in *The Frozen Deep*. In the preface to the novel he relates that he first conceived of the story while acting in Collins's play and states, ambiguously, that a 'strong desire was upon me then, to embody [the idea] in my own person'—as if he meant either to write such a story of his own or to act out the role in real life. 'I have so far verified what is done and suffered in these pages,' he continues, 'as that I have certainly done and suffered it all myself.'[23] Dickens's capacity for self-pity is recognized by all twentieth-century students of his life, and it is surely true that self-pity can be warmed by a profusion of forgiveness of others, whereas to be forgiven is almost an affront to self-pity. When a whole culture preaches that the powerless are better off than the powerful, the doctrine of forgiveness becomes a particularly attractive refuge for the secretly powerful man, like Dickens. But this reduction of the difficulty to biographical terms, without really simplifying anything, also fails to take into account the dominant morality of his time. The problem of forgiveness for the Victorians is analogous to the problem of

[22] *TTC*, Bk. III, ch. ix, p. 298, citing John 11:25–6.
[23] *TTC*, p. xiii. See Johnson, II, 866–8, 873–4, 876–8.

charity. Just as one may give but never receive, so one may forgive but can never be forgiven.

It must be asked whether forgiveness is merely an attitude, an emotional or even verbal tolerance of the sins of others, or whether it is an actual commitment to alter the consequences of moral acts, to remit punishment. If one distinguishes between debts owed to God and those obtaining between men, then 'forgive us our debts, as we forgive our debtors' may be interpreted as committing one to a certain attitude only. Under this interpretation God may remit sins, but men may only respect and worship this divine prerogative from afar. Christians are not likely to advocate forgiveness in the literal sense of refraining from the punishment of wrong-doing. Yet that is what forgiveness literally means; like charity, it is an abridgment of justice. It is this abridgment of justice that makes forgiveness so difficult to comprehend on the human scale. The Puritan religion that exults in God's power to impose or remit penalties at will, is precisely the religion that finds it impossible to compromise justice among men. For religious and other reasons justice, the morality of strict consequences, the morality of obligation and duty, are sanctions much more weighty in the nineteenth century than forgiveness.

Forgiving without forgetting bespeaks an objective moral principle. Far from being suspect in Victorian eyes, this principle was celebrated for its objectivity and defended on the grounds of social necessity. In the *Idylls of the King* Arthur is able to forgive his adulterous queen, and part from her, without deviating from justice one iota.

> Yet must I leave thee, woman, to thy shame.
> I hold that man the worst of public foes
> Who either for his own or children's sake,
> To save his blood from scandal, lets the wife
> Whom he knows false, abide and rule the house . . .
> Better the King's waste hearth and aching heart
> Than thou reseated in thy place of light,
> The mockery of my people, and their bane!

In his long compassionate speech, the king entertains and repudiates the thought of compromising justice for the sake of the wronged parties ('his own or children's sake') but does not even

consider compromise for Guinevere's sake. The assumption of
Tennyson and his audience is that Guinevere has placed herself
beyond help from others. There is no way to right her sin, and
this is what makes Arthur's beautiful speech of forgiveness so
important and so vain. 'Lo, I forgive thee, as Eternal God /
Forgives!' he pronounces, but he is forbidden to translate this
forgiveness into practical measures.[24] If it is true that eternal God
can forgive sins in the sense of altering their consequences, man
can only emulate God in some symbolic sense. And in view of
Arthur's own godlike status in the *Idylls*, it seems unlikely that
even God can do anything substantial for Guinevere. Dickens
on his part 'doubt[ed] if anything were ever done finer' as a
work of art than Tennyson's 'Guinevere'.[25] He also shared the
Poet Laureate's assumptions about forgiveness. The inner certainty that forgiveness cannot alter the practical consequences of
a moral act makes the need to forgive, as a gesture, that much
more compelling. The gesture of forgiveness is the *only* thing
the wronged party, or the bystander, can do for the trespasser.
'Yes, Steerforth, long removed from the scenes of this poor
history!' writes David Copperfield, 'My sorrow may bear
involuntary witness against you at the Judgment Throne; but
my angry thoughts or my reproaches never will, I know!'[26]

Victorians of all persuasions were genuinely hard pressed to
explain what could be done about sins once they had been committed. In *Social Statics* the young Spencer found it astonish-
ingly easy to construct a science of morality, but 'whether it is
possible to develop scientifically a Moral Therapeutics seems
very doubtful'.[27] To mitigate the consequences of wrong acts
would be vainly to interfere with nature. But Ruskin, too, at the
very opposite political pole, when asked whether there are not
some degrees of wrong-doing which one might adjust through
repentance, could only reply, 'You have no business at all to do
wrong.' The idea of remission of sins makes some Christianity
suspect for Ruskin: 'Pure Christianity gives her remission of

[24] 'Guinevere', ll. 508–12, 521–3, 541–2.
[25] To Wilkie Collins, 16 Aug. 1859, *Letters*, III, 116. On the popularity of King
Arthur's moral position see Michael Wolff, 'Victorian Reviewers and Cultural
Responsibility', in *1859: Entering an Age of Crisis* (Bloomington, 1959), pp. 273–
274, 284–6.
[26] *DC*, ch. xxxii, p. 455.
[27] *Social Statics*, p. 58.

sins only by *ending* them.'[28] Dickens resolves the problem in the only way that makes sense to him: the way to correct a wrong is to make reparations for it, to pay for it as nearly as possible in like coin. The principle is fully enunciated by the hero of *Little Dorrit*: 'Duty on Earth, restitution on earth, action on earth; these first, as the first steep steps upward. Strait was the gate and narrow was the way; far straiter and narrower than the broad high road paved with vain professions and vain repetitions, motes from other men's eyes and liberal delivery of others to the judgment—all cheap materials costing absolutely nothing.'[29] The discussion of duty in terms of cost and materials is still Puritan in spirit, despite this novel's attack on nonconformity in the person of Mrs. Clennam. So similar is Arthur's thinking to that of his putative mother, in truth, that this bookkeeping principle might be named, after mother and son, 'Clennam's Law'.

This law interprets justice as reparation in kind or in cash, almost by analogy to exchange economics. The law is rigidly invoked even in defence of one of Dickens's hated institutions, imprisonment for debt. 'It seems to me hard,' protests Little Dorrit, 'that [my father] should have lost so many years and suffered so much, and at last pay all the debts as well. It seems to me hard that he should pay in life and money both.' Her argument, too, is based on justice, and would seem plausible enough if Dickens did not immediately categorize it as confused. Mr. Dorrit has not really paid twice for his debt, however, because his creditors did not benefit from his payment in life—his imprisonment—but only from his payment in money. Imprisonment for debt may not be the most practicable institution in the world, but justice forbids that the Father of the Marshalsea should be forgiven his debts. 'The prison, which could spoil so many things, had tainted Little Dorrit's mind no more than this. Engendered as the confusion was, in compassion for the poor prisoner, her father, it was the first speck Clennam had ever seen, it was the last speck Clennam ever saw, of the prison atmosphere upon her.'[30] Whatever little irony may have played around

[28] *The Ethics of the Dust*, in *Works*, XVIII, 264; *The Crown of Wild Olive*, in *Works*, XVIII, 447.
[29] *LD*, Bk. I, ch. xxvii, p. 319.
[30] *LD*, Bk. I, ch. xxxv, p. 422.

Dickens's pen as he wrote Little Dorrit's protest is lost in this apology, in which the points of view of the hero, the novelist, and his readers are mingled.

The discussion of guilt in *Little Dorrit* centres about those mysterious apprehensions of the hero that prove to be groundless. Dickens gets over the case of Arthur's real crime, his speculation with other people's money, rather easily. The hero takes the only permissible attitude toward his fault: he must make restitution for the loss he has caused others. 'I must work out as much of my fault—or crime—as is susceptible of being worked out, in the rest of my days.' If Doyce's firm can survive its losses, Arthur, 'at as small a salary as he could live upon, would ask to be allowed to serve the business as a faithful clerk'. Nor will he try to avoid his creditors, though as a practical matter they are likely to prevent him from working out his debts as a faithful clerk. 'I must take the consequences of what I have done. . . . The writs will find me here.'[31] As soon as the hero has expressed these intentions—and gone to the Marshalsea, where he cannot carry them out—Daniel Doyce returns and makes reparations on his behalf, so that it is impossible for the reader to measure the depth of Clennam's fault.

That Doyce should so happily assume the burden of the hero's fault makes him a sort of fairy godfather. The hero's rescue seems luckily foredestined. To understand Dickens's moral position fully, therefore, we have to look for Clennam's counterpart in the decent non-heroic class who are damned until proved otherwise. One such, who has also been allowed at small salary to serve the business as a faithful clerk, is John Carker in *Dombey and Son*. In John Carker the reader can observe, in word and deed, and without heroic distortion, the correct stance of a man who has sinned and repented. He is a man who has undergone, in his sister's words, 'the humility of many years, the uncomplaining expiation, the true repentance, the terrible regret, the pain I know he has even in my affection', a man who takes care lest innocents like Walter Gay become his friend and suffer from his contagion. The sister, Harriet Carker, pleads the virtues of forgiveness with little variation: 'oh, Sir, after what I have seen, let me conjure you, if you are in any place of power, and are ever wronged, never, for any wrong, inflict a punish-

[31] *LD*, Bk. II, ch. xxvi, pp. 713, 716, 717.

ment that cannot be recalled; while there is a GOD above us to
work changes in the Hearts he made.' But as for one who commits wrong, like her brother John, he must not be deprived of
'any fragment of the merit of his unassisted, obscure, and forgotten reparation'. And therefore Harriet refuses the strange
gentleman, Mr. Morfin, who, like Daniel Doyce, is ready to
render assistance.[32]

Two years after *Dombey and Son* Dickens wrote 'Pet Prisoners' for *Household Words,* in which he compared the diet of
convicts favourably to that of paupers in the St. Pancras workhouse, the cost of keeping convicts unfavourably to the cost of
private lodgings, and belittled the sanctimonious 'pattern penitence' with which he would invest Heep and Littimer at the end
of *David Copperfield.* As a constructive alternative to the coddling
of convicts, he offers what he considers to be an ideal expression
of penitence in a letter from an imaginary convict to *his* Harriet
Carker:

My dear sister, I feel that I have disgraced you and all who should be
dear to me, and if it please God that I live to be free, I will try hard to
repair that, and to be a credit to you. My dear sister, when I committed
this felony, I stole something—and these pining five months have not
put it back—and I will work my fingers to the bone to make restitution,
and oh! my dear sister, seek out my late companions, and tell Tom
Jones, that poor boy, who was younger and littler than me, that I am
grieved I ever led him so wrong, and I am suffering for it now![33]

Unintentionally Dickens makes his model prisoner sound like
Uriah Heep. But the model prisoner makes his point about restitution and voluntarily accedes to the double jeopardy of payment in life and in money that Little Dorrit so timidly protests.

When he treats of crime, Dickens's conviction of the irrever-
sibility of moral acts is most evident. At the end of *Great
Expectations* Pip says he 'sometimes derived an impression . . .
that [Magwitch] pondered over the question whether he might
have been a better man under better circumstances'. This
thought agrees well with Dickens's own perception of causes
of crime that lie outside the criminal, and with his hopes of
preventing crime by treating those causes. But once the crime
is committed, it is too late. And Pip makes it a point of con-
gratulation that Magwitch, a morally sensitive criminal, 'never

[32] *D & S,* ch. xxxiii, pp. 476–8.   [33] *Collected Papers,* I, 286–7.

justified himself by a hint tending that way, or tried to bend the past out of its eternal shape'.[34] Dickens might as well agree with Spencer that crime, in this sense, is 'incurable';[35] his reflection on the eternal shape of the past reminds one of Spencer's friend George Eliot. Early in the novel Pip and Joe regard the convicts sympathetically and even hope that they will escape; much later the narrator explains: 'At that time, jails were much neglected, and the period of exaggerated reaction [to inadequate prisons] . . . was still far off. So, felons were not lodged and fed better than soldiers (to say nothing of paupers), and seldom set fire to their prisons with the excusable object of improving the flavour of their soup.'[36] Dickens's irony, which had touched on the pampering of prisoners as early as *Pickwick*, returned frequently to this subject in his last two decades. In two heavily ironic articles he even contended that the practice of criminal law was 'grounded on the profound principle that the real offender is the Murdered Person; but for whose obstinate persistency in being murdered, the interesting fellow-creature to be tried could not have got into trouble'.[37] These articles protest, in effect, that too little regard is paid those who are wronged by the criminal. They argue, logically enough, that even the execution of a murderer cannot redress the injury he has done to the person or persons he has murdered.

In Ruskin's words, 'the very definition of evil is in this irremediableness'.[38] The morality of consequences, the deep sense that choices are irretrievable, that deeds are done and never undone, results from a confluence of Puritanism, economic theory, historicism, and science in the nineteenth century. If instruction in what Smiles called 'the national code of Duty'[39] was harsh in the Puritan tradition, it was no less so in classical economic theory, including population theory, which also taught that actions were everywhere circumscribed by consequences, consequences of the direst kind. The rise of historicism fixed a temporal dimension on this tightening universe, by which not only moral acts but all events came to be seen as irreversible.

[34] *GE*, ch. lvi, p. 432.
[35] *Social Statics*, p. 351.
[36] *GE*, ch. xxxii, p. 246.
[37] 'Five New Points of Criminal Law', 24 Sept. 1859, in *Collected Papers*, II, 12–13; cf. 'The Murdered Person', 11 Oct. 1856, in *Collected Papers*, I, 660–5.
[38] 1871 Preface to *Sesame and Lilies*, in *Works*, XVIII, 42.
[39] *Self-Help*, p. 23.

What few spaces of untrammelled action were left to the imagination were rapidly filled in by discoveries in science. 'Throw up a handful of feathers, and all fall to the ground according to definite laws,' wrote Darwin, and modestly asserted that his own researches into the causes and effects of apparently haphazard events, over centuries of time, were even more complex.[40] Darwin, of course, was conscious of his debt to Malthus's vision of the jostling and competing for the finite sources of life. It may even be that another nineteenth-century discovery that tended to restrict the physical universe, the law of conservation of energy, also owed its inspiration to economic thought: by coincidence, the experiments by James Prescott Poule leading to its formulation were conducted in Manchester in the 1840s. Dickens is so remote intellectually from these developments that it hardly seems important to trace them in detail here. Yet without some appreciation of this broad growth in determinist ways of thinking, and their coincidence with the renewal of Puritan ethics, it would be difficult to comprehend the morality of consequences and the difficulties with forgiveness that follow from it. Nor would it be wise to underestimate the degree to which Dickens was aware of the intellectual ferment of his time, however little thought he gave to it. When writing of the chemist Redlaw, at least, an analogy to scientific law (the law of conservation of matter, it seems) comes readily enough to Dickens's pen: 'In the material world, as I have long taught, nothing can be spared,' concludes the professor; 'no step or atom in the wondrous structure could be lost, without a blank being made in the great universe. I know, now, that it is the same with good and evil, happiness and sorrow, in the memories of men.'[41]

[40] *The Origin of Species by Means of Natural Selection*, Modern Library (New York, n.d.), p. 60.
[41] *CB*, p. 374.

VIII

SOJOURNERS IN THE CITY

THE good people of Dickens's novels dwell in the earthly city without being of it. They are unselfish and earnest, but work is not their true aim; they are charitable, but do not receive charity unless from fairy godparents or ministering angels; they forgive their enemies, but are not importantly in need of forgiveness. They await the outcome of their lives; like Abel, they are only sojourners. 'They went quietly down into the roaring streets, inseparable and blessed,' in the concluding sentence of *Little Dorrit*; 'and as they passed along in sunshine and shade, the noisy and the eager, and the arrogant and the froward and the vain, fretted, and chafed, and made their usual uproar.'[1] The verb that Dickens employs is significant: Arthur and Little Dorrit— it is hard to think of them as 'Mr. and Mrs. Clennam' —do not purchase a house or even live in the city; they 'passed along'. They are 'blessed' among those who are unblessed, 'inseparable' from each other but very much separated from the crowd in Vanity Fair. Whether in sunshine or in shade they are neither eager nor fretful, because they are saved.

The good in Dickens are sojourners also in the literal sense of St. Augustine and St. Paul. They are travelling beyond the earthly city, beyond death. The odd humour of Jenny Wren in *Our Mutual Friend* renders this meaning explicit. On the roof of Pubsey and Company, Fledgeby's financial house in the City, she and Lizzie Hexam ironically discover a 'garden' in which they can withdraw from the earthly city, and there Jenny plays that she is dead. From the stairwell old Riah 'saw the face of the little creature looking down out of a Glory of her long bright radiant hair, and musically repeating to him, like a vision: "Come up and be dead! Come up and be dead!"' As in the ending of *Little Dorrit*, the blessed, few in number, are within the city but not of it. When you feel you are dead, says Jenny,

[1] *LD*, Bk. II, ch. xxxiv, p. 826.

'you hear the people who are alive, crying, and working, and calling to one another down in the close dark streets, and you seem to pity them so!'[2]

The studied pilgrimage of *The Old Curiosity Shop* makes Little Nell and her grandfather the most obvious sojourners in Dickens. Forster tells us that these two were drawn toward death with little 'direct consciousness of design' on Dickens's part, and claims that he himself had to point out the end to which the novel was logically tending.[3] If such is the case, even before the death of Nell and her grandfather became fixed in Dickens's mind, he conceived of them passing somewhere beyond the city. For Nell this goal consists of some rural place of the imagination: 'Let us be beggars. . . . Let us walk through country places, and sleep in fields and under trees, and never think of money again. . . . Let us never set foot in dark rooms or melancholy houses, any more, but wander up and down wherever we like to go; and when you are tired, you shall stop to rest in the pleasantest place that we can find, and I will go and beg for both.'[4] Nothing could express her antipathy to the city more than this proposal to become beggars, to leave 'money' behind them, and to escape the commotion of London. For Dickens does not morally countenance begging as a means of livelihood. Subconsciously, at least, he already realizes that Nell is on her way beyond this life—the life in the city that is defined by death in the final, destructive sense. The death in the country by which Nell will escape from life and death is merely a passage.

In a later dialogue with her grandfather Nell exclaims, 'Let me persuade you, then—oh, do let me persuade you . . . to think no more of gains or losses, and to try no fortune but the fortune we pursue together.' Her use of 'fortune' here is analogous to Paul Dombey's use of the word 'Bank': both usages hint at spiritual alternatives to the grandparent's or parent's fixation on gambling or business, institutions of worldly loss and gain. *The Old Curiosity Shop* is built around a whole series of such dialogues, in which the reader is asked to see through the superficial meanings to the religious implication. Nell explains to the fireman who has allowed them to sleep by his furnace that

[2] *OMF*, Bk. II, ch. v, pp. 281–2.
[3] Forster (Bk. II, ch. vii), I, 117, 123.
[4] *OCS*, ch. ix, p. 71.

she and her grandfather seek 'some distant country place remote from towns or even other villages':

> 'I know little of the country,' he said, shaking his head, 'for such as I, pass all our lives before our furnace doors, and seldom go forth to breathe. But there *are* such places yonder.'
>
> 'And far from here?' said Nell.
>
> 'Aye, surely. How could they be near us, and be green and fresh? The road lies, too, through miles and miles, all lighted up by fires like ours—a strange black road, and one that would frighten you by night.'
>
> 'We are here and must go on,' said the child boldly; for she saw that the old man listened with anxious ears to this account.
>
> 'Rough people—paths never made for little feet like yours—a dismal blighted way—is there no turning back, my child?'
>
> 'There is none,' cried Nell, pressing forward. 'If you can direct us, do. If not, pray do not seek to turn us from our purpose. Indeed you do not know the danger that we shun, and how right and true we are in flying from it, or you would not try to stop us, I am sure you would not.'[5]

Literally the danger that they flee is the gambling mania of her grandfather, which has by now driven him to steal—though so far only from Nell herself and (by borrowing and being unable to pay his debt) from Daniel Quilp. But to read 'the danger that we shun' and Nell's determination so narrowly is as unsatisfactory as to reduce Quilp's motives in the novel to a desire for money. Money means about as much to Quilp as it does to the devil in numerous stories of European folklore—a devil insidiously willing to lend his capital to those whose credit is weakest. The danger that they flee, the grandfather almost reluctantly and the child with heroic determination, can be more clearly described as the loss of salvation. It has to be expressed negatively because the alternative, damnation, is not conceived in *The Old Curiosity Shop* as parallel to salvation, a condition commencing with death, but as a disaster in life: the disgrace of the grandfather (Dickens seems to care little about his guilt) or the sexual violation of Nell. Since life threatens only evil, the heroine, who is nearly crippled with pain, walks inexorably toward death. 'Oh! if we live to reach the country once again, if we get clear of these dreadful places, though it is only to lie down and die, with what a grateful heart I shall thank God for so much

---

[5] *OCS*, ch. xxxi, pp. 232–3; ch. xliv, pp. 332–3.

mercy!' Though Nell's progress seems humanistically and psychologically perverse, it is justified as long as she and her grandfather are to be saved. She acts on that assumption, at least, and takes 'the road that promises to have that end':

'It was a dreary way he told us of,' returned her grandfather, piteously. 'Is there no other road? Will you not let me go some other way than this?'

'Places lie beyond these,' said the child, firmly, 'where we may live in peace, and be tempted to do no harm. We will take the road that promises to have that end, and we would not turn out of it, if it were a hundred times worse than our fears lead us to expect. We would not, dear, would we?'[6]

No other novel of Dickens has so obvious a religious design as *The Old Curiosity Shop*—though *Little Dorrit* makes a quieter use of the same wayfaring metaphor.[7] But novels have other conventional ways of touching on religious themes. The hero of *Martin Chuzzlewit*, for example, undergoes a distinct conversion. Before his illness and near death in far-off Eden young Martin is insufferably selfish; that he is almost as insufferable in his converted as in his unconverted state merely underlines the point: if ever a hero was saved arbitrarily, by grace, it is he. The episode of his illness, near death, and recovery has its parallel in romance literature, in which such an experience regularly contributes to the hero's elevation over ordinary men. Rather coyly, Dickens stresses the religious experience:

[Martin] had sat the whole time with his head upon his hands, gazing at the current as it rolled swiftly by; thinking, perhaps, how fast it moved towards the open sea, the high road to the home he never would behold again. . . .

'Don't give in, sir,' said Mr. Tapley.

'Oh, Mark!' returned his friend, 'what have I done in all my life that has deserved this heavy fate?'. . .

'I said you must be ill,' returned Mark, tenderly, 'and now I'm sure of it. A touch of fever and ague caught on these rivers, I dare say; but bless you, *that's* nothing. It's only a seasoning; and we must all be seasoned, one way or another. That's religion, that is, you know,' said Mark.[8]

---

[6] *OCS*, ch. xlv, p. 334. Steven Marcus argues that this novel assumes a typically Calvinist idea of 'the unbridgeable duality of salvation and damnation': *Dickens: From Pickwick to Dombey* (London, 1965), pp. 163–4.

[7] Cf. Miller, *Charles Dickens*, p. 235.   [8] *MC*, ch. xxiii, pp. 382–3.

Martin Chuzzlewit teaches not only this gospel according to
Mark, but providence according to Dickens. The false and the
misled in the novel foolishly believe that they are the children
of Providence; to surprise and punish them Dickens has Martin
Chuzzlewit senior play the role of God. This role is revealed
suddenly in the chastisement of Pecksniff at the end of the novel,
but revealed as a role that has been only just hidden from the
reader throughout, and altogether hidden from the adherents
of the earthly city. Dickens argues, in fact, that the long sup-
pression of old Martin's judgement causes it to burst forth that
much more wrathfully in the end. All along Martin has understood the principle that has opposed him but has not outwardly
intervened in its operation. 'In every single circumstance,
whether it were cruel, cowardly, or false, he saw the flowering
of the same pregnant seed. Self; grasping, eager, narrow-rang-
ing, over-reaching self; with its long train of suspicions, lusts,
deceits, and all their growing consequences; was the root of the
vile tree.' The reprisal, when it comes, has a brutality that ex-
ceeds the needs of comedy or even of poetic justice. (Only the
irrepressible Pecksniff saves the scene for Dickens.) The dis-
penser of justice, now revealed as the designer of the action as a
whole, defends his action, like Milton's God, with two further
arguments. 'If he had offered me one word of remonstrance, in
favour of the grandson whom he supposed I had disinherited; if
he had pleaded with me . . . I think I could have borne with him
for ever afterwards. But not a word, not a word.' Secondly, he
calls on Pecksniff 'to remember that there again he had not
trapped him to do evil, but that he had done it of his own free
will and agency'.[9] In the illustration for the scene Phiz portrays
a number of books being scattered in the vehemence of old
Martin's attack: one is *Tartuffe* and the other *Paradise Lost*.
The fortunate falls of young Martin in Eden, America, and of
Tom Pinch's expulsion from the false paradise in Wiltshire
(Pecksniff's country home) are apparently rounded out by the
unfortunate fall of the Satanic imposter.

The snaring of Pecksniff is carried out without the knowledge
or help of Pinch or young Martin. These two, the unsuccessful
and the successful devotee of the single heroine, may not contribute actively to their own salvation. John Westlock and Mark

[9] *MC*, ch. lii, pp. 796, 805, 809.

Tapley do contribute, the latter once again specifically inter-
ceding for the hero, persuading old Martin to admit that the
grandson's faults are 'in some degree, of my creation'. Ostensibly, the only need for young Martin in the scene of chastisement is to make Pecksniff suffer more acutely: '"Look there!"
said the old man, pointing at [Pecksniff], and appealing to the
rest. "Look there! And then—come hither, my dear Martin—
look here! here! here!" At every repetition of the word he
pressed his grandson closer to his breast.' Dickens seems unaware
of the distasteful position in which he is placing his hero. The
indelicacy might be said to be as puritanical as the sharp division
between the elect and the damned. Dickens may also be uncertain
of how to manage that difficult question of free will. Old Martin
has secretly designed his ward Mary Graham as the bride of
young Martin, but the young hero also loves Mary of his own
free will. The figure standing in for Providence in this novel is
a jealous god: 'it was little comfort to him to know that Martin
had [already] chosen Her, because the grace of his design was
lost.'[10]

Since the novelist, by the nature of his task, takes command of
the accidents and rewards of life, typically with one eye on the
moral deserts of his characters, literary history long ago observed that novels present a kind of secular paradigm of the
workings of Providence. This old idea of the English novel, in
particular, should not be underestimated. The novel, like the
institution of life insurance satirized in *Martin Chuzzlewit*, coincides historically with the weakening of faith in divine Providence under the impact of science and scepticism. By carefully
matching material rewards to birth, good works, or apparent
grace (in the sense of manners for one school of fiction and in
the Calvinist sense for another) novels helped fill the partial
vacuum of faith. Moreover, Dickens himself understood some
such relation between Providence and the art of the novel, even
though he expressed no theory of the relation. In reply to some
criticism of *A Tale of Two Cities* he wrote to Wilkie Collins:

I think the business of art is to lay all that ground [the exact nature of
Collins's criticism is not clear] carefully, not with the care that conceals itself—to show, by a backward light, what everything has been

10 *MC*, ch. lii, pp. 798, 803, 808.

working to—but only to *suggest*, until the fulfilment comes. These are the ways of Providence, of which ways all art is but a little imitation.[11]

Months later he wrote to another novelist, Bulwer-Lytton, with regard to the same novel:

I am not clear, and I never have been clear, respecting that canon of fiction which forbids the interposition of accident in such a case as Madame Defarge's death. Where the accident is inseparable from the passion and emotion of the character, where it is strictly consistent with the whole design, and arises out of some culminating proceeding on the part of the character which the whole story has led up to, it seems to me to become, as it were, an act of divine justice.[12]

Dickens does not explain the principle of justice involved. Madame Defarge's death is merely stated to be 'inseparable' from her passion and emotion, 'strictly consistent with the whole design', and 'led up to' by 'some culminating proceeding'. (The next sentence in the letter does state that her 'mean death' and the 'half-comic intervention' of Miss Pross are intentionally contrasted with the 'dignity of Carton's wrong or right'.) The meaning of 'inseparable', 'consistent', and 'led up to' depends on assumptions shared with Bulwer-Lytton and other readers about Providence: roughly, that Madame Defarge is damned because a Madame Defarge deserves to be damned; and that as long as the novelist has control of events, she shall be damned in art.

Distribution of rewards and punishments is the major index of providential design in fiction. But this design is likely to impose itself even before the action commences. Characters are apparently committed to the earthly city or, in the case of a few, to be sojourners, well before the opportunity to display merit or demerit arises. And in this respect such novels are specifically Calvinist rather than broadly Christian. The opening paragraph of *Martin Chuzzlewit* ironically balances a common motif in English fiction, family snobbery, against the Christian exegesis of the Old Testament, originated by St. Paul, that assigns the population of each spiritual city its own family history. 'As no lady or gentleman, with any claims to polite breeding, can possibly sympathise with the Chuzzlewit Family without being first assured of the extreme antiquity of the race,' the novel

[11] 6 Oct. 1859, *Letters*, III, 125.   [12] 5 June 1860, *Letters*, III, 162–3.

begins, 'it is a great satisfaction to know that it undoubtedly descended in a direct line from Adam and Eve; and was, in the very earliest times, closely connected with the agricultural interest.' Given the concern of so much nineteenth-century fiction with family and 'breeding', the first sentence of Dickens's novel is already mischievous. For the two families traced by Christian hermeneutics are spiritual classifications that cut across blood relationships. The point is driven home in Dickens's second paragraph: 'It is remarkable that as there was, in the oldest family of which we have any record, a murderer and a vagabond, so we never fail to meet, in the records of all old families, with innumerable repetitions of the same phase of character.'[13] The record of the Chuzzlewit family in the novel will display the same distribution of good and evil.

Predetermination to good or evil is most apparent in villains, whose often motiveless malignity suggests that they are not really moral agents at all—that is, do not make moral choices. Cain, according to Augustine, had no readily understandable motive in slaying Abel:

the founder of the earthly city was a fratricide. Overcome with envy, he slew his own brother, a citizen of the eternal city, and a sojourner on earth. . . . Now these brothers, Cain and Abel, were not both animated by the same earthly desires, nor did the murderer envy the other because he feared that, by both ruling, his own dominion would be curtailed,— for Abel was not solicitous to rule in that city which his brother built,— he was moved by that diabolical, envious hatred with which the evil regard the good, for no other reason than because they are good while themselves are evil.[14]

Many villains in Dickens fit this description: Monks and Bill Sikes, Ralph Nickleby and Squeers, Rudge (Barnaby's father) and Sir John Chester, James Carker, Uriah Heep, Tulkinghorn, Rigaud (alias Blandois), Madame Defarge, Orlick, Drummle, and Compeyson, Rogue Riderhood. True, for every hardened character of this type there are a dozen rascals, whose damnation, like that of Bunyan's Ignorance, is more lightly handled; and a few villains, like Fagin and Quilp, are more like devils incarnate. The Cain-like villains may be human enough, but are originally and irrevocably committed to evil, as if from spite. In the end Dickens can think of no appropriate fate for them except exter-

[13] *MC*, ch. i, p. 1.   [14] *The City of God*, Bk. XV, ch. v.

mination, and the increasing severity of his attitude toward the
hardened criminal in real life can be felt in his fiction. He explicitly compares Rigaud to Cain in *Little Dorrit*, and in the
same chapter the landlady of the Break of Day types this character as follows:

And I tell you this, my friend, that there are people (men and women
both, unfortunately) who have no good in them—none. That there are
people whom it is necessary to detest without compromise. That there
are people who must be dealt with as enemies of the human race.
That there are people who have no human heart, and who must be
crushed like savage beasts and cleared out of the way. They are but
few, I hope; but . . . this man—whatever they call him, I forget his
name—is one of them.[15]

And clearly the landlady of the Break of Day speaks for the
novelist: being crushed to death and cleared out of the way is
Rigaud's eventual fate.

Identifying the descendants of Abel in Dickens's novels presents more difficulties—but the identification of the elect among
the Puritans, too, was always a momentous question. Generally
speaking, heroes, heroines, and, more questionably, those whom
heroes and heroines befriend and are befriended by, are 'the
elect'. The way in which heroes are in certain respects exempt
from the official doctrine of work, their measure of prosperity
and the way they receive favours without being pauperized, the
frequency with which they are wronged and their capacity to
forgive, are ambiguous but positive signs of their salvation.
That some—young Martin, Bella Wilfer, Pip, certainly Mr.
Dombey—do not morally deserve to be saved, merely under-
scores their privileged state. Comparison of such characters with
others of similar situation but divergent rewards betrays the
predetermination of their respective fates. For example, there
are similarities of character and situation between Bella Wilfer
and Silas Wegg in *Our Mutual Friend*: one is inordinately selfish and the other a monomaniac in this respect; both are the
chosen victims of Boffin's pretended miserliness. The climax of
the elaborate hoax carried out by Boffin and Harmon is timed
for the maximum discomfiture and exposure of Wegg, just as it
is timed for the maximum surprise and happiness of Bella; but
she is converted by means of the hoax, whereas he is thrown in

[15] *LD*, Bk. I, ch. xi, p. 127.

a dust-cart and carried off. (Bella is also predestined in old Harmon's will to marry the son, just as Mary is destined by old Martin to marry his grandson in *Martin Chuzzlewit*, but she must still experience conversion and learn to live *as if* she were saved.) In the same novel, a blow on the head and near-drowning convert Eugene Wrayburn at the very moment he decides to seduce Lizzie Hexam; but the near-drowning of Rogue Rider-hood has the contrary effect of making him more presumptuous and unprepared for his real end.

It may be objected that Dickens despised, along with Sabbatarians and prohibitionists, religionists who had the temerity to boast of their election. But his heroes and heroines do not so presume, though the grimly pompous Mrs. Clennam does: 'I take it as a grace and favour to be elected to make the satisfaction I am making here . . . and to work out what I have worked out here.'[16] Nothing is more common in Puritan literature than the berating of precisely those individuals who, like Mrs. Clennam, rashly believe themselves saved. One of the chief practical issues of this faith from the beginning was to avoid the extremes of presumption and despair in the matter of election. Dickens's sensitivity to this issue was no more acute than that of his Puritan forbears, though his talent for belittling presumption is unsurpassed.[17]

In a sense, any novelist who employs a hero or heroine in the conventional way (making the reader's interest hinge on his or her fate) assumes the 'election' of these leading figures in a manner analogous to the Calvinist idea. In *A Tale of Two Cities*, when Charles Darnay has been saved (temporarily) by Doctor Manette, we are told that 'it was . . . impossible [for Lucie] to forget that many as blameless as her husband and as dear to others as he was to her, every day shared the fate from which he had been clutched'.[18] That may be true—for Lucie. But novels have an insidious way of making the reader forget such truths. At the end of *A Tale of Two Cities* the reader is not beset by the thought that many as blameless as Darnay have been guillotined; the suspense of the action has been built up entirely around the expectation and doubt that Lucie and Charles will be

[16] *LD*, Bk. I, ch. xxx, p. 357.
[17] See Haller, *The Rise of Puritanism, passim.*
[18] *TTC*, Bk. III, ch. vii, p. 274.

saved, and whether the sacrifice of Sydney Carton can be sucess-
fully carried out. No matter what Dickens tries to tell us of the
French Revolution in general, the fiction he has composed tells
us to be happy that those who are elected are indeed saved.

The routine of election, suspense, and denouement is not a
monopoly of Dickens among the novelists, but Dickens boldly
intensified the routine. Orwell noted that his heroes inevitably
speak correct English, from the beginning, though in some cases
their class or provincial origin makes this impossible:

A comic hero like Sam Weller, or a merely pathetic figure like Stephen
Blackpool, can speak with a broad accent, but the *jeune premier* always
speaks the then equivalent of B.B.C. This is so, even when it involves
absurdities. Little Pip, for instance, is brought up by people speaking
broad Essex, but talks upper-class English from his earliest childhood;
actually he would have talked with the same dialect as Joe, or at least
as Mrs. Gargery. So also with Biddy Wopsle, Lizzie Hexam, Sissie
Jupe, Oliver Twist—one ought perhaps to add Little Dorrit. Even
Rachel in *Hard Times* has barely a trace of Lancashire accent, an impossibility in her case.[19]

If this argument is extended to morality, and from consideration
of social class to religious destination, then training and early
environment seem even more irrelevant to heroic behaviour.
The child of the Marshalsea—'born there', etc.—has moral
qualities opposite to what her family and environment would
lead one to expect. Though Dickens subscribed to the theory
that many vices and failures were caused by poverty or early
associations, his heroes and heroines seem utterly immune from
such influences: on the contrary, the more difficult their paths in
life, the more exalted their goodness. Early deprivation or repression would seem to be a bad thing in Dickens's social theory,
yet a habit of 'dreaming' and the 'belief in all the gentle and
good things his life had been without' have enabled Arthur
Clennam, for example, to overcome his severe upbringing, and
have 'rescued him to judge not, and in humility to be merciful,
and have hope and charity'.[20] Whatever Dickens may refer to
by 'dreaming' in this context (the sentiments seem vaguely
autobiographical), the explanation in most cases seems to be

[19] Orwell, 'Charles Dickens', pp. 82–3.
[20] *LD*, Bk. I, ch. xiii, p. 165.

that a few persons enjoy a special state of grace, which is confirmed in the denouement of each fiction. What it all may come down to, of course, is that the arbitrariness of Calvinist election has always been similar to the arbitrary goodness or evil in fairy-tales, whose kinship with the novels of Dickens has often been casually noted and then forgotten.

The doctrine of election is peculiarly satisfying to the elect in part because, as in the original case of Cain and Abel and as in many fairy-tales, it is thoroughly unafraid of distinguishing among members of the same family. In *The Pilgrim's Progress*, when Christian decides to leave his wife, who is 'afraid of losing this world', and his children, who are 'given to the foolish delights of youth', the character Charity—oddly enough—draws the moral: 'Indeed Cain hated his brother, "because his own works were evil, and his brother's righteous"; and if thy wife and children have been offended with thee for this, they hereby show themselves to be implacable to good, and "thou hast delivered thy soul from their blood".'[21] In what is surely the most ambitious celebration of the state of grace in English secular fiction, Clarissa Harlowe can enjoy her persecution by her brother James and sister Arabella, and all her other relatives, as a prelude to her death and triumph over the whole family. Dickens, too, presents families that are inexplicably divided between the very, very good and the downright wicked. Little Nell has a gratuitously wicked brother, Frederick Trent; Paul and Florence are so different from the rest of their family that Mrs. Chick cannot believe they are Dombeys; Louisa and Tom Gradgrind have entirely different moral propensities; Little Dorrit's sufferings are compounded by her brother and sister; and Lizzie Hexam suffers from one of the most selfish brothers imaginable. The law of primogeniture introduced still another form of sibling rivalry in English fiction, and novelists, favouring the underdog, typically make heroes of younger sons. Fairytales share this tendency, however, and so was Abel younger brother of the first-born, who belonged to the city of men. Because Dickens often projects his remembered feelings as a child into his fiction, the apartness and righteousness of his heroes is uncommonly intense. More than any major novelist he resorts

21 John Bunyan, *The Pilgrim's Progress*, Everyman's Library (London, 1948), pp. 59–60.

to orphans as heroes, and so little is he concerned with property and primogeniture in this world that he would sometimes rather prove, contrary to the direction of so many English novels, that his protagonists are illegitimate.

The special apartness of Dickensian heroes, analogous to a state of grace, is seriously compromised, however, by a fictional construction that indirectly relates certain of the heroes to the villains. The construction in question mediates between the Calvinist idea of the absolute difference between Cain and Abel and a romantic idea of personality in which evil is always threatening from within. The *Doppelgänger* of German romantic fiction thus facilitated the projection of two sides of a single personality upon two characters, who ordinarily struggle against one another.[22] Dickens followed this construction closely in the relation of Bradley Headstone and Rogue Riderhood in *Our Mutual Friend*, and even more obviously in ' No Thoroughfare ', the long Christmas story in which he collaborated with Wilkie Collins. Stories of doubles are dream-like fictions that depend on a function analogous to 'displacement' in Freudian dream logic.[23] But some uses of displacement in Dickens are overt and others not. By dividing the heroic prerogatives between a pair of identical but unrelated twins in *A Tale of Two Cities*, for example, Dickens makes it possible both to live and to die for love. The impossibility of a single hero both living and dying for love is obvious, and Dickens goes about the task of making it possible in fiction with full deliberation. Some potential contradictions within a single hero, however, would be improper, and Dickens accommodates them in fiction only unconsciously. He divides the contradictory impulses between two characters but conceals, even from himself it appears, their original connection. These are the contradictions that seem to us most modern. The resulting psychological complexity of the novels taken as a whole undermines the strict division of characters good and bad, blessed and unblessed. In a few novels Cain and Abel are strangely allied.

---

[22] See Ralph Tymms, *Doubles in Literary Psychology* (Cambridge, 1949). The device may be studied in E. T. A. Hoffmann, Gogol, and Dostoevsky.

[23] Other dream-like constructions in Dickens's novels, notably 'secondary elaboration', have been pointed out by Taylor Stoehr, *Dickens: the Dreamer's Stance* (Ithaca, 1965).

Julian Moynahan has demonstrated such an alliance in *Great Expectations*.[24] Orlick and Drummle have no motives independent of the hero of this novel. Like Cain, they have no motive for the enmity that they direct at the hero, and, strangely enough, toward others they act as if they had motives that might be ascribed to the hero. Their enmity takes the curious form, in action, of wreaking vengeance on others who have offended or rejected Pip. Orlick murders the hero's termagant sister and lusts after Biddy—whom Pip, without loving, would like to be loved by. To Pip's old enemy Pumblechook he administers an appropriately comic punishment. Drummle, for his part, beats Estella, who has rejected Pip. The two, Orlick and Drummle, are related in appearance and in the mysterious way in which they cross and depart from the hero's life. The wild confrontation of Orlick and Pip at the limekiln, an excrescence in the workmanship of *Great Expectations*, makes sense to the plot only if they are doubles, two aspects of the same ego.

'Wolf!' said he, folding his arms again, 'Old Orlick's a going to tell you somethink. It was you as did for your shrew sister.' . . .
'It was you, villain,' said I.
'I tell you it was your doing—I tell you it was done through you,' he retorted, catching up the gun, and making a blow with the stock at the vacant air between us. 'I come upon her from behind, as I come upon you to-night. I giv' it her! I left her for dead, and, if there had been a limekiln as nigh her as there is now nigh you, she shouldn't have come to life again. But it warn't Old Orlick as did it; it was you. You was favoured, and he was bullied and beat. Old Orlick bullied and beat, eh? Now you pays for it. You done it; now you pays for it.'[25]

That Pip was favoured, or Orlick bullied and beat in that household, is absurd. The whole fantastic scene has the dream-like purpose of disguising the relation of Pip and Orlick—by making

24 'The Hero's Guilt: The Case of *Great Expectations*'. Jonathan Bishop has outlined an even stranger alliance of Oliver Twist and Bill Sikes, in 'The Hero-Villain of *Oliver Twist*', *Victorian Newsletter* (Spring, 1959), 14–16.
25 *GE*, ch. liii, pp. 404–5. Cf. Smerdyakov's accusation of Ivan Karamazov: '*You* murdered him; you are the real murderer, I was only your instrument, your faithful servant, and it was following your words I did it.' *The Brothers Karamazov*, trans. Constance Garnett, Modern Library (New York, n.d.), Bk. XI, ch. viii, p. 758.

the villain this time threaten vengeance on the hero—even while it reveals their alliance.

Dickens perhaps tacitly recognized the relation of David Copperfield and Steerforth as one of displacement, since Steerforth's affair with Emily arouses such ambivalent feelings in the hero. The possibility that Uriah Heep is also a double for the hero was surely unconscious on the novelist's part and has been raised by one or two critics only to be discounted.[26] The parallel experience of the two characters is admittedly very slim: Uriah sleeps in David's old room at the Wickfield's and, after Uriah is disposed of, Agnes remarks that they still think of it as David's room. The two are at least rivals for the same woman, and Uriah has one remote connection with the Steerforth story. (David dreams that Uriah 'had launched Mr. Peggotty's house on a piratical expedition' and 'was carrying me and little Em'ly to the Spanish Main, to be drowned'.) The plot of the novel requires the hero to love Agnes Wickfield without knowing it, and the first man to love her consciously is Uriah, who insists that David foresaw his partnership with Mr. Wickfield and was 'the first to kindle the sparks of ambition in my umble breast'. 'Something in the emphasis he laid upon the kindling of those sparks, and something in the glance he directed at me as he said it, had made me start as if I had seen him illuminated by a blaze of light.'[27] The 'sparks' and the glance at David are the first revelation of Uriah's desire. He goes on to make David, of all people, the confidant of his love. The hero reports that he 'understood' the motive of this confession, but does not specify it. Even if the motive is simply to preclude David's interference, the method is to make him a party to the scheme. Uriah's practical malevolence is directed against the Wickfields, but his wickedness is always experienced as a personal affront to David. Still, in the long run, Uriah is useful to David. He crushes Mr. Wickfield to a shadow of his former self, and until Mr. Wickfield is crushed, no one can marry his daughter.

Uriah's habit is to make a personal appeal to David for his advice and patronage, an appeal that fascinates the hero while it

[26] Leonard Manheim, 'The Personal History of David Copperfield', *American Imago*, IX (1952), 32; Mark Spilka, *Dickens and Kafka* (Bloomington, 1963), pp. 193, 228, and 291 n. 6.
[27] *DC*, ch. xxxv, p. 511; ch. lx, p. 840; ch. xvi, p. 236; ch. xxv, p. 379.

fills him with loathing and hatred. Their relation comes to a climax when Uriah tries to turn Dr. Strong against his wife. He has only the sketchiest motive for this hateful project, but his method is once again to make David his ally. When the scheme is rebuffed by Dr. Strong and they are left alone, David turns on Uriah in a fury: 'You villain . . . what do you mean by entrapping me into your schemes . . . as if we had been in discussion together?' And without waiting for an answer, David strikes him:

> As we stood, front to front, I saw so plainly, in the stealthy exultation of his face, what I already so plainly knew; I mean that he forced his confidence upon me, expressly to make me miserable, and had set a deliberate trap for me in this very matter; that I couldn't bear it. The whole of his lank cheek was invitingly before me, and I struck it with my open hand with that force that my fingers tingled as if I had burnt them.
>
> He caught the hand in his, and we stood in that connexion, looking at each other. We stood so a long time; long enough for me to see the white marks of my fingers die out of the deep red of his cheek, and leave it a deeper red.

The action is quite extraordinary. Smollett, for example, might have consented to the egocentric reduction of evil to a trap 'for me' and an attempt 'to make me miserable', but would never have left the hero hand in hand with his antagonist, watching the marks of his fingers die and then deepen in the other's cheek. The hero's outburst resolves nothing and leaves their relations exactly as before. In the subsequent dialogue (they go right on talking) David swears that he will 'know no more of' Uriah, and Uriah that David 'won't be able to help it'. Uriah more than holds his own. He argues that David is in a wrong position—'which I felt to be true'! David recalls, 'I felt only less mean than he. He knew me better than I knew myself.'[28] The truth is that Uriah also knows Agnes better than David does: at least he recognizes in her a marriageable woman. One would hesitate to connect this knowledge with the foregoing scene if it were not for the way Dickens has confused the sexual desires of his hero and his antagonist in the first place by borrowing their names from II Samuel. King David was a great man and Uriah the Hittite a lesser, but it was Uriah who was legally married to Bathsheba and David who lusted after her.

[28] *DC*, ch. xlii, pp. 619–21.

The case of Rigaud in *Little Dorrit* offers a final instance of
our difficulty. *Little Dorrit* has not the clearest of plots, but even
so the function of Rigaud as a villain is extraordinary. He keeps
turning up in various places; but what, aside from murdering
his wife, has he done? Suddenly he disappears, and Arthur Clennam becomes excited. He reasons that his mother (he presumes
Mrs. Clennam to be his mother) may be suspected of murdering
or otherwise disposing of Rigaud, and to counter this suspicion,
which seems to have occurred to no one but himself, he sends
Cavalletto to find the villain and thereby prove that he has suffered no harm from the house of Clennam. Cavelletto somehow
accomplishes this mission—there is no suggestion of what legal
or other authority the hero has to order Rigaud hunted down,
or why this formidable villain should come along back to London
so peacefully. Rigaud, alias Blandois, alias Lagnier, now turns
up in the Marshalsea, where Arthur is imprisoned for debt.
'Salve, fellow jail-bird! . . . You want me, it seems. Here I am!'
This is the scene that corresponds to the limekiln in *Great
Expectations* and the paralysing confrontation of David and
Uriah. Given the plot that Dickens is committed to, and his
apparent uncertainty as to the purpose of these scenes, it is understandably difficult for him to write sensible dialogue for his
hero. '"You villain of ill-omen!" said Arthur. "You have pur-
posely cast a dreadful suspicion upon my mother's house. Why
have you done it? What prompted you to the devilish invention?"' Rigaud chatters obnoxiously for a while, and Arthur
speaks again: '"I want to know," returned Arthur, without
disguising his abhorrence, "how you dare direct a suspicion of
murder against my mother's house?"' There follows more
chatter, Rigaud boasting over and over that he is a gentleman,
and that Arthur is not. The confrontation is altogether inconclusive, except for this: Arthur at one point says in disgust to
Rigaud, 'Do you sell all your friends?' and Rigaud is quick to
reply, 'How do you live? How do you come here? Have you
sold no friend?'[29] This time Arthur is silent, for the one thing
he has done wrong in his life (he feels guilty about many
things) is to ruin Daniel Doyce and other friends through speculation. With Rigaud's constant talk of being a 'gentleman', one
wonders whether this scene did not inspire the confrontation,

[29] *LD*, Bk. II, ch. xxviii, pp. 742, 744, 749.

conclusive and consciously handled, at the end of *Lord Jim*, in which the guilt of Conrad's hero is suddenly touched by 'Gentleman Brown', his double.

If Rigaud is Clennam's double, the plot of *Little Dorrit* makes a little more sense, and the hero's question, 'Why have you done it?' becomes self-accusing. Superficially, as in the case of *Great Expectations* and *David Copperfield*, the two are contemptuous enemies. In terms of practical activity, the substantially motiveless Rigaud, who is likened to Cain, behaves as if he obeyed motives that logically belong to the hero. Mrs. Clennam and Pet Meagles, two women who have offended against Arthur Clennam, are treated in *Little Dorrit* almost exactly the way Miss Havisham and Estella are treated: the older offender is stricken with paralysis and death and the younger married to a wife-beater. Rigaud operates against both these women, not against the hero. He blackmails Mrs. Clennam and finds out, in the ` end, exactly what Arthur has been trying to discover throughout the novel; he is employed against the Gowans by Miss Wade. When he perishes in the ruins of the house of Clennam, Arthur is freed from the Marshalsea and passes down through the streets with Little Dorrit.

Contrary to the mortal facts of the ancient story, but in keeping with the traditional interpretations, the descendents of Abel in the novels of Dickens always triumph over the descendants of Cain. Yet Cain, with human blood on his hands, seized power over life and death—the manifest power of the murderer, power subconsciously respected, whether from fear or envy, by the rest of mankind. A few novels of Dickens are constructed almost as if the heroes secretly envied Cain's power to manipulate others—especially others of the same family—through violence. Among the community of the elect, some apparently have secret relations to the damned. This romantic consideration carries Dickens far along the road toward *The Interpretation of Dreams* and ideas of personality prevalent in the twentieth century. It does not make any clearer the advantages of belonging, in the nineteenth century, to that lingering community of sojourners.

The determination of heroes and heroines and their friends to hold themselves aloof from the earthly city had already been sufficiently weakened by the gradual fading of their goal, the heavenly city of God. Like the cross on the summit of St. Paul's in *Bleak House*, the promise of the city of God may be 'the crowning confusion of the great confused city'. Even the common pastoral equivalent of a heavenly city seems 'unregainable and far away' in the nineteenth century: when Rosa Bud and Mr. Grewgious return from an excursion up the Thames, in almost the last pages that Dickens wrote, 'all too soon, the great black city cast its shadow on the waters, and its dark bridges spanned them as death spans life, and the everlastingly green garden seemed to be left for everlasting, unregainable and far away'.[30] The rare glimpses of another city are glimpses only, like the 'mirage' that Sydney Carton experiences amid the desert of London. 'In the fair city of this vision, there were airy galleries from which the loves and graces looked upon him, gardens in which the fruits of life hung ripening, waters of Hope that sparkled in his sight. A moment, and it was gone.' Though Dickens may have intended this mirage to be a prevision of Carton's sacrifice of his life at the end of *A Tale of Two Cities*, it shines very dubiously against the cold air, dull sky, dim river, and imaginary sand storm that 'had begun to overwhelm the city'.[31] Moreover, in the end Carton vests his immortality not in the hope of a Christian heaven, but in the memory of Lucie Darnay and her children.

In the nineteenth century it was much easier to accept the reality of the earthly city than to trust in the promise of a heavenly one. Victorian religious treatises made progressive concessions to historical criticism of the Bible and to a second 'revelation' of science. John Robert Seeley's *Ecce Homo* concluded almost apologetically: 'No man saw the building of the New Jerusalem, the workmen crowded together, the unfinished walls and unpaved streets; no man heard the clink of trowel and pickaxe; it descended *out of heaven from God*.'[32] In the *Idylls of the King* Arthur opposes the quest for the Holy Grail, and only Galahad attains the heavenly city. As Sir Percivale watches Galahad flee over the wasteland, over a thousand piers, every one of which bursts into flame as he passes, the spiritual city appears the size

[30] *MED*, ch. xxii, p. 254.
[31] *TTC*, Bk. II, ch. v, pp. 84–5.
[32] *Ecce Homo, a Survey of the Life and Work of Jesus Christ*, 2nd ed. (London, 1866), p. 330.

of a single pearl—'No larger, though the goal of all the saints'. Tennyson pointedly juxtaposes this brief vision with descriptions of a humble village, 'with gossip and old wives, / And ills and aches, and teethings, lyings-in, / And mirthful sayings', and of a town where Sir Percivale might have found domestic happiness with his childhood sweetheart, if he had not vainly pursued the Grail.[33]

[33] 'The Holy Grail', ll. 528, 553–5.

Part Three

THE BRIDE FROM HEAVEN

In old days there were angels who came and took men by the hand and led them away from the city of destruction. We see no white-winged angels now. But yet men are led away from threatening destruction: a hand is put in theirs, which leads them forth gently towards a calm and bright land, so that they look no more backward; and the hand may be a little child's.

GEORGE ELIOT, *Silas Marner*

IX

THE HEARTH

THE Christian tradition of two cities is inseparable from Dickens's fiction and yet unsatisfactory as an informing principle. The earthly city is unmistakably present, reinforced by a satiric tradition and the daily experience of the surrounding metropolis; but the promise of the heavenly city is muted or even denied. The same must be concluded of Christian concepts generally as they inform Dickens's work: they are inescapably there and yet finally elusive. The principle of grace is wishfully operative in the fiction yet not formally admitted; Christianity apparently contributes more to the complexity of social questions than it does to their solution; the teachings of Christ on charity and forgiveness run into unforeseen contradictions. 'We'll drink the daisies of the field, in compliment to you,' Steerforth moodily addresses David—whom he likes to call 'Daisy'; 'and the lilies of the valley that toil not, neither do they spin, in compliment to me—the more shame for me!' Apparently both Steerforth's conscience and the novelist labour under the impression that scripture reproves those lilies.[1] As so often, Dickens's Puritan ethic fails to come to grips with Christ's teaching. The fault is not Dickens's alone; that teaching was hard enough to comprehend even before the rapid ebbing of the sea of faith in the nineteenth century. The age as a whole, by means of a resurgence of religious feeling, vainly struggled to encircle and conceal its increasing secularism. If we can persuade ourselves to begin afresh the search for a religious centre in Dickens, however, the picture may clear. And to a large degree the difficulties of this search turn out to be difficulties of the too obvious.

The problem that challenges the imagination of Dickens can be named the city: the city condemned by satirists and sanitary engineers, overpopulated and undergoverned—above all, the city of death. And the Church, perplexed with the charge of

[1] *DC*, ch. xx, p. 295; cf. Matthew 6:25–31; Luke, 12:22–30.

supernaturalism, was less well equipped to cope with death than
in the past. The problem was in many ways unanswerable; the
future of individual life, as of the city, was obscure. Confronted with this problem, however, the nineteenth century developed a homely remedy of its own—so snug, so cherished, so
endlessly invoked, that we are apt to discount its importance and
its considerable success. The practical extension of this remedy
was the conviction that clean and tidy homes were the most prom-
ising answer to urban poverty and desolation. The sentimental
side was the celebration, as the antithesis of the city, of the fireside at home. 'A cheerful fire was blazing on the hearth, my lamp
burnt brightly, my clock received me with its old familiar wel-
come,' writes Master Humphrey; 'everything was quiet, warm
and cheering, and in happy contrast to the gloom and darkness
[of the city] I had quitted.'[2] No writer was fonder of exploiting
this contrast than Dickens; if the problem that besets him can
be called the city, his answer can be named the hearth. Surrendering to the obvious, we need to explore this antithesis, which can
be found everywhere in the nineteenth century and has survived
as an important expression of our own values.[3]

    The Dickensian celebration of hearth and home is so familiar
that it requires little documentation in itself. The celebration
begins memorably with Christmas at Dingley Dell and continues most notably in the Christmas books, where scoffers like
Tackleton in *The Cricket on the Hearth* and Dr. Jeddler in *The Battle
of Life* are betrayed by their anti-domestic sentiments—'Bah!
what's home? . . . Four walls and a ceiling!' or, 'a real home is
only four walls; and a fictitious one, mere rags and ink'.[4] With
Scrooge, these are the unbelievers in the religion of Dickens.

    [2] *OCS*, ch. i, p. 13.

    [3] Cf. Gordon N. Ray, *The Buried Life* (Cambridge, Mass., 1952), p. 14:
'Thackeray came to see life permanently in terms of a dichotomy between the
warmth and trust of a happy home circle and the brutality or indifference of the outside world.' Ruskin's lecture, 'Of Queens' Gardens', a central repository of Victorian ideas on women and home, makes the general point: 'This is the true nature
of home . . . the shelter, not only from all injury, but from all terror, doubt, and
division. . . . so far as the anxieties of the outer life penetrate into it, and the incon-
sistently-minded, unknown, unloved, or hostile society of the outer world is
allowed by either husband or wife to cross the threshold, it ceases to be home; it is
then only a part of the outer world which you have roofed over, and lighted a fire
in.' *Sesame and Lilies*, in *Works*, XVIII, 122. See also Houghton, *The Victorian
Frame of Mind*, pp. 343–8.

    [4] *CB*, pp. 176, 269.

But more effective than the propaganda of home in these stories are the domestic scenes, the firesides and family circles that are defended against the surrounding city. For Dickens makes us feel the Cratchits' home, or the Nubbles's home in *The Old Curiosity Shop*, or the instrument maker's in *Dombey and Son*, as sanctuaries; beyond them the streets are places of alienation or even physical danger. The phenomenon is a common one in modern literature, and *Ulysses* without the kitchen at 7 Eccles Street would be as intolerable as *A Christmas Carol* without the Cratchits' fire; it is only when these few saving interiors fail the protagonists, as is likely to be the case in Kafka, that the urban setting becomes traumatic. Dickens applied this felt antithesis between the hearth and the city to his concern for the nameless poverty of London; and in so doing spelled out its ultimate implications. 'Bleak, dark, and piercing cold,' he writes in *Oliver Twist*, 'it was a night for the well-housed and fed to draw round the bright fire and thank God they were at home; and for the homeless, starving wretch to lay him down and die.'[5] Given the premises of London life and of the earthly city, home represents nothing less than life in the midst of death.

Dickens's portrayal of the clerk Wemmick in *Great Expectations* is meant to be humorous, yet nowhere in literature is the modern segregation of hearth and city, of personal life and business, so sharply and consciously drawn. Wemmick's tiny home in Walworth is a castle defended against the city. The eccentricity of its owner, his moat and drawbridge and secret communication with the outside, his livestock and cucumber frame, express the peril and safety of urban life: 'if you can suppose the little place besieged, it would hold out a devil of a time in point of provisions.' The whole conception of Wemmick's castle looks forward to that moment in the twentieth century when the advent of the hydrogen bomb caused a wave of shelter-building and stockpiling of powdered milk in the cities of the West. More obviously, the home life of John Wemmick uncannily resembles that of today's suburbanite: 'I am my own engineer, and my own carpenter, and my own plumber, and my own gardener, and my own Jack of all Trades.' The flash of Dickens's imagination in 1861 suddenly illuminates, in the midst of the division of labour on which the modern city is founded, that curious domestic and

5 *OT*, ch. xxiii, p. 165.

defensive regression to a past in which individuals performed all such tasks for themselves. This surge of independence in one aspect of the worker's life merely accentuates, and probably responds to, the increasing separation of his home from his economic function in the city. Wemmick, with his two personalities, is the very symbol of this separation. 'No; the office is one thing, and private life is another. When I go into the office, I leave the Castle behind me, and when I come into the Castle, I leave the office behind me.'[6] That Wemmick adheres to this divided life with such conscious solemnity makes the point that much more universal and prophetic. For the joke is that he regards his radically divided life as perfectly natural.[7]

What the hearth signifies for Dickens is primarily the family, not the sprawling household of earlier centuries, in which numerous collateral relatives and others carried on part or all of their day's work on the premises, but the modern conjugal family, in which refuge is sought from the day's work. Master Humphrey, who has no family, but who must hide from the city at his fireside like everyone else, imagines his room peopled with companions. Relations with family and friends are the only relations in the city that are not commercial. The other human being or beings at each hearth differentiate it from streets, and they are chiefly remarkable for the selfless sacrifices they perform. As Master Humphrey reflects in his solitude and imaginary companionship, 'Amid the struggles of this struggling town what cheerful sacrifices are made; what toil endured with readiness; what patience shown and fortitude displayed for the mere sake of home and its affections!'[8] Work that Dickens really celebrates is 'sacrifice'—work dedicated to some loved one.

[6] GE, ch. xxv, pp. 196, 197.

[7] In the first volume of the History of England (1849) Macaulay wrote of the adverse effect of this division of life on the government of the City of London: 'This revolution in private habits has produced a political revolution of no small importance. The City is no longer regarded by the wealthiest traders with that attachment which every man naturally feels for his home. It is no longer associated in their minds with domestic affections and endearments. The fireside, the nursery, the social table, the quiet bed are not there. Lombard Street and Threadneedle Street are merely places where men toil and accumulate. They go elsewhere to enjoy and to expend. . . . The chiefs of the mercantile interest are no longer citizens. They avoid, they almost contemn, municipal honours and duties.' Works, ed. Lady Trevelyan, 8 vols. (New York, 1897), I, 275.

[8] MHC, p. 113.

The hearth is a symbol of these close relations. 'When I speak of home,' explains Nicholas Nickleby, 'I speak of the place where, in default of a better, those I love are gathered together.'[9] This symbol, with its peculiar moral and sentimental overtones, becomes a cliché of Victorian literature. Arthur Pendennis, the Thackerayan counterpart of David Copperfield, addresses his friend Bows: 'I do not mind telling you, sir, that on this Sabbath evening, as the church bells were ringing [when else?], I thought of my own home [what else?], and of women angelically pure and good, who dwell there [who else?]; and I was running hither as I met you, that I might avoid the danger which besets me [the temptation of Fanny Bolton's love], and ask strength of God Almighty to do my duty.'[10]

That the literature of home so often expresses itself as a series of clichés makes it all the more imperative that we examine it seriously. Northrop Frye believes that the comic action in Dickens 'moves toward a regrouping of society around the only social group that Dickens regards as genuine, the family'.[11] Many persons, outside literature, continue to find the family the only society that matters—with all the safeguards and dangers that assumption affords. The family as we know it is a comparatively recent institution, an institution that matured in the nineteenth century.[12] As the historian Philipe Ariès has argued, the modern family does not have to be regarded as a vestigial institution struggling against the inroads of modern individualism but may be seen as a product of individualism itself, and a reaction to industrial and urban experience. Instead of the natural focus of a loosely bounded social life, the modern family faces outward in a defensive posture, as if the foremost purpose of life were the nurture and education of children who will continue to guard the hearth and home. So far has this institution advanced today that it almost conflicts with wider habits of

[9] *NN*, ch. xxxv, p. 443.
[10] *The History of Pendennis*, ch. xlix, p. 487. Quotations from Thackeray are from the Biographical Edition, 13 vols. (Toronto, 1899).
[11] 'Dickens and the Comedy of Humors', in *Experience in the Novel*, ed. Roy Harvey Pearce (New York, 1968), p. 63.
[12] A critical distinction is drawn between the ancient and modern family in Sir Henry Maine, *Ancient Law*, 4th ed. (London, 1870), p. 133; the first edition appeared in 1861. Cf. Émile Durkheim, 'La Famille conjugale' (1892), in *Revue philosophique*, XCI (1921), 1–14.

sociability.[13] Mark Spilka has suggested, writing specifically of
Dickens, that an almost mechanical relation obtains between
urban life and this family. The felt hostility of the city intensifies
the need for both love and discipline at home, and the inevitable
contradiction of the two parental roles thus exaggerated ('maternal love' and 'paternal rule') in effect prevents the nineteenth-century child from growing to adulthood.[14] Such interpretations of Dickens and his contemporaries, including the
reduction of Victorian sexuality to a regressive interest in childhood, are frankly Freudian in orientation; but Freud's discoveries would hardly have been made if he had lived two centuries
earlier. The assumptions we make today about the rather heated
relations of parent and child, and indeed our experience of these
relations, are themselves outgrowths of the Victorian hothouse,
as it has been called: the family in its closed, inward aspect.

'Before marriage and afterwards, let [young couples] learn
to centre all their hopes of real and lasting happiness in their own
fireside,' is the early advice of Dickens, in *Sketches of Young
Couples*; 'let them cherish the faith that in home, and all the
English virtues which the love of home engenders, lies the only
true source of domestic felicity; let them believe that round the
household gods, contentment and tranquility cluster in their
gentlest and most graceful forms; and that many weary hunters
of happiness through the noisy world, have learnt this truth too
late, and found a cheerful spirit and a quiet mind only at home
at last.' He backs up this advice with a timely recommendation
(it is 1840) of the example of Queen Victoria and Prince Albert.[15]
These sentiments seem dated to us, not because we no longer
enjoy gazing at children, or warming ourselves at fires, or eating
dinner, nor because we do not easily put such feelings into words,
but because of the incantation of such sentiments that the Victorians required, as if they were at once more confident of such
values than we are and more desperate to affirm them. Religious
doubt in some way contributed to this ritual sentiment, as if the
need for spiritual comfort, too, turned inward on the family. The

[13] *L'enfant et la vie familiale sous l'ancien régime* (Paris, 1960); translated as
Centuries of Childhood (New York, 1962). On the newness of the modern family in
relation to the novel as a genre, see Ian Watt, *The Rise of the Novel* (Berkeley and
Los Angeles, 1957), pp. 139–41.
[14] *Dickens and Kafka*, p. 14.
[15] *SB*, pp. 602–3.

scenes of domestic life in *In Memoriam*—genre sketches in which
the poet becomes, by analogy, the husband or the bride of his
lost friend, and which nearly embarrass the twentieth-century
reader—are in a sense replies to the religious doubts of Tennyson's poem. So is the celebration of Edmund Lushington's marriage in the epilogue.[16] In an earlier poem, 'The Two Voices',
a tedious night of doubting is resolved by church bells and the
sight of a family of three proceeding to church:

> One walked between his wife and child,
> With measured footfall firm and mild,
> And now and then he gravely smiled.
>
> The prudent partner of his blood
> Leaned on him, faithful, gentle, good,
> Wearing the rose of womanhood.
>
> And in their double love secure,
> The little maiden walked demure,
> Pacing with downward eyelids pure.

It seems unlikely that such an image can balance successfully the
long wakeful night of discursive doubt that has preceded it, yet
the image is surely more affirmative than the mere whisper of
the second voice, 'Be of better cheer.'[17] I have just recalled how
Tennyson, in the *Idylls of the King*, pointedly contrasts Sir
Percivale's vain quest for the holy grail with the opportunity of
domestic happiness that might have been his if he had not been
bound by his unfortunate vow. The opposition of hearth and
home to doubts of personal immortality is especially logical;
for the family confers both biological and legal means of coping
with death, in the survival of one's progeny and in their title to
one's property.

The intensified celebration of the family can be interpreted
as part of an effort to substitute for transcendental beliefs values
that could be experienced in this life. For the traditional religion
such values were merely shadows of a life to come. According to
Augustine, 'There was indeed on earth, so long as it was needed,
a symbol and foreshadowing image of [the heavenly city],

16 E.g., *In Memoriam*, xl, lx, xcvii.

17 'The Two Voices', ll. 412–20, 429. These are the lines that T. S. Eliot cited
in 'The Metaphysical Poets' to call attention to 'something which had happened
between the time of Donne . . . and the time of Tennyson': *Selected Essays* (London, 1966), p. 287.

which served the purpose of reminding men that such a city was to be, rather than of making it present; and this image was itself called the holy city, as a symbol of the future city, though not in itself the reality.' Nineteenth-century positivism undermined the very premise of this argument. If there was a holy city, it should preferably not be the image of some other place, but the thing itself. Essentially, that city would either have to be discovered in the here and now or else foregone forever. 'In the earthly city,' Augustine continues, '. . . we find two things—its own obvious presence, and its symbolic presentation of the heavenly city.'[18] Of the earthly city there was more evidence than ever in the nineteenth century; but rather than surrender the heavenly city altogether, this century would find both its symbolic presentation and its reality in the family surrounded by the earthly city. So Dickens writes in *The Cricket on the Hearth* that the steam from the Peerybingles' kettle 'hung about the chimney-corner as its own domestic Heaven'.[19]

Instead of a Christian symbolism the hearth suggests a more primitive symbolism. Shelter and warmth, after all, are human needs that antedate Christianity. More importantly, these needs were met by human ingenuity long before cities came into being. The very outward shape and appearance of cities differ so from more primitive dwellings that cities seem hostile to earlier communities. The hostility was perceived (and returned) by Spengler:

The village, with its quiet hillocky roofs, its evening smoke, its wells, its hedges and its beasts, lies completely fused and embedded in the landscape. . . . It is the Late city that first defies the land, contradicts Nature in the lines of its silhouette, *denies* all Nature. It wants to be something different from and higher than Nature. These high-pitched gables, these Baroque cupolas, spires, and pinnacles, neither are, nor desire to be related with anything in Nature. And thus begins the gigantic megalopolis, the *city-as-world*, which suffers nothing beside itself and sets about *annihilating* the country picture.

A few pages later Spengler holds out this hope: 'So long as the hearth has a pious meaning as the actual and genuine centre of a family, the old relation to the land is not wholly extinct.'[20]

[18] *The City of God*, Bk. XV, ch. ii.
[19] *CB*, p. 161.
[20] *The Decline of the West*, trans. Charles Francis Atkinson, II (New York, 1928), pp. 94, 100.

8. *Little Nell*, by Willis Maddox

9. *Under the Arches*, by Gustave Doré

Freudian logic interprets such symbolic forms—harsh lines, spires and pinnacles on the one hand, curves and enclosures on the other—as male and female. Though it is difficult to believe that cities and homes can be unconsciously experienced as male and female, or were ever so experienced by man, Mumford has very suggestively contrasted the functional differences of the earliest cities from those of more primitive enclosures in sexual terms.[21] A passage in *Oliver Twist* makes even village graves contrast comfortably with the city. Oliver 'seemed to enter on a new existence there. . . . Hard by, was a little churchyard; not crowded with tall unsightly gravestones, but full of humble mounds, covered with fresh turf and moss: beneath which, the old people of the village lay at rest.'[22] It is very like Mumford's contrast between neolithic and later, urban cultures.

Many descriptions of the city in Dickens bristle with chimneys, steeples, and masts: these are standard props of satiric descriptions of the city generally, and they afford a respectable contrast with more intimate scenes. After his accidental incarceration for the night in the Marshalsea, Arthur Clennam has an interview with Little Dorrit in which she cannot help crying a little as she talks of her father—'Such a good, good father!'

He let the little burst of feeling go by before he spoke. It was soon gone. She was not accustomed to think of herself, or to trouble any one with her emotions. He had but glanced away at the piles of city roofs and chimneys among which the smoke was rolling heavily, and at the wilderness of masts on the river, and the wilderness of steeples on the shore, indistinctly mixed together in the stormy haze, when she was again as quiet as if she had been plying her needle in his mother's room.[23]

There is no comfort whatever in the typical cityscape that meets Clennam's eye as he turns away from Little Dorrit. With measured pace Dickens is already developing the personal relation that will be Arthur's salvation. Little Dorrit weeps selflessly for her father, whose room in the Marshalsea and place in her affections the hero will one day occupy; and he sees her once more as he saw her the first time in his mother's room. What seems irrefutable, on evidence entirely independent of Freudian

---

[21] *The City in History*, chs. i–ii.
[22] *OT*, ch. xxxii, p. 238.
[23] *LD*, Bk. I, ch. ix, p. 99.

symbolism, is that for Dickens, at least, the principle opposed to the city resides in some relation with the female sex. But to arrive at this conclusion is to open a critical problem that may be aptly called Pandora's box.

Presiding over each hearth is a cheerful female eidolon. Rose Maylie, to take an early example, 'was in the lovely bloom and spring-time of womanhood; at that age, when, if ever angels be for God's good purposes enthroned in mortal forms, they may be, without impiety, supposed to abide in such as hers'. Her attributes are all such that 'earth seemed not her element', and all, especially her cheerful smile, 'were made for Home, and fireside peace and happiness'. Yet it cannot be said that married love is celebrated very directly in *Oliver Twist*. The main affective relation with Rose is Oliver's rather than Harry Maylie's. She turns out to be Oliver's aunt in actuality and his 'sister' by preference: '"Not aunt," cried Oliver, throwing his arms about her neck; "I'll never call her aunt—sister, my own dear sister, that something taught my heart to love so dearly from the first! Rose, dear, darling Rose!"' And for that matter, she has been brought up as Harry's sister, too.[24] In *Martin Chuzzlewit* the love of Ruth Pinch and John Westlock is explicitly celebrated as a magic equivalent of the heavenly city that transforms the London scene:

They went away, but not through London's streets! Through some enchanted city, where the pavements were of air; where all the rough sounds of a stirring town were softened into gentle music; where everything was happy; where there was no distance, and no time. There were two good-tempered burly draymen letting down big butts of beer into a cellar, somewhere; and when John helped her—almost lifted her—the lightest, easiest, neatest thing you ever saw—across the rope, they said he owed them a good turn for giving him the chance. Celestial draymen![25]

But that is not the whole story, for again the main affective relation is not between these two, who are about to be married, but between Ruth and her brother Tom, who have already set up housekeeping in Islington. If anyone, it is really Tom who has discovered the sexual attraction of his sister: 'how altered you are, Ruth! . . . You are so improved . . . you are so woman-

[24] *OT*, ch. xxix, p. 212; ch. li, p. 401.
[25] *MC*, ch. liii, p. 817.

ly'; and he tenderly embraces her and smooths down her hair.
A whole chapter has been devoted to their domestic life in 'two
small bedrooms and a triangular parlour,' where she brushes
'Tom's old hat round and round and round again, until it was
as sleek as Mr. Pecksniff', and glances 'demurely every now and
then at Tom, from under her dark eye-lashes' while she and he
play at making pudding. In fact, they are caught making pudding
when John Westlock walks in for the first time, and Ruth
'started and turned very red'. The novel is designed so that the
love of brother and sister appears to outlast that of husband and
wife, and the final paragraphs play on the heavenly theme, not
of celestial draymen in the enchanted city of romantic love, but
of Ruth and Tom Pinch.

And coming from a garden, Tom, bestrewn with flowers by children's
hands, thy sister, little Ruth, as light of foot and heart as in old days,
sits down beside thee. From the Present, and the Past, with which she
is so tenderly entwined in all thy thoughts, thy strain soars onward to
the Future. As it resounds within thee and without, the noble music,
rolling round ye both, shuts out the grosser prospect of an earthly
parting, and uplifts ye both to Heaven![26]

The conjugal family celebrated by Dickens, without losing anything of its warmth and sense of enclosure, exhibits a tendency
to take in additional female relatives that seems historically conservative and sexually ambiguous.

Often enough, to address a Victorian heroine as 'sister' is
merely the prelude to a warmer theme. When Florence Dombey
pledges Walter Gay, 'I'll be your sister all my life', or when
Agnes Wickfield and David Copperfield begin to 'brother' and
'sister' each other in earnest, the rest of the story is clear.[27]
But a literal *ménage à trois* is by no means looked down upon
either. As Esther Summerson prates of Ada Clare and Richard
Carstone in *Bleak House*, 'I was to live with them afterwards;
I was to keep all the keys of their house.' Since Carstone dies,
the roles of the two girls are reversed at the end, and Ada becomes housekeeper to Jarndyce; but a pleasing memento of the
original plan is left in the person of little Richard, Ada's child
by Carstone, who 'says that he has two mamas, and I [Esther]

[26] *MC*, ch. xxxvi, pp. 570, 576; ch. xxxix, pp. 600, 603, 604; ch. liv, p. 837.
[27] *D & S*, ch. xix, p. 264; *DC*, ch. lx.

am one'.[28] As soon as Ruth Pinch and John Westlock enter the triangular parlour alone, for once, to seal their engagement, 'They soon began to think of Tom again': 'I am never to leave him, *am* I dear? I could never leave Tom. I am sure you know that.'[29] It is customary to refer such cozy arrangements of hearth and home to Dickens's frustrations with his own marriage. The trail left behind by that particular unhappiness shows the novelist projecting his need for sympathy on both sisters-in-law, Mary and Georgina Hogarth (the latter was the effectual manager of the household throughout his marriage). He wrote to Miss Coutts of his separation from Mrs. Dickens, 'No one can understand this but Georgina, who has seen it grow from year to year, and who is the best, the most unselfish, and most devoted of human Creatures. Her sister Mary, who died suddenly and who lived with us before her, understood it as well in the first months of our marriage.'[30] These personal considerations, once again, have to be judged in the light of cultural sanctions that were partly responsible for the presence of Dickens's sisters-in-law in his home in the first place. The constraining influence of the modern family had not yet eliminated every single relative but the wife and child from its company; and sisters or others bound to this family were part of the enclosed circle around the fire, not representatives of the urban and industrial world outside. Female relatives were inevitably bound closer to the home than males, but fiction also sentimentalized and exaggerated their role while tending to leave their male counterparts unnoticed. Thackeray had no sisters-in-law in his home: in *The History of Pendennis*, however, after the hero has engaged himself to Blanche Amory, the true heroine does not hesitate to ask if she may live with the couple after their marriage—and Laura Bell is a very model Victorian young lady. The hero replies affirmatively: 'I . . . want my wife on one side of the fire and my sister on the other.' Later he writes to Blanche that they might occupy rooms over the offices of the *Pall Mall Gazette*: 'there are four very good rooms, a kitchen, and a garret for Laura.'[31]

[28] *BH*, ch. xiv, p. 182; ch. lxvii, p. 879. Cf. James Broderick and John Grant, 'The Identity of Esther Summerson', *Modern Philology*, LV (1958), 257.

[29] *MC*, ch. liii, p. 819.

[30] 9 May 1858, *Coutts Letters*, p. 355.

[31] *Pendennis*, ch. lxvi, p. 658; ch. lxxii, p. 709.

Regarding a marriageable woman as a ward or daughter is not unlike regarding her as a sister. Little Dorrit 'thought what a good father [Clennam] would be. How . . . he would counsel and cherish his daughter', and Clennam reciprocates this view. 'Thinking of her, and of the possibility of her father's release from prison by the unbarring hand of death . . . he regarded her, in that perspective, as his adopted daughter, his poor child of the Marshalsea hushed to rest.'[32] It often happens in stories of romantic love that suitors must await a change in attitude or even the death of the loved one's father, but in *Little Dorrit* the supplanting of the father is so thorough that it culminates in the hero's occupation of the father's exact room in the prison, with all the ministrations that the heroine earlier devoted to the Father of the Marshalsea. In *Martin Chuzzlewit* the heroine is literally the adopted daughter of the man who, sometimes confusingly, bears the same name as the hero. In *A Tale of Two Cities* and *Our Mutual Friend* much is made of accommodating a father instead of a sister at the side of the fire. '"Look here, Pa!" Bella put her finger on her own lip, and then on Pa's, then on her own lip again, and then on her husband's. "Now we are a partnership of three, dear Pa."'[33] More remarkably, the physical byplay of Bella and her father, whom she calls Rumpty, is more pronounced throughout the novel than are any of the caresses exchanged with John Harmon. Bella and her father openly discuss the unsatisfactoriness of Mrs. Wilfer as a companion for him, and the chapter that describes their intimate dinner at Greenwich is entitled, 'In which an Innocent Elopement Occurs'. Before the triangular affair of Rumpty, Bella, and Harmon is put down to the disparity in age of Dickens and Ellen Ternan, it should be remembered how Dolly Varden and her father hugged and kissed long ago in *Barnaby Rudge*, with asides on the imagined jealousy of any lover. Part of Florence Dombey's unhappiness, too, is that she has been deprived of this relation: she gazes enviously at the family next door, who have lost their mother, but in which the eldest daughter is always sitting by the father's side, 'or on his knee, or hanging coaxingly about his neck'. This child, though younger than Florence, has become her father's 'little housekeeper'.[34] The most general conclusion that

32 *LD*, Bk. I, ch. xiv, p. 168; ch. xvi, pp. 187–8.
33 *OMF*, Bk. IV, ch. iv, p. 668.   34 *D & S*, ch. xviii, pp. 247–8.

emerges from these transmutations and incestuous games is
simply the fondness for portraying the heroine as both woman
and child. Other evidences of the same syndrome are the ambiguous ages of the child heroines and the epithet 'Little', which had
special connotations of innocence.[35] Little Nell is fourteen, and
therefore either child or woman as one pleases; Little Dorrit is
twenty-two at the commencement of the story and sometimes
annoyed at not being recognized as a woman by the hero, yet
she is thought by everyone to be a child and signs herself, in a
letter to Clennam, 'Your poor child, LITTLE DORRIT'.[36]

At Dingley Dell the frolic and joking chiefly concern love and
matrimony, yet curiously enough the host on that famous occasion, Mr. Wardle, has, in number of female relations, a mother,
a sister, and daughters but no wife. The Peggotty family in
David Copperfield is even more studiously asexual in its family
relations. Such friendly fireside groups, together with the tendency to make children out of grown women and the residence of
sisters and fathers in the conjugal family—to say nothing of the
way the latter are likely to be more caressed than wives and
sweethearts—suggest the repression of 'normal' relations between adults of the opposite sex: a diagnosis that has often been
applied to both Dickens and his audience. Spilka, for example,
believes that Dickens's 'unhealthy predilection for sexless love
. . . was reflected in his novels by his concentration on the love
of fathers and daughters, uncles and nieces, sons and mothers,
or brothers and sisters, and by his sentimentalization of adult
romance', though he adds somewhat cryptically that the Victorians were our superiors at keeping alive 'the quality and
worth of childhood love'.[37]

But repression of sexuality is not a sufficient explanation of
such phenomena in any case. A novel of what is today called
'adult sexuality' is, in the first place, of no more intrinsic value
than a novel, say, of paternal love. Nor is a novel about paternal
love necessarily dishonest because it is not explicit about the
sexual component of the love. Oddly enough, we wish just as

[35] Compare Little Dorrit's preference for this name (*LD*, Bk. II, ch. xi, p. 552)
with Little Em'ly's guilty objections to the same: 'You need not call me Little,
you need not call me by the name I have disgraced' (*DC*, ch. xl, p. 587).

[36] *LD*, Bk. II, ch. iv, p. 471.

[37] 'Little Nell Revisited', *Papers of the Michigan Academy of Science, Arts, and
Letters*, XLV (1960), 432, 437; cf. *Dickens and Kafka*, pp. 47–8.

much to read about passions in their multiform disguises as we do of passions in naked genital embraces; passions are more often than not disguised in real life, and their extraordinary complexity, and even their universality, are often a function of the disguise. For that matter, a longing for an admiring sister-in-law may be just as real as a longing for a wife or mistress—and is almost certain to be more dangerous.

The main error of reducing all the varieties of incestuous sentiment in Victorian fiction to repression, of seeing the triangular parlours of Victorian culture as evasions of sexuality, is that this negative explanation conceals from view the positive aim of such arrangements. The pressures on hearth and home are such that much more is longed for than sexual pleasure, much more is hoped for than domestic comfort. The heroines of hearth and home bear the modern burden of a relationship that has been construed in Christian times as incompatible with sex. The present critical tendency to treat nineteenth-century novelists— more especially nineteenth-century audiences—as afraid of sex misses even the traditional argument for repression: namely, that in quest of the heavenly city, sexuality, like every other aspect of the earthly city, must be left behind.

The point of transmuting sweethearts and wives into sisters and daughters, or of living snugly with sisters and daughters as well as wives, was not necessarily to substitute one for the other female relation, but ideally to enjoy both, or all three relations in the enclosure of the hearth. The ritual language of the hearth often strives to combine these roles in a single sentence. When Annie Strong publicly embraces Dr. Strong in *David Copperfield*, she incants: 'this dear face, revered as a father's, loved as a husband's, sacred to me in my childhood as a friend's'.[38] In the emotional interview of *A Tale of Two Cities* in which Darnay confesses his love for Lucie Manette to her father, he solemnly avers, 'I know that when she is clinging to you, the hands of baby, girl, and woman, *all in one*, are round your neck.' And he adds, almost mystically, 'I know that in loving you she sees and loves her mother at her own age, sees and loves you at my age, loves her mother broken-hearted, loves you through your dreadful trial and in your blessed restoration.' Lucie thus becomes the hopeful counterpart of the peasant girl whose rape by

[38] *DC*, ch. xlv, pp. 662–3.

Darnay's uncle destroyed her senses and who kept repeating wildly to the young Dr. Manette, 'My husband, my father, and my brother!' and no other words.[39]

The convergence of the available intimate family relations—daughter, sister, wife, mother—can also be observed in the novels of Thackeray. In *Pendennis*, after the hero is finally straightened away, Laura has an opportunity to say to Fanny Bolton, 'I am—that is, I was—that is, I am Arthur's sister.' But in addition to sister and fiancée, 'She was his mother's legacy to him.' And this relation obtains, not only because Helen Pendennis always wished that her son would marry her adopted Laura (the child of her first lover by another woman, and in that sense, too, Arthur's sister), but mystically, symbolically: when Laura and the hero embrace for the first time as lovers, 'Come and bless us, dear mother,' he prays, 'and arms as tender as Helen's once more enfold him.'[40] In the more heated adventures of *Henry Esmond* the hero-narrator writes of 'his beloved mistress, who had been sister, mother, goddess to him during his youth'. '"I think the angels are not all in heaven," Mr. Esmond said. And as a brother folds a sister to his heart; and as a mother cleaves to her son's breast—so for a few moments Esmond's beloved mistress came to him and blessed him.' When Mr. Esmond finally married Lady Castlewood, some reviewers thought Thackeray had gone too far.[41]

The effect of this convergence of roles is often to make a single heroine function as if she belonged to more than one generation of the family. Even outside fiction, in a public address at Leeds in 1847, Dickens defined women as 'those who are our best and dearest friends in infancy, in childhood, in manhood, and in old age, the most devoted and least selfish natures that we know on earth, who turn to us always constant and unchanged, when others turn away'.[42] He thus hints of a divinity that can be experienced 'on earth', and a principle 'constant and unchanged' that ministers to our mortal needs. This ministry, from infancy to old age, would seem to require a series of

---

[39] *TTC*, Bk. II, ch. x, p. 126, italics added; Bk. III, ch. x, p. 305.

[40] *Pendennis*, ch. lxxiv, p. 728; ch. lxvi, p. 655; ch. lxxiv, p. 725.

[41] *The History of Henry Esmond*, Bk. II, ch. vi, pp. 192, 196. For the reviews see John E. Tilford, Jr., 'The "Unsavoury Plot" of *Henry Esmond*', *Nineteenth-Century Fiction*, VI (1951), 121–30.

[42] *Speeches*, p. 83.

ladies in separate roles, and yet 'constant and unchanged, when others turn away', implies that they are one. In a related passage on the prehistory of Little Nell he writes: 'If you have seen the picture-gallery of any one old family, you will remember how the same face and figure—often the fairest and slightest of them all—come upon you in different generations; and how you trace the same sweet girl through a long line of portraits—never growing old or changing—the Good Angel of the race—abiding by them in all reverses—redeeming all their sins.' By appealing to an ancestral line, he rationalizes the multiple role of the angel in the modern family. The portraits enable Nell and her mother, and her mother before that, never to grow old or change. 'In this daughter the mother lived again,' the passage continues.[43] The timelessness of the female principle is important, and a factor that in itself opposes the finite experience of the city and legislates against the sexuality of heroines. Sexuality brings only the survival of the race, not their redemption. Moreover, sexuality cannot bring personal survival to the individual, the male individual who is at the centre of this myth. It implies, on the contrary, his biological death. And it is against death, I shall argue, that the heroines of the hearth are finally enlisted.

The proposition, 'In this daughter the mother lived again,' requires special comment, for it is not immediately evident that mothers have a positive role in the novels of Dickens. The inclusion of 'sons and mothers' in Spilka's list of the sexless relations in Dickens, for instance, might be questioned. The mothers who first come to mind, Mrs. Nickleby, Mrs. Micawber, and Mrs. Wilfer, are hilarious caricatures. Lady Dedlock and Mrs. Steerforth are not calculated to engage our sympathies, and there are a host of minor, officious matrons in the canon that nearly set one's teeth on edge: Mrs. Varden in *Barnaby Rudge* and Mrs Fielding in *The Cricket on the Hearth*; and in *Bleak House*, not only Mrs. Jellyby but the mother of Allan Woodcourt and the offensive Mrs. Guppy. A note preserved in the number plans for *David Copperfield*—'Young mother—Tendency to weakness and vanity'—makes Dickens's intention for Mrs. Copperfield unmistakable.[44] More extraordinarily, both sexual aggressors in that novel, Uriah Heep and Steerforth, have mothers who

[43] *OCS*, ch. lxix, p. 524.
[44] See Butt and Tillotson, *Dickens at Work*, p. 117.

abet their favourite children, and Annie Strong's mother, Mrs.
Markleham, is similarly inclined. Against such a tribe as these
a handful of trustful lower-class women such as Mrs. Rudge,
Mrs. Toodles, and Mrs. Nubbles, show rather weakly, as do
the occasional asides praising mothers as a class or the toast of
the Cheeryble brothers to 'The Memory of our Mother'.[45] It
has sometimes been conjectured that the mothers in Dickens
reflect his childhood disappointment in his own; but of course
Dickens is not alone among the novelists in neglecting or belittling mothers, or even in portraying them as hostile. The most
prominent mother in Scott's novels, for example, Lady Ashton
in *The Bride of Lammermoor*, might easily qualify for the title
of greatest villain. The best general explanations of this treatment of mothers are that they have too many conflicting roles
in real life to enter gracefully into fiction, that they are further
encumbered by social and legal prejudices against them, that they
are too biological a thought for ideal fictions. Mothers suggest too unmistakably that their children were born, and will
subsequently die. With few exceptions (notably in Thackeray
and D. H. Lawrence) English fiction has failed to look mothers
steadily in the eye.

But if one has faith in the return of the repressed, the mothers
in Dickens are not hard to discover. 'In this daughter the mother
lived again,' in the words of *The Old Curiosity Shop*. The ideal of
motherhood, which Dickens in one place calls 'the nearest and
dearest of human relations',[46] turns up in other guises, in the
deliberate confusion of female roles at the hearth. When Grace
Jeddler becomes a mother to her sister Marion, in *The Battle of
Life*, then Dickens can exclaim, 'Great character of mother, that,
even in this shadow and faint reflection of it, purifies the heart,
and raises the exalted nature nearer to the angels!'[47] Dickens
is nearly as explicit at the end of *Little Dorrit*. Clennam's supposed mother is fortunately not his at all; the only true mother
of his childhood was 'great Nature'. 'But, in the tones of the voice
that read to him [Little Dorrit's voice, in the Marshalsea],
there were memories of an old feeling of such things, and echoes
of every merciful and loving whisper that had ever stolen to him

45 *NN*, ch. xxxvii, p. 476.
46 'No Thoroughfare', *CS*, p. 579.
47 *CB*, p. 244.

in his life.'[48] Little Dorrit as Mother Nature is only less con-
spicuous than the conception of Jenny Wren in *Our Mutual
Friend*, who has become the mother of her own father. With true
insight Chesterton saw that Dickens's childlike heroines were
'little mothers' rather than children:

in many parts of Dicken's work there is evidence of some peculiar affection on his part for a strange sort of little girl; a little girl with a premature sense of responsibility and duty; a sort of saintly precocity.
Did he know some little girl of this kind? Did she die, perhaps, and
remain in his memory in colours too ethereal and pale? In any case
there are a great number of them in his works. Little Dorrit was one of
them, and Florence Dombey with her brother, and even Agnes in infancy; and, of course, Little Nell. And, in any case, one thing is evident;
whatever charm these children may have they have not the charm of
childhood. They are not little children: they are 'little mothers.'[49]

Though the answer to Chesterton's questions is Mary Hogarth,
we have no reason to believe that Miss Hogarth herself was a
little mother. The source of Chesterton's insight is *Little Dorrit*,
in the curious introduction of Maggy, the imbecile of twenty-
eight whose consciousness has been arrested by disease at the
age of ten, and who addresses the heroine as 'little mother'.
When Clennam sees, at their interview in his Covent Garden
rooms, that he has distressed Dorrit by calling her 'my child',
he asks if he may call her Little:

'. . . let me call you Little Dorrit.'
'Thank you, sir, I should like it better than any name.'
'Little Dorrit.'
'Little mother,' Maggy (who had been falling asleep) put in, as a
correction.
'It's all the same, Maggy,' returned Dorrit, 'all the same.'
'Is it all the same, mother?'
'Just the same.'[50]

Shortly after this interview in *Little Dorrit* the heroine is
mistaken for a child by the prostitute who stops her in the streets
at dawn and asks for her blessing. When she discovers that
Maggy's companion is not a child, the prostitute recoils; she is
one of those fallen creatures who are good enough not to want to
contaminate pure women. She urges Little Dorrit to go home to

[48] *LD*, Bk. II, ch. xxxiv, p. 815.
[49] Chesterton, *Charles Dickens*, p. 122.
[50] *LD*, Bk. I, ch. xiv, pp. 167–8.

her father and 'be afraid of me'.[51] This is not the place to enter
into that bewildering subject of fallen women in the Victorian
age, except to note how the common expression of their fall
returns to the basic antithesis of home and the streets. When
another such woman, apparently better off than the prostitute
who accosts Little Dorrit, encounters Little Nell at the races,
the same point is made: she 'bade her go home and keep at home
for God's sake'.[52] Women of the streets are regularly designated also by phrases that invert the quasi-religious position of
women in the home. A prostitute in *The Haunted Man* is duly
referred to as 'the ruined Temple of God'; in Alice Marwood of
Dombey and Son shines 'a ray of the departed radiance of the
fallen angel'.[53] Even in a letter Dickens will speak of fallen
women as 'tarnished and battered images of God'.[54] It is sufficient to note that the Victorians did not speak of any class of men
in this fashion.

The religion of the hearth is strangely pre-Christian. It often
seems closer to the worship of Lares and Penates than to
Christianity. One of the signatures of Victorian literature, in
truth, is the frequent reference to 'household gods'. The phrase
is invoked casually, for the most part, but is worth stopping for.
In 'What Christmas Is As We Grow Older' the household gods
are linked with the memory theory: 'Be all ungentleness and
harm excluded from the temples of the Household Gods, but be
those remembrances admitted with tender encouragement!'[55]
The same gods are supposed especially dear to the family of
humble circumstances. According to *The Old Curiosity Shop*, the
poor man's 'household gods are of flesh and blood, with no alloy
of silver, gold, or precious stone; he has no property but in the
affections of his own heart; and when they endear bare floors
and walls, despite of rags and toil and scanty fare, that man has
his love of home from God, and his rude hut becomes a solemn
place.' The moral is that the truly valuable relations are those
family relations available to rich and poor alike. 'The ties that
bind the wealthy and the proud to home may be forged on earth,
but those which link the poor man to his humble hearth are of

51 *LD*, Bk. I, ch. xiv, p. 175.
52 *OCS*, ch. xix, p. 151.
53 *CB*, p. 366; *D & S*, ch. xxxiv, p. 489.
54 3 Nov. 1847, *Coutts Letters*, p. 103.
55 *CS*, p. 25.

the truer metal and bear the stamp of Heaven.'[56] Similarly, according to Ruskin:

so far as [a home] is a sacred place, a vestal temple, a temple of the hearth watched over by Household Gods, before whose faces none may come but those whom they can receive with love,—so far as it is this, and roof and fire are types only of a nobler shade and light,—shade as of the rock in a weary land, and light as of the Pharos in the stormy sea;—so far it vindicates the name, and fulfills the praise, of Home.[57]

The ritual of the hearth and worship of the female figure presiding there are concentrated especially in Dickens's Christmas books. Thus the cricket discourses to John Peerybingle on the merits of the latter's wife and deliberately puns on the ritual meanings of the word 'sacrifice':

The hearth she has—how often!—blessed and brightened . . . the hearth which, but for her, were only a few stones and bricks and rusty bars, but which has been, through her, the Altar of your Home; on which you have nightly sacrificed some petty passion, selfishness, or care, and offered up the homage of a tranquil mind, a trusting nature, and an overflowing heart; so that the smoke from this poor chimney has gone upward with a better fragrance than the richest incense that is burnt before the richest shrines in all the gaudy temples of this world!—Upon your own hearth; in all its quiet sanctuary; surrounded by its gentle influences and associations; hear her! Hear me! Hear everything that speaks the language of your hearth and home![58]

The conception is a very common one in this period. The image of sacrificial fires is quite as determinedly exploited by clerical interpreters of the religion of home. The Victorian preacher J. Baldwin Brown contends that 'There is an altar of sacrifice whose fire is ever burning in every household, and all the richest and purest joys of the household spring out of the offerings which are laid upon its shrine.'[59] Coventry Patmore employs the same image in *The Angel in the House*:

[56] *OCS*, ch. xxxviii, pp. 281–2.
[57] *Sesame and Lilies*, in *Works*, XVIII, 122. Cf. Isaiah, 32:2.
[58] *The Cricket on the Hearth*, *CB*, pp. 210–11.
[59] *The Home Life: in the Light of Its Divine Idea* (London, 1866), p. 45. Cf. the same writer's *Young Men and Maidens: a Pastoral for the Times* (London, 1871), pp. 32–3: 'It belongs mainly to the women to keep alive on the world's hearth the sacred fire. The earthly fire the men will look to: remember, young girls, it is yours specially to look to the Divine. The German races, as you know, were from the very first distinguished by a kind of religious reverence for woman. They believed there was a sacred element in her composure which made her, in a measure

> And I perceiv'd, (the vision sweet
> Dimming with happy dew mine eyes,)
> That love and joy are torches lit
> From altar fires of sacrifice.[60]

George Eliot, who felt very deeply about the unsung heroism of humble places, also wrote of the household gods; she understood better than Brown or Patmore the historical mixture of old and new in the domestic religion. Silas Marner 'loved the old brick hearth as he had loved his brown pot—and was it not there when he had found Eppie? The gods of the hearth exist for us still; and let all new faith be tolerant of that fetichism, lest it bruise its own roots.'[61]

The rediscovery of the religion of the hearth in the nineteenth century is as important to the history of sentiment as the rediscovery of the idea of natural right in the seventeenth century is to political thought. Dickens's scornful contrast of the hearth to gaudy temples is a contrast natural to Puritanism; but the same contrast is invoked by Fustel de Coulanges in his history of the domestic religion of archaic Greece and Rome: 'religion dwelt not in temples, but in the house; each house had its gods; each god protected one family only, and was god only in one house'. The many half-serious allusions to household gods in nineteenth-century literature reflect a popular interest in ancient history; but it might also be argued that Fustel exaggerates the role of domestic religion in the ancient world because that religion especially appealed to his own time. The ancient religion of the hearth was intimately associated with the worship of the dead, and came to be centred about the chaste goddess Vesta, before whom sexual intercourse was not permitted to take place. According to Fustel, 'Ancient morality, governed by this [domestic religion], knew no charity; but it taught at least the domestic virtues. Among this race the isolation of the family was the commencement of morals. Duties,

---

which man as man with difficulty attains to, the mouthpiece of the gods. The classical nations were not without some glimpses of the same great truth. A woman was regarded as the organ of the Divinity in their most noted oracle, and women, virgin women, were trusted with the guardianship of the sacred fire on the hearth of Vesta at Rome.'

[60] Bk. II, Canto x, in *The Poems of Coventry Patmore*, ed. Frederick Page (London, 1949), p. 193.

[61] *Silas Marner*, Bk. II, ch. xvi, p. 212.

clear, precise, and imperious, appeared, but they were restricted within a narrow circle.'[62]

But in Greek and Roman society the religion that Fustel describes merged successfully, for a time, with the state religion of the cities; whereas the domestic religion of the nineteenth century, despite the appeals of patriotism, grew inward and apart from the city. This was one of the legacies of Christianity, that all spirituality, even of pagan origin, must develop in isolation from the earthly city. The Puritan strain of Christianity redoubled this tendency to separateness. As a sociologist Herbert Spencer was familiar with the new critical distinction, which he found in Sir Henry Maine, between the ancient and the modern family. Spencer's ideal was 'that medium state in which there has been finally lost the compound family-group, while there is a renovation of the family-group proper, composed of parents and offspring'. His respect for the modern family was balanced, however, against the Puritan ethic of individualism. Therefore, and somewhat ironically, the 'cardinal distinction between the ethics of the Family and the ethics of the State' must be maintained at all costs.[63]

[62] *The Ancient City*, trans. Willard Small (New York: Anchor Books, n.d.), pp. 38, 100. *La Cité antique* was first published in 1864; this English translation, in 1873.

[63] *The Principles of Sociology*, Pt. III, ch. ix (1876); 3 vols. (New York, 1916), III, 719.

X

THE SPIRIT OF LOVE AND TRUTH

The Cricket on the Hearth is potentially another story of January and May; but when John Perrybingle doubts his young wife, the voice of the cricket reassures him: 'All things that speak the language of your hearth and home, *must* plead for her! . . . For they speak the truth.' Likewise, the nimble fairies in their home 'never showed her, otherwise than beautiful and bright, for they were Household Spirits to whom falsehood is annihilation'.[1] Oblique references to truth abound in such homely contexts of Dickens's fiction, and they are scattered about (often with a capital letter) among his efforts to find words for the brides he has missed in real life. In a letter to a stranger hinting that the death of Mary Hogarth inspired *The Old Curiosity Shop* he writes: 'The grave has closed over very deep affection and strong love of mine. So far, and no farther, there is Truth in it.' The solemn reference to 'Truth' echoes a passage in the novel on the death of Nell.[2] Again, to his friend T. J. Thompson he writes of the imagined death of Christiana Weller, 'As I live, I write the Truth, and feel it.'[3]

Dickens tenders a similar sentiment in a late defence of his treatment of Nancy in *Oliver Twist*, in which he concludes: 'It is useless to discuss whether the conduct and character of the girl seems natural or unnatural, probable or improbable, right or wrong. IT IS TRUE.' One can smile at Dickens's tenacity here and judge that he asserts only the verisimilitude of his art— except that he has just said that he cares not whether the fiction is 'natural or unnatural, probable or improbable', or even whether it is 'right or wrong'. And he continues illogically that his treatment of Nancy 'is emphatically God's truth, for it is the

---

[1] *CB*, pp. 211, 212.

[2] To Jos. S. Smith, 12 Feb. 1842, *Letters*, I, 382; cf. *OCS*, ch. lxxii, p. 544.

[3] 11 Mar. 1844, *Letters*, I, 580. For Christiana Weller, see Johnson, I, 497–504, 572–3.

truth He leaves in such depraved and miserable breasts; the hope
yet lingering there; the last fair drop of water at the bottom of
the weed-choked well'.[4] Somehow 'IT IS TRUE' refers not only
to Dickens's artistic achievement but to Nancy's truth, her
loyalty, presumably, to Sikes and to Oliver. Moreover, his elaboration in terms of truth at the bottom of a well calls up a host
of proverbial and allegorical associations. This unfortunate girl,
though fallen, is the embodiment of truth. She is a distant relative—very distant, to be sure—of Laura Bell in *Pendennis*:
'How was it that a simple country-girl should be the object of
fear and trembling to such an accomplished gentleman as Mr.
Pen? . . . As he rode from Clavering to Baymouth, he felt as
guilty as a schoolboy who doesn't know his lesson, and is about
to face his master. For is not Truth the master always, and does
she not have the power and hold the book?'[5]

The imprecision of these sentiments is forbidding; yet in a
sense the responsibility for this imprecision is no longer Dickens's
or Thackeray's, but ours: we can either leave it alone or try its
depths. At least a name for the sentiment is available: the spirit
of love and truth. In the late Christmas story 'Mrs. Lirriper's
Legacy', Jemmy Jackman, in his idealized version of his parents'
relations, imagines them saying, 'Unchanging Love and Truth
will carry us through all!'[6] Here and elsewhere love and truth
are sounded as the slogan of domestic trials, but the epithet 'Unchanging' hints (compare the 'constant and unchanged' nature
of the women in our lives) that love and truth are identified with
the heroine or some other angelic figure in Victorian fiction.[7]

The unchanging heroine of *Little Dorrit* embraces her father
in his newly discovered good fortune just as 'she had in the long
years of his adversity encircled him with her love and toil and
truth'. She will continue that embrace (to the extent that he will
permit her) until he dies in her arms. Meanwhile, in 'the old
room' in the Marshalsea, arrives Arthur Clennam, and 'Her
absence in his altered fortunes made it, and him in it, so very
desolate and so much in need of such a face of love and truth,
that he turned against the wall to weep, sobbing out, as his heart

---

[4] *OT*, Preface, p. xvii.

[5] *Pendennis*, ch. lxvi, p. 655.

[6] *CS*, p. 431.

[7] The present chapter occasionally borrows from my earlier essay, 'The Allegory of Truth in English Fiction', *Victorian Studies*, IX (1965), 7–28.

relieved itself, "O my Little Dorrit!"' Again the heroine proves constant amid inconstant fortunes, and when she becomes poor again, she vows in that room to serve Arthur 'with all my love and truth'.[8] Agnes Wickfield, who represents the same principle and devotes herself with similar constancy to both a father and a hero, addresses herself more nearly to a doctrine of love and truth. Her ministrations are less active than Little Dorrit's, the faith she avows more abstract: 'if any fraud or treachery is practising against [my father], I hope that simple love and truth will be stronger in the end . . . than any evil or misfortune in the world.' David, who is engaged to Dora Spenlow at this time, is forced to acknowledge 'how strong [Agnes] was, indeed, in simple love and truth'.[9] Similarly, though he is still engaged to 'Blanche' Amory, Pendennis cannot refrain from exclaiming to Laura: 'Ah, sister . . . how spotless, and full of love and truth, Heaven made you!' Earlier in the novel, when the city has come between Pen and his mother in the country, Thackeray asks if his hero is 'the only one, who in his progress through this dark life goes wilfully or fatally astray, whilst the natural truth and love which should illumine him grow dim in the poisoned air, and suffice to light him no more?'[10] In the end Pen does marry Laura, his mother's candidate and replacement; he continues to speak of 'the love and truth glowing in her face' in *The New-comes*, and again of her 'love and truth' in *The Adventures of Philip*.[11] Pendennis's career as the narrator of the later novels perhaps unfairly allows Laura to outlive Agnes as a spirit of love and truth. But the most persevering Victorian heroine is Mabel Stanley of *The Pirates of Penzance*, who plights her troth until 1940, when Frederic, the unfortunate apprentice who was born in leap year, will come of age:

> Oh, here is love, and here is truth,
>   And here is food for joyous laughter.
> He ⎱
> She ⎰ will be faithful to ⎰ his ⎱ sooth
>   ⎱ her ⎰
>   Till we are wed, and even after.

---

[8] *LD*, Bk. I, ch. xxxv, pp. 418–19; Bk. II, ch. xxvi, p. 719; ch. xxxiv, p. 817.
[9] *DC*, ch. xxxv, pp. 511–12. Cf. ch. xlii, p. 613; ch. xlix, p. 707.
[10] *Pendennis*, ch. lxxi, p. 704; ch. xlv, p. 452.
[11] *The Newcomes*, ch. lix, p. 630; *Philip*, ch. xiii, p. 242.

That truth should be stressed in domestic contexts and linked so persistently to love is not surprising. The English definition of truth is very ample: contrary to the usage of most European languages the English word stands for both loyalty, in a whole range of personal relations, and truth-telling, the correspondence of words or other signs to facts. The faithful correspondence of words to reality, and of persons to each other, was vividly present to the Victorians as the secure basis of science and commerce as well as love. Devotion to truth in this sense has remained one of the common denominators, sometimes the only common denominator, of modern values. Truth-telling was defended against expediency by utilitarian ethics.[12] It was defended intuitively by Joe Gargery: 'There's one thing you may be sure of, Pip . . . namely, that lies is lies.'[13] It was incised in the morality of consequences by Joe's creator, who directed in his 'Appeal to Fallen Women', Polonius-fashion, 'Above all things, to be truthful in every word you speak.' In the mark system that Dickens devised for the inmates at Shepherd's Bush a bad mark was always to be given cautiously, 'but when it is deserved under the head of "truthfulness", by any wilful falsehood, no matter what, it is never to be foregone'.[14] Truthfulness was in many ways thought of as a peculiarly nineteenth-century virtue. The new sociology confirmed that increased truthfulness was one of the important differences between an 'industrial' and a 'military' society. W. E. H. Lecky ventured that 'industrial veracity' was the *only* positive contribution of the growth of manufactures to morals.[15] But science and commerce held no monopoly in the field; gentlemanly interests also championed truth. Thackeray asserted the prerogative of the gentleman 'through evil or good to maintain truth always'; and Trollope held that 'true honour, true love, true worship, and true humanity' were the proper themes of literature.[16] In these polite contexts the twin imperatives of loyalty and truth-telling become one. The more publicly and sonorously truth is celebrated, the

[12] Mill, *Utilitarianism* (London, 1863), pp. 31–3.
[13] *GE*, ch. ix, p. 65.
[14] 28 Oct. 1847; 29 Aug. 1848; *Coutts Letters*, pp. 100, 125.
[15] *History of European Morals*, 2 vols. in one (London, 1913), I, 138–9. This work was first published in 1869.
[16] Concluding paragraph to *The Four Georges*; Trollope, *Autobiography*, Oxford World's Classics (London, 1961), p. 186.

greater the tendency to subsume all its meanings under one word. As Arthur himself intones in the *Idylls of the King*, 'Man's word is God in man.'[17] Truth becomes the single value of widest currency in the nineteenth century. The religious overtones of this value are due as certainly to the resurgence of Puritanism as to romantic nostalgia. Milton was hardly the only voice in the seventeenth century to make truth strong, next to the Almighty; the history of truth in the eighteenth and nineteenth centuries is that of steady secularization, a process that paradoxically enhances the value and may even render it more nearly absolute. 'Your honesty is *not* to be based either on religion or policy,' according to Ruskin. 'Both your religion and policy must be based on *it*.'[18]

Novelists naturally stress the personal relation of truth. In this sense they may be seen as the most conservative and traditional of the celebrants of truth, since etymologically the word first meant loyalty or good faith (Old English *tríewe*, *tréowe*), and the cognates that preserve the original meaning (*trow*, *troth*, *betrothal*) came to be used exclusively for the relation of marriage. 'If I can teach politicians that they can do their business better by truth than by falsehood, I do a great service, but it is done to a limited number of persons,' Trollope rationalized. 'But if I can make young men and women believe that truth in love will make them happy, then, if my writings be popular, I shall have a very large class of pupils.' He follows up this argument with a paragraph in praise of Laura Bell.[19] English heroines of the nineteenth century typically obey and advertise both imperatives of truth. Jeanie Deans, whose 'love of truth' became a legend, would not tell a lie to save her sister from death; yet her loyalty inspired her epic journey to London and saved her sister after all. In *Middlemarch* the story of Mary Garth and Fred Vincy is by far the most conventional action. In spite of every temptation Mary remains loyal to Fred and becomes, in effect, his salvation; but she is also the strict proponent of the other meaning of truth: 'honesty, truth-telling fairness, was Mary's reigning virtue'.[20] In *The Spoils of Poynton*, by James,

---

17 'The Coming of Arthur', l. 132.
18 *Time and Tide*, in *Works*, XVII, 348.
19 *Autobiography*, pp. 192–3.
20 *Middlemarch*, Bk. I, ch. xii, p. 169.

the heroism of Fleda Vetch consists in keeping the hero to his word; her loyalty must be compatible with his engagement to the other girl. 'You mustn't break faith. Anything's better than that. . . . The great thing is to keep faith.' Mona Brigstock contemptuously refers to Fleda as the hero's 'Mummy', and no doubt there is something maternal in Fleda's love. Like Laura Bell, she is closely allied with the hero's actual mother, and her way of loving Owen Gareth differs from Mona's in its respect for truth. 'Nobody had a right to get off easily from pledges so deep and sacred [as a betrothal]. . . . Of a different manner of loving she herself was ready to give an instance, an instance of which the beauty indeed would not be generally known.'[21]

The heroine of truth has a distinguished history, and she is always a woman who makes no outward show or sexual appeal.[22] She participates in one or the other of two traditional plots that may be thought of as allegories. In one tradition she is opposed by a figure of falsehood, who does make a superficial appeal to the hero. Jane Austen's *Mansfield Park*, Mrs. Gaskell's *Wives and Daughters*, James's *The Wings of the Dove* and *The Golden Bowl* have opposed heroines of this kind. Their contest goes back to that of Una and Duessa in the first book of *The Faerie Queene*, but in some ways seems to have been most meaningful to the nineteenth century. Tennyson, significantly, began to construct the *Idylls* around the stories of Enid and Vivien, and the early trial copies of the poem were subtitled 'The True and the False'. In the novel, the contest of truth and falsehood is the special province of Thackeray. Each of his first three major novels employs a true and a false heroine, both in respect to truth-telling and loyalty: Becky and Amelia, 'Blanche' and Laura, Beatrix and Lady Castlewood. *The History of Pendennis*, in particular, is cast into allegorical shape: the design for the covers of the monthly parts showed the hero torn between domestic virtue and the more flashy figure of falsehood.[23] More obviously allegorical is the Trollope novel with a similar plot, *The Eustace Diamonds*, in which Lucy Morris contends with the flashy and stupendously deceitful Lizzie Eustace. 'How unlike she was to Lucy!' The

---

[21] *The Spoils of Poynton*, ch. xvi, pp. 196–7; ch. xiv, p. 167; ch. ix, pp. 106–7.

[22] A possible exception as to sex is Tom Pinch, who 'might have been the Spirit of Truth, in a homely dress'. *MC*, ch. l, p. 763.

[23] Cf. Gordon N. Ray, *Thackeray: the Age of Wisdom, 1847–1863* (London, 1958), p. 108.

hero 'knew that the difference was that between truth and false-hood'.[24] And though few Victorian heroines can be reduced to allegorical figures, none of the good heroines, who triumph in the end, offends against truth. As Bella Wilfer says to Lizzie Hex-am, 'I have no more of what they call character, my dear, than a canary-bird; but I know I am trustworthy.'[25]

A second tradition represents truth as the daughter of a diffi-cult old man, a daughter who will not flatter or tell lies, but whose loyalty is unswerving. This martyrdom of truth, as dis-tinct from her rivalry with falsehood, is the special province of Dickens in the nineteenth century. *The Old Curiosity Shop*, in particular, is a redaction of *The Tragedy of King Lear*. The sins of the old man have evolved from misrule to gambling and spending of other people's money—sins of the bourgeois imag-ination; and he has been insulated from the heroine by a missing generation. She accordingly has become younger and more frail, with none of the ordinary humanity of Shakespeare's heroine. But like Cordelia, Nell's only dower is truth. Some internal evidence—a storm and snatches of phrase like 'I will be pa-tient'[26]—suggest that Dickens unconciously shaped the novel under the influence of Macready's production of *King Lear*; while the parallel to *The Pilgrim's Progress* and the continual reference to the principals as 'the child' and 'the old man' give it a more pronounced allegorical cast than most novels of its time. These are not hard and fast lines. Lord Jeffrey declared that there had been 'nothing as good as Nell since Cordelia'; Forster compared her to Una.[27] Other novels, *Wives and Daughters* and *The Golden Bowl*, more obviously put together both traditional representations of truth. The latter, especially, balances the con-test of true and false heroines with the loyalty of daughters to fathers, and does so with an almost Dickensian sense of the child mothering her parent.

According to Sleary in *Hard Times*, 'there ith a love in the world, not all Thelf-interetht after all, but thomething very dif-ferent'.[28] When Dickens sets out to demonstrate this love, he typically concentrates on the love of a daughter for her father.

[24] *The Eustace Diamonds*, Modern Library (New York, n.d.), ch. xix, p. 176.
[25] *OMF*, Bk. III, ch. ix, p. 524.
[26] *OCS*, ch. liv, p. 407.
[27] Forster (Bk. II, ch. x), I, 147; (Bk. VI, ch. ii), II, 33.
[28] *HT*, Bk. III, ch. viii, pp. 292–3.

In fact Sleary is led to this reflection by observing the devotion of Sissy Jupe to her departed father. Sissy Jupe and Lizzie Hexam, Madeline Bray and Lucie Manette in the genteel class, all exemplify scrupulous and highly conventional fidelity to fathers. When Nicholas Nickleby discovers Miss Bray's domestic history, for example—her incredible loyalty to a wretched father who is prepared to sell her person—he is able to appreciate 'the truth and purity of her heart'; and this in turn enables him to avoid 'such a passion as young men attracted by mere beauty and elegance may entertain'.[29] This relation is extremely conventional and can be met with almost anywhere in novels and romance. The case of four heroines of Dickens, however, is altogether of a different order. The loyalty of Little Nell, Florence Dombey, Agnes Wickfield, and Little Dorrit assumes mythic proportions. The fathers of these four behave with utmost perversity; the redemptive powers of the spirit of love and truth expand to meet this opportunity; and the conventional transference of loyalty from father to husband becomes a ritual of salvation. For it will be noted that after *The Old Curiosity Shop* Dickens gradually permits more and more of the love and truth to flow toward the younger hero. This in itself increases the intensity of the heroine's service, since the process refuses to acknowledge any lesser commitment to the father.

Little Dorrit focuses more deliberately than any previous novel of Dickens on the relation of this heroine to the hero, yet none of the novels makes more of her relation to her father. The extravagance and unworthiness of William Dorrit, and his callousness towards his daughter, make the truthfulness of Little Dorrit irrational but heroic: 'What affection in her words, what compassion in her repressed tears, what a great soul of fidelity within her, how true the light that shed false brightness round him!' Yet this truth is also unheroic, because it is lowly and domestic. Dickens has in mind an emblematic, classical figure; he has in mind his own conception of the child-mother; he joins Scott and George Eliot, Thackeray and Trollope in the quest of an unheroic heroine of home, and outdoes them all by choosing the humiliated home of the debtor's prison. 'There was a classical daughter once—perhaps—who ministered to her father in his prison as her mother had ministered to her. Little Dorrit,

29 *NN*, ch. xlviii, p. 625.

though of the unheroic modern stock, and mere English, did much more, in comforting her father's wasted heart upon her innocent breast, and turning to it a fountain of love and fidelity that never ran dry or waned, through all his years of famine.'[30] The unusual imagery here, transforming Little Dorrit to a veritable fountain of love and truth, obliges us to return to Chesterton's insight that these child-like heroines are 'little mothers'. Dorrit is the miraculous child who ministers to her father 'as her mother had ministered to her'. Once again we have the convergence of generations upon a single heroine, and in the heroine of truth it is entirely appropriate that this convergence should stress her maternal aspect. A mother is, universally, the first inspirer of confidence in a child and the image of what the child may trust. If twentieth-century corroboration of this symbolic relation is needed, it can be found in the contention of Erik Erikson that the earliest stage of infancy is crucial to the establishment of 'basic trust', including trust in God or a cosmic order.[31] Though Little Dorrit's innocent breast is featured here, more commonly the heroine's face symbolizes love and truth to the hero ('so much in need of a face of love and truth', 'the love and truth glowing in her face'). The prominence of the face, however, also confirms the maternal aspect of the heroine. Nor is the face to be understood, in this context, as a substitute for some more intimate contact with a mother, but as the first part of the world outside of itself that a child can recognize and respond to.[32]

Exactly midway in the action of *Little Dorrit*, by an involuntary identification of the hero with the father, the heroine announces the transference of her intense fidelity. As Clennam breaks the news of the Dorrits' changed fortunes and kisses her,

[30] *LD*, Bk. I, ch. ix, p. 97; ch. xix, p. 229.

[31] *Childhood and Society*, 2nd ed. (New York, 1963), pp. 247–51. Cf. Brown, *The Home Life*, p. 126: 'Perhaps, though, I have spoken hastily in saying that the child's first discovery is that hands and feet belong to it. The first thing which an infant discovers in the universe is love. God's order of the world is in every possible form a protest against isolation, a witness against the self as the starting-point of life. The first impression on the young child's heart, as the mother's proud and tender glances rest upon it, is the sense of belonging . . . the mother's love, from the first moment, begins its training for the love of man and the love of God.'

[32] See Erikson's *Young Man Luther* (New York, 1962), pp. 115–19. I am grateful to William Kessen for acquainting me with the experimental work that has been done on early responses to the mother's face.

'she turned her head towards his shoulder, and raised her arm towards his neck; cried out "Father! Father! Father!" and swooned away'. When the hero is subsequently imprisoned, he realizes that 'One weak girl' is superior to 'an army of received heroes and heroines'; and when she returns in person, it is as his 'own poor child come back!' 'So faithful, tender, and unspoiled by Fortune. In the sound of her voice, in the light of her eyes, in the touch of her hands, so Angelically comforting and true!' And Little Dorrit 'laid his head upon her bosom, put a hand upon his head, and resting her cheek upon that hand, nursed him as lovingly, and God knows as innocently, as she had nursed her father in that room when she had been but a baby, needing all the care from others that she took of them.' It is all Arthur can do 'to believe that all the devotion of this great nature was turned to him in his adversity, to pour out its inexhaustible wealth of goodness upon him'.[33]

In his essay on *Mansfield Park* Trilling remarks that the heroines of Dickens are representative of a type that includes Fanny Price, Clarissa Harlowe, and Fielding's Amelia, and 'perhaps came to an end for literature with the death of Milly Theale' at the end of *The Wings of the Dove*. Such heroines—I should wish to exclude Clarrisa—are characterized by Trilling as 'poor in spirit' and specifically Christian.[34] They are obviously composed of ambiguous strength and weakness. As Dickens writes of Little Nell, 'With failing strength and heightening resolution, there had sprung up a purified and altered mind; there had grown in her bosom blessed thoughts and hopes, which are the portion of few but the weak and drooping.'[35] We have just witnessed some of Little Dorrit's extraordinary powers, but she is presented first, in the turmoil of the city and of nature both, as very frail:

Thus they emerged upon the Iron Bridge, which was as quiet after the roaring streets, as though it had been open country. The wind blew roughly, the wet squalls came rattling past them, skimming the pools on the road and pavement, and raining them down into the river. The clouds raced on furiously in the lead-coloured sky, the smoke and mist raced after them, the dark tide ran fierce and strong in the same direc-

33 *LD*, Bk. I, ch. xxxv, p. 415; Bk. II, ch. xxvii, p. 720; ch. xxix, pp. 756, 758.
34 *The Opposing Self*, pp. 213–14.
35 *OCS*, ch. lii, p. 388.

tion. Little Dorrit seemed the least, the quietest, and weakest of Heaven's creatures.[36]

Somehow this frailty converts to strength. At first a hero may underestimate even the moral strength of the young lady, as Geraint worries about Enid's association with Queen Guinevere, or David about Agnes's 'ill-assorted' friendship with Annie Strong. Yet before long, in the devotion of this child, or this woman, from whom every personal quality has been drained except unchanging love and truth, the hero finds his salvation.

Among Victorian critics Ruskin has the clearest vision of the heroine whose function it is to save the hero. Ruskin interpreted the heroines of any artist—of any artist whom he approved—in just this way. Of Shakespeare he noted, 'The catastrophe of every play is caused always by the folly or fault of a man; the redemption, if there be any, is by the wisdom and virtue of a woman, and, failing that, there is none.' Scott's heroines possess 'a patient wisdom of deeply-restrained affection, which does infinitely more than protect its objects from a momentary error; it gradually forms, animates, and exalts the characters of the unworthy lovers, until, at the close of the tale, we are just able, and no more, to take patience in hearing of their unmerited success'.[37] Among twentieth-century critics of Dickens, J. Hillis Miller has seemed the most interested in heroines. But if Ruskin's pronouncements are often quaint or backward-looking, Miller's may be anachronistic in the other direction. He has had the courage to look the heroine in the eye, so to speak, while David Copperfield intones, 'Clasped in my embrace, I held the source of every worthy aspiration I had ever had; the centre of myself, the circle of my life, my own, my wife; my love of whom was founded on a rock!' And he has concluded that 'David has that relation to Agnes which a devout Christian has to God, the creator of his selfhood'.[38] Miller is interpreting David's words metaphorically here, but also anticipating his wider thesis concerning the Victorians in *The Disappearance of God*.[39] More recently he has broadened this view: Victorian fiction relates one

[36] *LD*, Bk. I, ch. ix, p. 96.

[37] *Sesame and Lilies*, in *Works*, XVIII, 113, 116.

[38] *DC*, ch. lxii, p. 864; Miller, *Charles Dickens*, p. 157.

[39] *The Disappearance of God: Five Nineteenth-Century Writers* (Cambridge, Mass., 1963).

self to another in 'an attempt to satisfy religious longings' and
explores 'ways in which a man may make a god of another person
in a world without God'.[40] Miller seems entirely correct as far
as the eventual tendency of this treatment of the 'self' is concerned. When Matthew Arnold resolves 'Dover Beach', his
short poem of religious doubt, with the practical, domestic
relation—'Ah, love, let us be true / To one another!'—he points
in the new direction. The outcome of it all will be E. M. Forster's
credo: 'I do not believe in belief,' but in 'personal relationships'.[41] What Miller's broader view neglects is the difference
between heroes and heroines, a difference that Ruskin and the
Victorian novelists insist upon.

An easy sentimental tradition links romantic love with the
practical guidance of young men in the world. As Smiles puts it,
'a pure and honourable attachment arms a young man against
the siren attractions of idleness, and "pleasures turned to pain,"
with which our crowded cities abound.'[42] And yet the same
sentiments might suddenly be translated into Christian heroics,
as in Ruskin's parting charge to women: 'in your cities, shall the
stones cry out against you, that they are the only pillows where
the Son of Man can lay His head?' Ruskin could take very
seriously the business of romantic love; he could Christianize it;
and Hellenize it, in the tradition of Alexandrine wisdom literature; and still see it as a practical issue. 'You cannot think that
the buckling on of the knight's armour by his lady's hand was a
mere caprice of romantic fashion. It is the type of an eternal
truth. . . .'[43] Within a more or less realistic frame, Dickens and
other novelists attempted to display this ideal function of women
in believable terms. Sometimes the relation of the heroine to the
hero is expressed temperately and, allowing for changes in
idiom, not very differently from subsequent celebrations of personal relations. 'Since I knew you,' Sydney Carton confesses to
Lucie Manette, 'I have been troubled by a remorse that I thought
would never reproach me again . . . I have had unformed ideas
of striving afresh, beginning anew, shaking off sloth and sen-
suality, and fighting out the abandoned fight.' When he adds,

40 *The Form of Victorian Fiction* (Notre Dame, Indiana, 1968), p. 96.
41 *Two Cheers for Democracy* (New York, 1951), p. 67.
42 George Moore, *Merchant and Philanthropist* (London, 1878), p. 83.
43 *Sesame and Lilies*, in *Works*, XVIII, 144, 120.

'In the hour of my death, I shall hold sacred the one good remembrance . . . that my last avowal of myself was made to you,
and that my name, and faults, and miseries were gently carried
in your heart,' it will be agreed that he depends on Lucie, in
comparatively abstract fashion, for a definition of his self.[44]

Yet novelists are hinting at more than just another person in
a heroine like Lucie, much more than a person in a heroine like
Little Dorrit. They are invoking something more nearly divine.
If the spirit of love and truth were merely a person, she would
not make her reappearance one day as an ironic type in the Intended of *Heart of Darkness*, or as Nancy Rufford, the imbecile
virgin in *The Good Soldier* who has lost all power of speech
except for the endlessly repeated 'Credo in unum Deum Omni-
potentem' and 'Shuttlecocks!' Courtship is the main action in
most nineteenth-century English novels, but so passive a courtship on the heroine's part that it might be said to be conducted
in the name of Agape rather than Eros. Such is one implication
of so many discriminations of a different, asexual love. In Dickens the description of Florence Dombey's grief after her brother's
death is a good example: 'it is not in the nature of pure love
to burn so fiercely and unkindly long. The flame that in its grosser
composition has the taint of earth, may prey upon the breast that
gives it shelter; but the sacred fire from heaven is as gentle in
the heart, as when it rested on the heads of the assembled
twelve, and showed each man his brother, brightened and unhurt.'[45]
The purpose of so many incantations of love and *truth* is partly
to distinguish between the courtship of desire and of faith. To a
Brighton clergyman Thackeray wrote, 'I want, too, to say in
my way [as a novelist], that love and truth are the greatest of
Heaven's commandments and blessings to us.'[46]

Trilling's comment that Little Dorrit is 'the Beatrice of the
Comedy, the Paraclete in female form'[47] obviously deserves
some consideration. The fourth gospel was theologically the
most difficult for the nineteenth-century to accept; yet the promise of the Comforter, the Spirit of truth, the aspect of God that

[44] *TTC*, Bk. II, ch. xiii, pp. 144, 145.   [45] *D & S*, ch. xviii, pp. 246–7.
[46] To Joseph Sortain, 15 May 1850, quoted by Anne Ritchie, Introduction to
The Newcomes, p. xxxix. Cf. Mrs. Gaskell's report of an opinion 'That "Love &
Truth" were the two qualities that formed the Essence of the Xtian religion', in
Letters, ed. J. A. V. Chapple and Arthur Pollard (Cambridge, Mass., 1967), p. 648.
[47] *LD*, Introduction, p. xvi; reprinted in *The Opposing Self*, p. 65.

abides with the faithful, comes especially close to the needs of a
domestic religion. 'If ye love me, keep my commandments. And
I will pray the Father, and he shall give you another Comforter,
that he may abide with you for ever; Even the Spirit of truth;
whom the world cannot receive, because it seeth him not,
neither knoweth him: but ye know him; for he dwelleth with you,
and shall be in you.'[48] It was apparently possible for the Victorians, perhaps easier for the Victorians, to confuse the ministrations of this Spirit with the ministrations of heroines. A
precedent for altering the gender of the Spirit of truth can be
found in the older wisdom literature, to which the promise in
the fourth gospel is historically related. The generative and
nurturing functions attributed to Wisdom in the apocryphal
book by that name, and in the book of Proverbs, are certainly
consonant with her sex. 'Say unto wisdom, Thou art my
sister';[49] more pertinently, the first nine chapters of Proverbs
repeatedly associated wisdom with the true wife, as against the
'strange' temptation of illicit sexuality.

Not to be discounted entirely is the possibility that Victorian
heroines owe something to the intercessory role of the Virgin;
though one would expect this analogy to be repressed or
guarded by the dramatic context. We recall Lydgate's thought
in *Middlemarch* that Dorothea Brooke possessed 'a heart large
enough for the Virgin Mary': the interview that precedes this
thought is replete with the 'trust' of Dorothea, her 'sweet
trustful gravity'. 'I am sure that the truth would clear you,' she
pleads; and 'Do trust me.'[50] We know that in Genoa in 1844
Dickens dreamt of Mary Hogarth in the blue drapery of the
Madonna, and that when he tried to ask her a leading question—
whether she agreed that the form of religion did not matter as
long as 'we try to be good'—she rather provokingly recommended Roman Catholicism.[51] Lecky believed that Puritanism,
in rejecting the intercession of the Virgin, became 'the most

[48] John 14: 15–17.
[49] Proverbs 7:4.
[50] *Middlemarch*, Bk. VIII, ch. lxxvi, pp. 361, 351–2. Cf. ch. lxxvii, p. 366:
'There are natures in which, if they love us, we are conscious of having a sort of
baptism and consecration: they bind us to rectitude and purity by their pure
belief about us; and our sins become that worst kind of sacrilege which tears down
the invisible altar of trust. . . . Dorothea's nature was of that kind.'
[51] Forster (Bk. IV, ch. v), I, 336–7.

masculine form that Christianity has yet assumed'.[52] It may be
that the price of this masculinity was the sentimental inflation
of the secular heroine's role.

Wisdom, the Paraclete, the Mother of God—all seem rhet-
orically remote from the sweet domestic figure of the Victorian
imagination. Call her simply an angel: 'A poor angel . . . but
faithful', Agnes will reply, modestly conceding the point.[53]
'That hackneyed simile of an angel', as Scott called it in *The
Pirate* in 1822, was still very much in use for heroines fifty years
later. Thinking back on his own novel James observed, in the
twentieth century, that Fleda Vetch sees and feels 'almost
demonically'.[54] This is only a more neutral way of stating a
quality of heroines that an earlier generation of novelists were
willing to praise effusively. In his childhood and youth Arthur
Pendennis thought of his mother 'as little less than an angel—a
supernatural being, all wisdom, love, and beauty'.[55] But Victorians—and James, too, was a Victorian in this respect—imaginatively elevated living women, also, and especially dead
women, to supernatural heights. We have only to think of the
treatment accorded by Dickens to Mary Hogarth, or by James
to Minny Temple, or the elevation of Elizabeth Barrett Browning in *The Ring and the Book* and of Harriet Taylor in Mill's
Autobiography. In the dedication to *On Liberty* Mill memorial-
ized the 'exalted sense of truth and right' and 'all but unrivalled
wisdom' of his personal helpmate.

The most remarkable elevation was that of Clothilde de Vaux,
who in one short year before her death inspired the religion of
humanity of Auguste Comte. The peculiar hold of this religion,
or Positivism, really deserves an explanation.[56] Though Positivism had not many adherents in England, it had important
friends, and the domestic religion that Comte tried to inculcate

[52] *History of European Morals*, II, 368.

[53] *DC*, ch. xlii, p. 612.

[54] *The Spoils of Poynton*, Preface, p. xv.

[55] *Pendennis*, ch. ii, p. 13.

[56] Cf. W. M. Simon, *European Positivism in the Nineteenth Century* (Ithaca,
1963), pp. 9–10. The best short exposition of the cult of Positivism is Mill, 'Later
Speculations of M. Comte', *Westminster Review*, 1865, reprinted in *Auguste Comte
and Positivism* (Ann Arbor, 1961), Pt. II. For the religious extravagance of the
original relation, see the *Testament d'Auguste Comte, avec . . . pièces justificatives,
prières quotidiennes, confessions annuelles, correspondance avec Mme de Vaux* (Paris,
1884), published in accordance with Comte's last wishes.

epitomized the very sentiments we have been tracing; it suggests that the transformation of Mary Hogarth, or of Minny Temple, in the mind of a novelist was broadly sanctioned by the ethos of the nineteenth century. Women were the objects of adoration in this religion, and the chief ritual was commemoration, or the deliberate act of recalling the image of the dead. Adoration was deliberately plural: of the mother, the wife, and the daughter, who are 'les vrais anges gardiens'.[57] In this way Positivism, also, created woman constant and unchanged, and we can sympathize with its strained effort to buttress the worshipper's sense of identity by non-theistic means. The deliberate investment of the several female roles in a single heroine in this period makes a parallel effort.

In the book of Wisdom, when the author impersonates Solomon, he turns to Wisdom as soon as he is born. 'For all men have one entrance into life, and the like going out. Wherefore I prayed, and understanding was given me: I called upon God, and the spirit of wisdom came unto me.'[58] If in Proverbs Wisdom is represented as a sister and wife, in the apocryphal book she is represented as a mother; and indeed she is present at the creation of the universe. The image of Little Dorrit 'comforting her father's wasted heart upon her innocent breast, and turning to it a fountain of love and fidelity that never ran dry or waned', of her 'great nature . . . pour[ing] out its inexhaustible wealth of goodness' upon the hero, in its mixture of humanity and allegory, its claim to innocence and eternity, may be traced forward to psychoanalytic literature or back to the Old Testament. 'Drink waters out of thine own cistern, and running waters out of thine own well. Let thy fountains be dispersed abroad, and rivers of water in the streets. Let them be only thine own, and not strangers' with thee. Let thy fountain be blessed: and rejoice with the wife of thy youth. Let her be as the loving hind and pleasant roe; let her breasts satisfy thee at all times; and be thou ravished always with her love.'[59]

[57] 'As for the sister, the influence she exercises has hardly a very distinct character, and she may, in succession, be connected with each of the three essential types.' *The Catechism of Positive Religion*, trans. Richard Congreve (London, 1858), p. 121.
[58] Wisdom 7:6–7.
[59] Proverbs 5:15–19.

XI

TWO ANGELS OF DEATH

AND now, as I close my task, subduing my desire to linger yet, these faces fade away. But one face, shining on me like a Heavenly light by which I see all other objects, is above them and beyond them all. And that remains.

I turn my head, and see it, in its beautiful serenity, beside me. My lamp burns low, and I have written far into the night; but the dear presence, without which I were nothing, bears me company.

Oh Agnes, oh my soul, so may thy face be by me when I close my life indeed; so may I, when realities are melting from me like the shadows which I now dismiss, still find thee near me, pointing upward!

Such are the last words of David Copperfield and of the novel by that name. They are words that embarrass twentieth-century admirers of the novel; and the more they have been regretted, the less they have been examined. The final sentence alone touches on at least four significant motifs: the adoration of Agnes Copperfield, *née* Wickfield, as the 'soul' of the hero; the identification of this angel with her 'face'; the prayer that she will be near him at the moment of death; and the analogy of the close of the novel to the close of life, an analogy to which I shall need to return. The last two words of *David Copperfield* are 'pointing upward', the special Agnes motif that Dickens insists on as if its meaning were quite precise.[1]

The motif that now commands our attention is the prayer that Agnes will be near at the time of death. This prayer places the other attributes of the heroine in a new perspective. Her apparent relation to the divine ('like a Heavenly light'), her permanence and proof against change (she alone 'remains'), and

---

[1] He uses it elsewhere, with apparent reference to Mary Hogarth, in a letter to Forster from America: 'the presence and influence of that spirit which directs my life, and through a heavy sorrow has pointed upward with unchanging finger for more than four years past.' Forster (Bk. III, ch. ii), I, 182. It also occurs in *D & S*, ch. xiv, p. 194, as an attribute of Christ in the print by the stairs.

the specific nomenclature ('soul' rather than angel here) are all brought to bear on the problem of the hero's death. To borrow Miller's thesis, the definition of the hero's self ('without which I were nothing') becomes crucial at death, after which he will indeed be nothing unless the heroine can save him. In his play on the end of the novel as the end of life Dickens invites double readings: 'subduing my desire to linger yet' with his life story, subduing my desire to cling to life; the writing lamp burning low, the lamp of life burning low. What remains uncertain is the efficacy of David's prayer, or the degree of Agnes's power. Clearly she can be near him at his death, but does he hope that she can save him *from* death? One hesitates to attribute to any heroine, no matter how angelic, a power over death itself. Still, in the nature of things a power over death is mythical power only. In a novel that asserts the putative real-life existence of all the characters we must expect the heroine's mythical powers to be expressed only in hints, or in the configuration of events that the novelist selects. It is at least obvious that *David Copperfield* and many English novels work round to a permanent connection between the hero and his good angel.

David Copperfield contains passages suggesting that Agnes, whom the hero regularly associates with the 'tranquil brightness' of a church window, is a familiar of death. 'What is your secret, Agnes? . . . When I have come to you, at last (as I have always done), I have come to peace and happiness. I come home, now, like a tired traveller, and find such a blessed sense of rest!' After he is married to Dora, the old days with Agnes come to his mind 'like spectres of the dead, that might have some renewal in another world, but never never more could be reanimated here'. And when he watches her bending over her father, and thinks of her 'calm seraphic eyes', he first conceives of her final office: 'I pray Heaven that I never may forget the dear girl in her love and truth, at that time of my life; for if I should, I must be drawing near the end, and then I would desire to remember her best!'[2] His prayer in the last sentence of the novel specifically recalls her attendance upon the death of Dora, his 'child-wife'. The reference is to that moment in the action when Agnes descends the stair and signals with her 'solemn hand upraised towards Heaven' that Dora is dead. In the interval between

[2] *DC*, ch. xv, p. 223; ch. xxxix, p. 567; ch. xlviii, p. 697; ch. xxxv, p. 519.

Dora's death and his marriage to Agnes this incident and its symbolism are sufficiently belaboured. 'You remember, when you came down to me in our little room—pointing upward, Agnes? . . . Until I die, my dearest sister, I shall see you always before me, pointing upward!' 'Until I die' anticipates 'when I close my life' of his last prayer; he has studied Agnes's saving role from her behaviour with Dora. The interval before his second marriage permits David to exercise a purely spiritual love for his 'sister': 'I had faithfully set the seal upon the Past, and, thinking of her, pointing upward, thought of her as pointing to that sky above me, where, in the mystery to come, I might yet love her with a love unknown on earth. . . .'[3]

If a heroine can not only improve a hero—reform his character, give him a better life, fix his identity—but actually save him, however, she ought instinctively to be feared as well as worshiped. The power of an angel to save implies, even while it denies, the eventuality of death. Agnes cannot invite the hero to join her in the sky without at the same time inviting him to die. It is an invitation that one inevitably wishes to refuse as well as to accept. In short, a heroine who presides over the moment of death can be seen in two radically different ways, both prayerful, but one a prayer of hope and the other of fear. The ominous aspect of the heroine's power may even contribute to our resistance, as readers, to Agnes Wickfield and her sisters. Orwell thought Agnes 'the most disagreeable of [Dickens's] heroines, the real legless angel of Victorian romance, almost as bad as Thackeray's Laura'. Was this contempt or hostility? What is more surprising, Forster didn't like Agnes either.[4] Though Agnes, David, and Dickens are campaigning for some method of transcendence of death, they cannot and do not deny the fact of death. The fact of death is underlined by the convenience of Dora's demise, a convenience that simply would not obtain if death were not real. There is something terribly convenient in Dora dying alone with her rival in love; and something ludicrously convenient in Jip dying at the feet of his rival at the same moment. Do Orwell, Forster, and others (present company excepted) despise this angel merely as a matter of taste or because they are offended by the potentially two-sided

---

[3] *DC*, ch. liii, p. 768; ch. lx, pp. 843–4.
[4] Orwell, p. 109; Forster (Bk. VI, ch. vii), II, 109.

power of Agnes, who, in the language of detective fiction, was
the last person to see Dora Copperfield alive?

Angels are so supremely confident that a hero's happiness is
not of this world that one scarcely trusts oneself alone with them.
The point is humorously made by an exchange in *Jane Eyre*, in
which Rochester accosts Jane upon her return from her aunt's
deathbed:

'I have been with my aunt, sir, who is dead.'
'A true Janian reply! Good angels be my guard! She comes from the
other world—from the abode of people who are dead . . .'[5]

Rochester, with his Brontëan repartee, pretends that Jane is a
ghost or a bad angel. Reader, we know better—though Jane,
after all, had plenty of reason to wish her aunt dead; and though
Helen Burns has died in Jane's arms. The difficulty of assigning
this ominous character to David's angel is that between David
and Agnes there is no expressed hostility whatever, not even
of the jovial kind expressed by Mr. Rochester. To discover such
hostility in *David Copperfield* one has to resort to the interpretation that Uriah Heep, who lusts after Agnes and takes the
offensive against her father, is a double or private devil of the
hero.

Yet tension is possible between a fictitious angel, a spirit of
love and truth, and the object of her devotion. It is recorded
clearly in the case of John Carker. His sister has deliberately
gone to live with him because of his greater need, and the result
is to remind him of his crime as much as to comfort him:

The cordial face she lifted up to his to kiss him, was his home, his life,
his universe, and yet it was a portion of his punishment and grief; for
in the cloud he saw upon it—though serene and calm as any radiant
cloud at sunset—and in the constancy and devotion of her life, and in
the sacrifice she had made of ease, enjoyment, and hope, he saw the
bitter fruits of his old crime, for ever ripe and fresh.[6]

The tension of such a relation will be predictably more disguised from heroes than from poor Carker, who may or may not
be saved, but it is manifest dramatically in almost any nineteenth-century English novel. That is, in order to make a story
of the hero's salvation (or at least his happiness in the end), he

[5] Charlotte Brontë, *Jane Eyre* (Boston, 1959), ch. xxii, p. 232.
[6] *D & S*, ch. xxxiii, p. 474.

must resist for a certain time the true heroine. Consciousness of resistance varies, from the blindness of Edmund Bertram in *Mansfield Park*, to the stalling and delaying of a Pendennis or a Trollope hero, to the deliberate act of Amerigo in *The Golden Bowl*. In *David Copperfield* the resistance is that of 'an undisciplined heart', of one who is 'Blind! Blind! Blind!' to those seraphic eyes; but some later heroes of Dickens put up a conscious struggle against their salvation. Any degree of resistance makes the spirit of love and truth in part an adversary of the hero. Only in Dickens's two attempts at tragic themes does the resistance to the heroine reach the level of hostility. The grandfather in *The Old Curiosity Shop* is childishly and ineffectually hostile to Nell; the hero of *Dombey and Son* is concertedly and effectually hostile to Florence until the very end. The latter novel requires special attention.

Victorian novels would lead us to believe that it is the special office of young women to watch over the dying. Very likely in real life this office has always fallen to women, who are at home, caring for the family in health as well as in sickness. But novels dwell on the subject, celebrating the heroine's loyalty and courage and even hinting of some special efficacy in her services. Agnes Wickfield, Jane Eyre, Mary Garth, Margaret Hale, Little Dorrit, Esther Summerson, all figure in deathbed scenes and in some cases death occurs in their embrace. Florence Dombey is perhaps the most experienced of all such watchers at imaginative deathbeds, and she apparently assists in the translation of the dying to a future state. She assumes this role as a child at her mother's death, in the opening chapter of *Dombey and Son*;[7] and her part in the translation of her brother Paul is much more prominent. Florence does not merely comfort little Paul with her love: she welcomes him from the other side of death. Dickens's language discovers her drawing him toward death, a death that is embraced contentedly by Paul because of Florence. She is the boat, with 'sail like an arm, all silver', that beckons to him. He envisions death as a garden where he will live with her. He hears the fateful murmer of the waves in her song. And his dying imagination suggests to him a conceit that

[7] 'Thus, clinging fast to that slight spar within her arms [i.e., Florence], the mother drifted out upon the dark and unknown sea that rolls round all the world.' *D & S*, ch. i, p. 10.

seems to explain the part she is playing: 'Floy, are we *all* dead, except you?'[8] Such implicit statements of Florence's sacred office are reinforced by others of broadly hinted double meaning, such as 'I want Florence to come for me', and 'Take me home, Floy! take me home!'[9] In Florence Dombey Dickens presents a heroine who is not only near at the time of death but a power against death as a destructive force.

The deathbed of her mother is for Florence what the deathbed of Dora is for Agnes. It becomes the emblem of her office, like Agnes pointing upward. Paul tolerates his doctor, for example, because the doctor 'had been with his mama when she clasped Florence in her arms, and died', at Paul's birth. He thinks his mother 'must have loved sweet Florence better than his father did, to have held her in her arms when she felt that she was dying— for even he, her brother, who had such dear love for her, could have no greater wish than that'. The dying child-wife that Agnes Wickfield tends is at best a replica of David's childlike mother; the woman whom Florence watched over was her own and Paul's actual mother. The angel who beckons to Paul and oversees his death is closely associated with his mother and with his mother's face—which he has never seen. And this face, flickering between his sister and his mother, makes the hallowed portrait at school seem dim, and then brighter:

Sister and brother wound their arms around each other, and the golden light came streaming in, and fell upon them, locked to-gether. . . .

He put his hands together, as he had been used to do at his prayers. He did not remove his arms to do it; but they saw him fold them so, behind her neck.

'Mama is like you, Floy. I know her by the face! But tell them that the print upon the stairs at school is not divine enough. The light about the head is shining on me as I go!'[10]

From this point in the novel her ministration at Paul's death becomes the emblem of the heroine's office.

At the end of *Dombey and Son* this same child—now the mother of a second Florence—has one last interview with Edith Dombey, her adopted 'Mama'. Edith figuratively dies after

8 *D & S*, ch. xii, pp. 167–8; ch. xiv, p. 190; ch. xvi, p. 224.
9 *D & S*, ch. viii, p. 94; ch. xiv, p. 204.
10 *D & S*, ch. xvi, pp. 222, 223, 225–6.

Florence leaves the room: 'When you leave me in this dark room, think that you have left me in the grave.' Though she acknowledges Florence as 'My better angel!' however, it is not certain that Edith can be saved. The frenzied history of these two suggests that Edith might have been saved if she had been able fully to surrender to Florence. She is distraught, torn by pride and self-contempt, and yet was potentially able to help Dombey himself. When she first met him, she played at the piano 'the air that his neglected daughter sang to his dead son'. Yet she is never able to realize this potential; it would have been better for her to die while embracing Florence, at one of those moments in which her better self has surrendered.

Was this the woman whom Florence—an innocent girl, strong only in her earnestness and simple truth—could so impress and quell, that by her side she was another creature, with her tempest of passion hushed, and her very pride itself subdued? Was this the woman who now sat beside her in a carriage, with her arms entwined, and who, while she courted and entreated her to love and trust her, drew her fair head to nestle on her breast, and would have lain down life to shield it from wrong or harm?

Oh, Edith! it were well to die, indeed, at such a time! Better and happier far, perhaps, to die so, Edith, than to live on to the end![11]

The failure of their last meeting, and the hint that Florence leaves her 'in the grave', can be traced to this perverse refusal of the opportunity to die in Florence's arms.

Even Florence's relation to Walter Gay seems directed toward death. When he first goes off to sea, there is a kind of pre-engagement scene in which Florence looks upon him 'with confidence and truth' and promises to be 'your sister all my life'. For Walter, the face of Florence brings thoughts of the death of Paul. 'The purity and innocence of her endearing manner, and its perfect trustfulness, and the undisguised regard for him that lay so deeply seated in her constant eyes, and glowed upon her fair face . . . brought back to his thoughts the early deathbed he had seen her tending, and the love the child had borne her; and on the wings of such remembrances she seemed to rise up, far above his idle fancies, into clearer and serener air.' Their subsequent wedding commences with a visit to Paul's grave. The ceremony itself takes place in one of those dusty City churches,

[11] D & S, ch. lxi, pp. 871–2, 868; ch. xxi, pp. 296–7; ch. xxx, p. 423.

and Dickens pauses for his usual reflections on the relation of
the dust and the smell to those buried nearby. But the most
curious insistence on the parallel between Walter and Paul is in
the treatment of the sea. As they sail for the orient, Florence
recalls the association of the sea with Paul's death, and Dickens
intervenes almost as if to say that Walter, too, is being borne,
in marital embrace, toward death.

'As I hear the sea,' says Florence, 'and sit watching it, it brings so
many days into my mind. It makes me think so much——'
'Of Paul, my love. I know it does.'
Of Paul and Walter. And the voices in the waves are always whispering to Florence, in their ceaseless murmuring, of love—of love,
eternal and illimitable, not bounded by the confines of this world, or by
the end of time, but ranging still, beyond the sea, beyond the sky, to the
invisible country far away![12]

Though most readers do not consider this marriage of primary
importance in Dombey and Son, it anticipates the marriage of
Arthur Clennam and Little Dorrit. Walter's return from his
first voyage (and from supposed death—an experience that
qualifies him for Florence's embrace), looks forward to Clennam's return from the orient to begin life anew, and to the more
dramatic return and rebirth of John Harmon. It should be noted,
too, that Walter arrives in London at about the same hour at
which Florence is struck by her father and turned out to the
streets, a coincidence that anticipates the formal transference of
love and truth from father to husband in Little Dorrit.

These are the minor developments of the theme. The great
point of Dombey and Son is that the senior partner, Mr. Dombey
himself, must learn to embrace this child, with her specialized
experience and her premonitions, before he, too, shall die.

Awake, unkind father! Awake, now, sullen man! The time is flitting
by; the hour is coming with an angry tread. Awake! . . .
Awake, doomed man, while she is near. The time is flitting by; the
hour is coming with an angry tread; its foot is in the house. Awake! . . .
He may sleep on now. He may sleep on while he may. But let him
look for that slight figure when he wakes, and find it near him when
the hour is come!

Florence waits there, contemned but faithful. To her, looking

12 D & S, ch. xix, pp. 264, 262; ch. lvii, p. 811.

on, Dombey's sleep has 'the solemnity . . . of death and life in one'.[13] What will happen if he should die without surrendering to her love? And why had he better hope that she is near him when his hour is come? The role of Florence in the life of Paul and the others gives the answer, which is the only logical answer in a religion that does not believe in damnation. Unless he wakes and loves Florence, he will die. The heroine's power over death is confirmed by her dream, in which she has earlier sensed that her father is dead and she 'charged with something that would release him from extraordinary suffering'.

She dreamed of seeking her father in wildernesses, of following his track up fearful heights, and down into deep mines and caverns; of being charged with something that would release him from extraordinary suffering—she knew not what, or why—yet never being able to attain the goal and set him free. Then she saw him dead, upon that very bed, and in that very room, and knew that he had never loved her to the last, and fell upon his cold breast, passionately weeping. Then a prospect opened, and a river flowed, and a plaintive voice she knew, cried, 'It is running on, Floy! It has never stopped! You are moving with it!' And she saw him at a distance stretching out his arms towards her, while a figure such as Walter's used to be [Walter is presumed dead at this time], stood near him, awfully serene and still. In every vision, Edith came and went, sometimes to her joy, sometimes to her sorrow, until they were alone upon the brink of a dark grave, and Edith pointing down [the wrong direction], she looked and saw— what!—another Edith lying at the bottom.

It turns out well enough for Dombey. After his financial ruin, and when 'Death stood at his pillow', he does embrace his daughter and is granted unlimited reprieve as 'the white-haired gentleman' who murmurs to his grandchild, 'Little Florence! Little Florence!'[14]

Dickens designed the novel so that Florence would be Dombey's 'unknown Good Genius always' but also 'his bitterest reproach'.[15] Tension between hero and heroine mounts highest in *Dombey and Son*. The hero's resistance to his salvation begins abruptly with the birth of Paul and the death of his wife, when 'his previous feelings of indifference towards little Florence

13 *D & S*, ch. xliii, p. 609.
14 *D & S*, ch. xxxv, p. 508; ch. lxi, p. 860; ch. lxii, p. 878.
15 Forster (Bk. VI, ch. ii), II, 21.

changed into an uneasiness of an extraordinary kind. He almost felt as if she watched and distrusted him. As if she held the clue to something secret in his breast, of the nature of which he was hardly informed himself.' Dickens carefully and impressively motivates these feelings, but at the same time develops his theme. Dombey's uneasiness becomes hatred, and culminates in the heavy blow with which he wards his daughter off as she attempts to clasp him round the neck, when 'he told her what Edith was, and bade her follow her'. His passionate repudiation of his fate is imaged by the forceful ejection of the heroine from home and her abandonment to the streets. And 'Florence, with her head bent down to hide her agony of tears, was in the streets'.[16]

The hostility that rises to such a climax is all important to the most dramatic rendering of the allegory of death in *Dombey and Son*: the railway journey with Major Bagstock, soon after the death of Paul.

The very speed at which the train was whirled along mocked the swift course of the young life that had been borne away so steadily and so inexorably to its foredoomed end. The power that forced itself upon its iron way—its own—defiant of all paths and roads, piercing through the heart of every obstacle, and dragging living creatures of all classes, ages, and degrees behind it, was a type of the triumphant monster, Death.

There follow the memorable paragraphs that recreate the sensations of a rapid journey, each paragraph punctuated by the allegory: 'like as in the track of the remorseless monster, Death! . . . like as in the track of the remorseless monster, Death! . . . the indomitable monster, Death! . . . still like the way of Death.' For some reason the chapter has attracted more readers interested in railroading than in allegory or the death of Paul. Neglected altogether is the part Florence plays in the journey—or the part played by Florence's face, which becomes increasingly prominent as the pulsating engine of death fades from the foreground. She—the face—is not the monster Death, but is just as inexorable where Dombey is concerned.

There was a face . . . that often had attended him in fancy, on this ride. He had seen it, with the expression of last night, timidly pleading

16 *D & S*, ch. iii, p. 29; ch. xlvii, pp. 665–6.

to him. It was not reproachful, but there was something of doubt, almost of hopeful incredulity in it, which, as he once more saw that fade away into a desolate certainty of his dislike, was like reproach. It was a trouble to him to think of this face of Florence.

To Dombey's heated imagination—and this, the reader is to understand, has been his recurrent thought during the entire feverish journey—Florence appears as the armourer of Death: 'Because the face was abroad, in the expression of defeat and persecution that seemed to encircle him like the air. Because it barbed the arrow of that cruel and remorseless enemy on which his thoughts so ran, and put into its grasp a double-handed sword.' Though Florence is the angelic opponent of the monster Death, Dombey in his grief confuses her with Death's familiar and seeks to shield himself from her face.

Her loving and innocent face rising before him, had no softening or winning influence. He rejected the angel, and took up with the tormenting spirit crouching in his bosom. Her patience, goodness, youth, devotion, love, were as so many atoms in the ashes upon which he set his heel. He saw her image in the blight and blackness all around him, not irradiating but deepening the gloom. More than once upon this journey, and now again as he stood pondering at this journey's end, tracing figures in the dust with his stick, the thought came into his mind, what was there he could interpose between himself and it?[17]

Mr. Dombey will suffer more trials before his final near-death and reconciliation with Florence. The famous railway journey demonstrates the availability to the Victorian imagination of two angels of death, a saving angel as well as a destroying angel. The latter, the monster, usually spelled with a capital 'D', can be met most anywhere in Victorian letters, in serious non-literary contexts as well as in poetry and novels. He is the railway engine of Dombey's journey and of the mutilation of James Carker; the 'old, old fashion—Death!' who comes to Paul and who is fatuously resisted by Mrs. 'Cleopatra' Skewton. In *David Copperfield* he is 'that great Visitor, before whose presence all the living must give place'.[18] There is little point in multiplying instances, except to observe how different an idea this personification conveys from our abstract, twentieth-century idea of death. The vulgar personification of Death, whatever

17 *D & S*, ch. xx, pp. 280–3.
18 *DC*, ch. xxx, p. 438.

else one can say about it, is one of the marks that distinguish the literature of earlier generations from our own; and it cautions us to be open-minded about the other angel, who saves.

Both angels appear together, and are confused together, in Dombey's journey. Both angels appear at the deathbed of Dora Copperfield, the so-called angel of Death and the modest, faithful, persistent Agnes: 'When the Angel of Death alighted there, my child-wife fell asleep . . . on [Agnes's] bosom, with a smile.'[19] Both angels appear in the chapter on the death of Bessey Higgins in *North and South*. 'The dark shadow of the wings of the angel of death' crosses the bed, but the presence of Margaret Hale is a countervailing force. 'Margaret's voice broke upon the stillness of the room, with a clearness that startled even herself: "Let not your heart be troubled," it said; and she went steadily on through all that chapter of unspeakable consolation.'[20] Mrs. Gaskell's heroine is a very down-to-earth person, but for Bessey she is a saving angel. The gospel, in which Christ promises to send the Comforter, the Spirit of truth, breaks from her lips involuntarily. Moreover, Bessey has actually dreamed of Margaret before ever seeing her, and has desired to be buried in some of the heroine's clothing—not unlike the murdered Nancy holding Rose Maylie's handkerchief 'as high towards Heaven as her feeble strength would allow' in *Oliver Twist*.[21] Both angels, finally, are under consideration in this advice by Dickens to another storyteller:

surely in the close of this piece you have quite perverted its proper object and intention. To make that face his comfort and trust—to fill him with the assurance of meeting it one day in Heaven—to make him dying, attended, as it were, by an angel of his own creation [such as a daughter?]—to inspire him with gentle visions of the reality sitting by his bedside and shedding a light even on the dark path of Death—and so to let him gently pass away, whispering of it and seeking the hand to clasp in his—would be to complete a very affecting and moving picture. But, to have him struggling with Death in all its horrors, yelling about foul fiends and bats' wings, with staring eyes and rattles in his throat, is a ghastly, sickening, hideous end, with no beauty, no moral, nothing in it but a repulsive and most painful idea.[22]

[19] *DC*, ch. liv, p. 769.
[20] *North and South*, ch. xxx, pp. 285, 297; cf. John 14.
[21] *OT*, ch. xlvii, p. 362.
[22] To S. Harford (pseudonym for R. S. Horrell), 25 Nov. 1840, *Letters*, I, 279.

Personified death in the nineteenth century was not always seen as a masculine force or a robed and hooded skeleton of indeterminate sex. The remorseless monster, the destroying angel, to be sure, was not thought of as a woman; but a beckoning, welcoming, comforting figure definitely appeared as an angel of the softer sex. With the possible exception of *Love and Death*, in which the figure is seen from the back, the allegories of George Frederick Watts, for example, portray Death as a female. In his *Court of Death* and *The Messenger* she is a female of admittedly masculine proportions; but in *Death Crowning Innocence* and *Time, Death and Judgement* she is as feminine as any heroine of a novel.[23] The angel in John Tenniel's drawing for the little page of *The Haunted Man*, who clasps the right hand of the child while a hooded figure of death grasps the left (the whole encircled by a crown of roses and thorns), is also clearly female. Or the artist's rendering of death may merely suggest a female angel, without specifying the sex, as in the lines by Adelaide Anne Proctor quoted by Dickens in his introduction to her *Legends and Lyrics*:

> Why shouldst thou fear the beautiful angel, Death,
> Who waits thee at the portals of the skies,
> Ready to kiss away thy struggling breath,
> Ready with gentle hand to close thine eyes?[24]

Though not nearly as ostentatious as the threatening, dark-robed figure, this comforting angel often turns up in unexpected places. On his deathbed at the end of *The Portrait of a Lady* Ralph Touchett says that Isabel Archer is like the angel of death. Their last conversation touches on some of the very ambiguities we are examining.

'You've been like an angel beside my bed. You know they talk about the angel of death. It's the most beautiful of all. You've been like that; as if you were waiting for me.'

'I was not waiting for your death; I was waiting for—for this. This is not death, dear Ralph.'

'Not for you—no. There's nothing makes us feel so much alive as to see others die. That's the sensation of life—the sense that we remain. . . . Isabel,' he went on suddenly, 'I wish it were over for you.' . . .

'I would die if you could live. But I don't wish you to live; I

---

[23] A large version of *Time, Death and Judgement* hangs (1970) in the nave of St. Paul's Cathedral, London.

[24] *Collected Papers*, I, 108.

would die myself, not to lose you.' Her voice was as broken as his own and full of tears and anguish.

'You won't lose me—you'll keep me. Keep me in your heart; I shall be nearer to you than I've ever been. . . .[25]

When she strangely couples 'I don't wish you to live' with 'I would die myself, not to lose you', and he counters, 'I shall be nearer to you than I've ever been,' they together nearly confirm Ralph's comparison of Isabel to the angel.

Isabel Archer is one of the heroines who derive in part from James's special feelings for Minny Temple and her premature death. The idea of a heroine dying and giving life to a hero can be traced to this source, for we know that James felt, with something like supernatural force, that Miss Temple's death had given him life.[26] One of Dickens's early treatments of Mary Hogarth's death exploits a similar idea. In the tale of 'The Five Sisters of York' in *Nicholas Nickleby* the sisters resist the blandishments of the cloister and affirm life, in spite of difficulties, because they are inspired by the death of Alice, the youngest. A related idea teases Dombey's thoughts about Florence, who might have died so that Paul could live. 'Why was the object of his hope removed instead of her?'[27] One is struck by the apparent reversibility of the heroine's role, whereby the acts of dying and of saving someone from death seem confused. At the root of the problem is the irony that death defines life by negation. Stated bluntly by Ralph Touchett, 'There's nothing makes us feel so much alive as to see others die.' The two possible acts of the heroine are related by what Miller calls, in writing of *Our Mutual Friend*, 'the nonlogical derivation of one thing from its opposite'.[28] In either case the heroine saves a hero from death: either by dying instead or by protecting him from the destroying angel. This paradox is confirmed by the impression of most readers that Little Nell, who dies, is essentially the same heroine as Florence Dombey, who lives.

Recall that the real-life heroines of the period, Clothilde de Vaux chief among them, acquire their fullest significance in death. This may be due to a feeling of release from ordinary re-

[25] *The Portrait of a Lady*, ch. liv, pp. 413–14.

[26] See Leon Edel, *Henry James: The Untried Years* (Philadelphia, 1953), pp. 326–30.

[27] *NN*, ch. vi; *D & S*, ch. xx, p. 282.

[28] *Charles Dickens*, p. 316.

strictions on the love of a living person. Mary Hogarth's death
liberated Dickens psychologically by rendering her a safe object
of his emotional longing.[29] But Dickens's testimony also suggests a direct significance of her death. 'Thank God she died in
my arms, and the very last words she whispered were of me,' he
exclaims; and four years later he confesses to a constant desire
to be buried with her.[30] Was it merely frustrated love that made
it desirable to be 'with' Mary in this sense, or made it especially
fortunate that she died in his arms, whispering of him? In some
dimly understood way the dead girl represented for Dickens a
triumph over death, an idea that he incorporates in Nell and
Florence both. Liberation of emotion does not seem a sufficient
explanation of that special attitude toward a woman that in-
variably seems to heighten and become more extravagant at the
thought of death. In a letter to Mrs. Brookfield Thackeray
writes: 'I wonder if you remember the day we talked of death.
I thought of myself as damned, and of you as an angel full of pity.
. . . I long for you to give me your blessing, my angel.'[31]

Dickens's heroines have to be viewed against the backdrop of
Victorian angelology. Victorians did not precisely believe that
the dead became angels, but they made room for this idea in
their make-believe worlds and in their rituals of grief and condolence. Children and women, on these occasions, seem far more
likely to become angels than men are. Dickens's most obvious
contribution to make-believe angelology is 'A Child's Dream of
a Star'. The dreamer in this four-page story actually grows from
childhood to old age, while his dead sister, an angel associated
with the star of the title, waits to receive him. Thus the loved
one becomes not just any angel, but the angel in personal charge
of the hero's death. The story is offered, of course, as no more
than a dream.[32] Letters of condolence take a certain license from
the occasion of grief and push this dream toward an article of
faith: 'The certainty of a bright and happy world beyond the
Grave which such young and untried creatures (half Angels here)

[29] Cf. Johnson, I, 200.
[30] To Thomas Beard, 17 May 1837, *Letters*, I, 108; 25 Oct. 1841, Forster (Bk.
III, ch. i), I, 174.
[31] *The Letters and Private Papers of William Makepeace Thackeray*, ed. Gordon N.
Ray, 4 vols. (Cambridge, Mass., 1945–6), II, 453. The original letter was in
French.
[32] *RP*, pp. 387–90.

must be called away by God to people—the thought that in that blessed region of peace and rest there is one spirit who may well be supposed to love and watch over those whom she loved so dearly when on earth.'[33] This sentiment cannot really be called Christian, though it is one to which many Christians have lent themselves. No less devout a person than Samuel Johnson could pray that the soul of his wife might intercede for him. But Johnson was careful not to pray directly to his wife, or to presume anything about the arrangements that may obtain between the living and the dead. His yearning toward a domestic religion was strictly confined within the orthodoxy of the Church of England.[34]

Dickens seems to have dwelt primarily on the theory that dead children become angels.[35] At times the theory approaches something nearer primitive superstition than either classical or Christian religion, as when David Copperfield is made to kiss the hand of his dying brother: 'I wish I had died then, with that feeling in my heart! I should have been more fit for Heaven than I ever have been since.'[36] But it must be remembered that Dickens's most distinctive heroines, Nell, Florence, Agnes, and Dorrit—the little mothers—and a good many others, are in one degree or another children.

[33] To William Bradbury, 3 Mar. 1839, *Letters*, I, 202.
[34] Boswell, *Life of Samuel Johnson*, I, 139.
[35] E.g. *OCS*, ch. xxvi, p. 194; ch. liv, p. 406; *D & S*, ch. xvi, p. 226; ch. l, p. 708; *HT*, Bk. I, ch. xiii, p. 88; *Letters*, II, 86, 672. This sentiment may be regarded as the converse of a familiarity with death that is also alien to the twentieth century. Thus Dickens is able to joke about infant corpses that look like pigs' feet, or the corpse of a child (a real child) that has been sewn up like a feast for a giant: 'Dullborough Town', *UT*, pp. 118–19; 'Some Recollections of Mortality', *UT*, pp. 195–6.
[36] *DC*, ch. viii, p. 109.

XII

MEMORY AND DEATH

DICKENS does not believe in supernatural powers. His allusions
to Mary Hogarth's continued existence and guardianship are
spoken as fervent wishes, statements burdened with the consciousness of what cannot be proved—like the nagging thought,
'We have but faith: we cannot know,' of *In Memoriam*. His
letters of condolence proffer sentiments of what '*must*' be so,
but may not be. His most exuberant ghost stories, like most
stories of that kind, are bouts of indulgence in the supernatural.
Yet clearly there is a reason for these wishes, exhortations, and
indulgences, and a reason, too, for the make-believe powers
with which his heroines are endowed. Reminiscences of the
Paraclete or of Wisdom show the Victorians in general struggling with the irony of non-religious culture; the process of
secularization is never complete. In the words of Mircea Eliade,
the scholar who has made secularization his special study, 'religion is the paradigmatic solution for every existential crisis'.[1]
The crisis most difficult of all to manage, and impossible to
evade, is death. It is arguable that religion comes into being in
the first place in order to cope with death; certainly that secularization of belief leaves men dangerously exposed to death. *In
Memoriam*, almost exclusively concerned with death, is the
Victorians' major religious poem. House observes of Dickens,
'a religion in a state of transition from supernatural belief to
humanism is very poorly equipped to face death, and must dwell
on it for that very reason'.[2]

To a twentieth-century reader it may seem that 'Dickens,
Thackeray, George Eliot, and others, were abnormally sensitive about death'.[3] We are in some ways, however, less comfortable with death than the Victorians were. A further decline
in the belief in immortality has made the physical aspect of death

[1] *The Sacred and the Profane*, trans. Willard R. Trask (New York, 1959), p. 210.
[2] House, *The Dickens World*, p. 132.
[3] A. O. J. Cockshut, *Anthony Trollope* (New York, 1968), p. 89.

10. *Death Crowning Innocence,* by George Frederick Watts

11. Title drawing for *The Haunted Man*, by John Tenniel

still uglier. Whereas Dickens can bear to see the children dead (though not dying), we contemplate birth and copulation more readily than corpses.[4] Assigning an angel to oversee death, whether a living angel or a person who has experienced death, accomplishes more than a mere bath of sentiment. Even if the angel's powers are not fully believed in, she stabilizes the moment of death and makes it individual by sharing in it. In fiction, at least, every hero can have a death of his own. In the nineteenth century urbanization and industrialization were changing death into a statistic, confirming the myth of the city of destruction that religion had supposed. Twentieth-century death is still more impersonal and abstract, and more destructive. Thus Jerome S. Bruner has written of death as an illustration of the change in uses of metaphor from myths to novels, a change that he finds comparable to that between demonic possession and the concept of neurosis.[5] We have seen, however, that this change is not complete by the end of the nineteenth century; even a James heroine sees and feels 'demonically'. Victorian novels can be looked on as transitional documents in this respect: like twentieth-century novels, they are more concerned with the style of dying than the transcendent meaning of death; but like Christian and earlier myths, they cling to the demonic as a link to transcendence. Thus for her father Lucie Manette 'was the golden thread that united him to a Past beyond his misery, and to a Present beyond his misery'; and she becomes the same for two heroes.[6]

We need to investigate briefly the ideas Dickens entertained about death. If there is no longer a Christian heaven or hell, then the sojourners in the city are biding their time in vain. They may as well belong to the earthly city, since they dwell in it. But sometimes Dickens writes vaguely of far-away places, of what Miller calls 'a transcendent spirit, present in nature and reached through death, but apparently unattainable in this world'.[7] The far-away place is best typified by the vision of little Paul, who asks Florence about the sea:

[4] See Geoffrey Gorer, *Death, Grief, and Mourning in Contemporary Britain* (London, 1965), esp. Appendix 4, 'The Pornography of Death'.
[5] *On Knowing: Essays for the Left Hand* (Cambridge, Mass., 1962), pp. 55–7.
[6] *TTC*, Bk. II, ch. iv, p. 74.
[7] *Charles Dickens*, p. 148; cf. pp. 78–81, 238.

'What place is over there?'

She told him that there was another country opposite, but he said he didn't mean that: he meant farther away—farther away!

Very often afterwards, in the midst of their talk, he would break off, to try to understand what it was that the waves were always saying; and would rise up in his couch to look towards that invisible region, far away.[8]

In *Oliver Twist*, building on the satiric contrast of city and country, Dickens once associates the far-away place with an almost Platonic idea of a previous existence:

Who can tell how scenes of peace and quietude sink into the minds of pain-worn dwellers in close and noisy places, and carry their own freshness, deep into their jaded hearts! Men who have lived in crowded, pent-up streets, through lives of toil, and who have never wished for change. . . . The memories which peaceful country scenes call up, are not of this world, nor of its thoughts and hopes. Their gentle influence may teach us how to weave fresh garlands for the graves of those we loved: may purify our thoughts, and bear down before it old enmity and hatred; but beneath all this, there lingers, in the least reflective mind, a vague and half-formed consciousness of having held such feelings long before, in some remote and distant time, which calls up solemn thoughts of distant times to come, and bends down pride and worldliness beneath it.[9]

None of these imputations of another existence is very definite; the tone in each is that of indulged feeling. They are intimations, as in Wordsworth's immortality ode.

The passage in *Oliver Twist* is more central to Dickens's thought than its isolated Platonism would lead one to suspect. That the intimations are memories is important; and the efface-ment of 'old enmity and hatred', in particular, returns us to Dickens's special doctrine of memory. *The Haunted Man* is again useful here, for that story contains a motif that has yet to be explained: a portrait of one of the founders of Redlaw's college, with the inscription, 'Lord, keep my memory green'. The rele-vance of the portrait to Redlaw's wrongs and sorrows, or to the visitation of his ghost, is not immediately apparent; but the in-scription is repeated, and supplies the last words of the story: 'Lord, keep my memory green'. Dickens would not place the inscription so strategically if it did not have two meanings: both

[8] *D & S*, ch. viii, p. 109.   [9] *OT*, ch. xxxii, p. 237.

'let me remember', a prayer that corresponds to the moral theme of *The Haunted Man*, and 'let me be remembered after death', an expression of the common function of a portrait. This pun makes good sense: the memory of one's past and the memory of oneself preserved by others after death are both reassurances of individual existence. When Redlaw sees the mistake of surrendering his memory of the past, he exclaims, 'Give me back myself!' Once he has reconciled himself to his own past, Redlaw is prepared also to live in the memory of others; on these terms, like the subject of the portrait, he is prepared to die.[10]

Memory provides Dickens with an explicit accommodation with death, which he details in a number of places. This accommodation requires no supernatural belief, even though it may be expressed in a ghost story, as in *A Christmas Carol*:

Oh cold, cold, rigid, dreadful Death, set up thine altar here, and dress it with such terrors as thou hast at thy command: for this is thy dominion! But of the loved, revered, and honoured head, thou canst not turn one hair to thy dread purposes, or make one feature odious. It is not that the hand is heavy and will fall down when released; it is not that the heart and pulse are still; but that the hand *was* open, generous, and true; the heart brave, warm, and tender; and the pulse a man's. Strike, Shadow, strike! And see his good deeds springing from the wound, to sow the world with life immortal![11]

In other words, a Scrooge who has done no good deeds will fall victim to death because he will not be remembered; 'life immortal' is conferred in the remembrance of the living. The theory is a possible one for the nineteenth century because it defines immortality without recourse to the supernatural. The worship of the dead in the service of this idea is explored by James in 'The Altar of the Dead', a story of a deceased fiancée and friend who has wronged the hero that recalls *The Haunted Man*. And James points specifically to the secular advantages of this means of overcoming death: 'This was no dim theological rescue, no boon of a contingent world, [the dead] were saved better than faith or works could save them, saved for the warm world they had shrunk from dying to, for actuality, for continuity, for the certainty of human remembrance.'[12]

10 *CB*, pp. 330, 398, 360.
11 *CB*, pp. 64–5.
12 *The Altar of the Dead*, etc., p. 52.

Other passages in Dickens make clear that memory supplies this immortality, not the continuing benefit from the deeds of the deceased. The good deeds that spring from the wounds of the dead are deeds inspired in the living. Of the death of little Nell we are told:

Oh! it is hard to take to heart the lesson that such deaths will teach, but let no man reject it, for it is one that all must learn, and is a mighty, universal Truth. When Death strikes down the innocent and young, for every fragile form from which he lets the panting spirit free, a hundred virtues rise, in shapes of mercy, charity, and love, to walk the world, and bless it. Of every tear that sorrowing mortals shed on such green graves, some good is born, some gentler nature comes. In the Destroyer's steps there spring up bright creations that defy his power, and his dark path becomes a way of light to Heaven.

In a similar declaration the schoolmaster in *The Old Curiosity Shop* argues that memories of the dead are a frequent source of good deeds: 'Forgotten! oh, if the good deeds of human creatures could be traced to their source, how beautiful would even death appear; for how much charity, mercy, and purified affection, would be seen to have their growth in dusty graves!'[13] The theory recurs in Dickens in contexts that are not even sentimental. Later, wilier heroes can actually be caught manipulating the theory. John Harmon, by playing dead in *Our Mutual Friend*, has found 'the true friends of my lifetime still as true, as tender, and as faithful as when I was alive, and making my memory an incentive to good actions done in my name'.[14] At the funeral of his sister Pip reflects 'that the day must come when it would be well for my memory that others walking in the sunshine should be softened as they thought of me'. And confronting Orlick at the limekiln, he confronts 'the dread of being misremembered after death'.[15]

The softening and improving influence of the memory of death fits the category of 'sorrows' in the doctrine of memory that is elaborated in *The Haunted Man*. Moreover, the hero of that story has not only been wronged by a friend but has suffered the death of his sister, so that the second category of memories is illustrated as well as named in the story. But the doctrine is

13 *OCS*, ch. lxxii, p. 544; ch. liv, p. 406. Cf. *NN*, ch. xliii, p. 564.
14 *OMF*, Bk. II, ch. xiii, p. 372.
15 *GE*, ch. xxxv, p. 264; ch. liii, p. 404.

still more consistent than the dividing of memories into categories of wrongs and sorrows supposes. For it is also true that the dead, whom we have loved in life, have wronged us by dying. Not only do the dead succeed in wronging us by departing, but they depart with finality. Their wrong is irremediable; they, too, stand in need of our forgiveness, and yet they cannot receive it. There is no way for the dead to make restitution, in accordance with the morality of consequences, unless the memory of the dead inspires the moral life of the living.

Christmas is the festival of the hearth, the feast day of the religion of Dickens. It is also the day of the dead. In *A Christmas Carol* Scrooge's nephew remarks that Christmas is the one time of year when men and women 'think of people below them as if they really were fellow-passengers to the grave'.[16] Dickens associated Christmas, rather than Easter, with death and the remembrance of the dead. Three out of five Christmas books are ghost stories; *The Battle of Life*, one of the two exceptions, almost gratuitously opens with a discourse on the 'deep green patches' in the local landscape that mark places where corpses were buried long ago. As early as the celebration at Dingley Dell in *Pickwick* Dickens connects Christmas with death by comparing the 'happy state of companionship and mutual good-will' of the season with the 'first joys of a future condition of existence' hoped for by all peoples.[17] In 'What Christmas Is As We Grow Older', like Tennyson in *In Memoriam*, published the year before, he makes a studied use of this season as a time for the recollection of the dead, including one 'dear girl—almost a woman—never to be one' who is presumably Mary Hogarth. The low voice that begins a dialogue with the narrator in this story (which is hardly a story at all) is a device borrowed from Tennyson:

On this day we shut out Nothing!
'Pause,' says a low voice. 'Nothing? Think!'
'On Christmas Day, we will shut out from our fireside, Nothing.'
'Not the shadow of a vast City where the withered leaves are lying deep?' the voice replies. 'Not the shadow that darkens the whole globe? Not the shadow of the City of the Dead?'
Not even that. Of all days in the year, we will turn our faces towards

16 *CB*, p. 10.
17 *PP*, ch. xxviii, p. 374. Cf. 'A Christmas Dinner', *SB*, p. 220.

that City upon Christmas Day, and from its silent hosts bring those we loved, among us. City of the Dead, in the blessed name wherein we are gathered together at this time, and in the Presence that is here among us according to the promise, we will receive, and not dismiss, the people who are dear to us!

The home that serves as a shelter from the actual city apparently has a private entrance on Christmas to the city of the dead. The invitation to loved ones follows without transition the invitation to any living enemy who may have wronged us—'By Christmas Day we do forgive him!' [18]

The religion of Positivism regarded death as a sacrament, and interpreted it as a passage from life into the memory of a surviving friend or relation. *In Memoriam* records a ten-year effort to master death through an exercise in memory. Similarly, the key function in Dickens's Christmas books and stories is memory, whether of the dead or of those who have wronged us. In *A Christmas Carol* the recollection of the past is necessary to accomplish the conversion of Scrooge. 'Scrooge hung his head to hear his own words quoted by the Spirit, and was overcome with penitence and grief.' Memory operates, for once, on a person who is wrong rather than wronged. Then, by transporting the hero into the future, the story appeals to memory as it pertains to the dead. The method of the third ghost is to fill Scrooge with pity for his own death. He displays the corpse, and Scrooge, 'agonized', begs him to show 'any person in the town, who feels emotion caused by this man's death'. He is answered by a vision of a couple of debtors who are, indeed, relieved by his death.[19] By appealing to the second function of memory Dickens assures that Scrooge is a fairly typical hero after all, for the method of conversion is to bring Scrooge to the point where he is sorry, not so much for his deeds, as for himself. His is not fear of damnation, note, nor even strictly speaking the fear of death, but the fear of not being remembered.

Memory is characteristically manipulated in these tales: fantasy and dream intervene with time. Dickens can no more disbelieve in linear, historical time than any other man of the nineteenth or twentieth centuries, but the Christmas tales constitute his sportive revolt against time. *The Chimes*, in particular, is such a revolt: Dickens has Trotty Veck dream the inevitable

[18] *CS*, p. 23.   [19] *CB*, pp. 47, 65.

course of events, the moral ruin and descent to prostitution
caused by the conditions of the city, so that in the end he can
reverse the course of events and deny the theory of social causation. This is fundamentally a religious exercise; it is arguable
that all reading of fiction is an escape from time, and certain that
the Christmas books have this function.[20] *The Chimes* unabashedly puts two mutually exclusive courses of events side by side;
A Christmas Carol and *The Haunted Man* change a course of
events by manipulating the memory of the past. From here it is
a short step to a favourite pattern of Dickens's later works: the
fantasy of rebirth. This fantasy also provides an escape from
one's personal duration in time and an opportunity to live two
lives—but sequentially rather than contemporaneously. It is
closely related to the use of doubles in the same works; not the
inadvertent doubling of hero and villain, but the deliberate
decision to let the hero lead two lives, by resemblance to another
man in the case of Sydney Carton and Charles Darnay, by im-
personation of another in the case of John Harmon, and by proxy
in love in the case of George Silverman. It can be argued that the
literary invention of the *Doppelgänger* is itself an accommodation
of death, being merely a species of that psychological displacement that generates, from fear of death, the idea of an immortal
soul.[21]

In *Pickwick* Mr. Weller scorns the Reverend Stiggins's 'in-
wention for grown-up people being born again'; he would
'wery much like to see that system in haction, Sammy'.[22] What
would the sagacious Mr. Weller say of that system in action in
A Tale of Two Cities or *Our Mutual Friend?* The system seems
to have been invented in the Christmas story for 1854, which
relates the adventures of Richard Doubledick.[23] Briefly, Doubledick loses his girl-friend; joins the army in order to get killed;
meets a mentor and double who is killed instead; inherits the
mentor's mother; is wounded so seriously at the battle of
Waterloo that he loses consciousness for some months; 'comes
back to life' to find the mother and the girl-friend, who has

[20] See Eliade, *The Sacred and the Profane*, p. 205; and *The Myth of the Eternal
Return*, trans. Willard R. Trask (New York, 1954).
[21] See Otto Rank, *Beyond Psychology* (New York, 1958), ch. ii; and *Der
Doppelgänger, eine psychoanalytische Studie* (Leipzig, Wien, and Zurich, 1925).
[22] *PP*, ch. xxii, p. 297.
[23] 'The Seven Poor Travellers', *CS*, pp. 77–91.

married him while he lay at the point of death; and is enabled by this experience to forgive the Frenchman who killed his double. One of the provisional titles of *A Tale of Two Cities* was 'Buried Alive',[24] and the first book of the novel, with reference to Dr. Manette, is entitled 'Recalled to Life'. From the somnolent meditations of Jarvis Lorry on the state of being buried alive, to the English trial in which Darnay is 'recalled to life', and from Jerry Cruncher's profession as a 'resurrection man', to Carton's meditation, 'I am the resurrection and the life', the theme of rebirth crowds in on the original design of uniting, by the use of two heroes, the contradictory heroisms of living and dying for love. To reconcile love and riches in *Our Mutual Friend* Dickens is content with nothing less than the secret rebirth and double identity of Harmon-Rokesmith; a second, more wayward hero, Eugene Wrayburn is subjected to near drowning, Doubledickian marriage, and moral rebirth.

Continuation of life in the memory of others, the remembrance of the dead at Christmas time, and the symbolic rebirths in the late novels and stories are themes of Dickens that have another factor in common: in one way or another they all enlist the heroine of love and truth. The passages that detail the function of memory apply either directly to Little Nell or indirectly to Mary Hogarth; even Redlaw has a dead sister and Scrooge a lost love. The Christmas scenes, like fireside scenes generally in Dickens, tend to be dedicated to or presided over by a special female. Most obviously, the miraculous rebirths are conducted by some heroine: Mary Marshall in the case of Doubledick, Marguerite Obenreizer in 'No Thoroughfare', Lucie Manette in *A Tale of Two Cities*, Lizzie Hexam in *Our Mutual Friend*. Lucie, for example, not only nurses her father back to life and guards the immortal memory of Carton, but is partially credited with her husband's continued existence. Darnay loves her from the moment of his first trial for his life in England: 'he had never seen a face so tenderly beautiful, as hers when it was confronted with his own on the edge of the grave that had been dug for him'. Lucie is grotesquely linked to death from her first appearance in the 'large, dark room, furnished in a funereal manner' at the Royal George Hotel in Dover. The candles on the dark table burn 'as if *they* were buried, in deep graves of black mahogany',

[24] Forster (Bk. IX, ch. ii), II, 280.

and on the frame of the pier-glass behind Lucie 'a hospital procession of negro cupids, several headless and all cripples, were
offering black baskets of Dead Sea fruit to black divinities of the
feminine gender'.[25] Lizzie Hexam, a fisher of corpses from the
Thames with her father, is thought by Betty Higden to be an
angel when the latter dies in her arms; and just before Wrayburn
is struck by Headstone and rescued from the river by Lizzie,
'He held her, almost as if she were sanctified to him by death,
and kissed her once, almost as he might have kissed the dead.'[26]

That the spirit of love and truth is also an angel of death explains a great deal. The conjunction of truth and death is not
new: in the Garden of Eden Adam learned 'that suffering for
Truth's sake / Is fortitude to highest victorie, / And to the faithful Death the Gate of Life'.[27] But in the Victorian faith truth and
death are also peculiarly interdependent. Tennyson argues that
merely the existence of human love and truth is a reason for
believing in a future state:

> Contemplate all this work of Time,
>   The giant labouring in his youth;
>   Nor dream of human love and truth,
> As dying Nature's earth and lime.[28]

It is not a very strong argument: but the corollary is that love
and truth justify a future state of existence, bring about survival.
The persistence of the heroine of truth in English fiction raises
the question of her purpose. Clearly she is there to save the hero
in some sense; but the soteriology of the novel, and of the nineteenth century, is not the conventional Christian one that dis-
criminates among different after-lives. The real issue is whether
a hero, or an ordinary man, can escape death at all. If the heroine,
as the evidence suggests, is meant to save the hero, she must
save him from death. At the same time death is the sanction of
the heroine's moral influence: the hero and others must heed her
before it is too late.[29]

[25] *TTC*, Bk. II, ch. x, pp. 123–4; Bk. I, ch. iv, pp. 18–19.
[26] *OMF*, Bk. III, ch. viii, p. 512; Bk. IV, ch. vi, pp. 695–6.
[27] *Paradise Lost*, XII, ll. 569–71.
[28] *In Memoriam*, cxviii.
[29] Houghton, *The Victorian Frame of Mind*, pp. 389–93, makes the general point
that Victorian idealization of women was related to religious doubt, especially to
doubts of immortality. Cf. also Humphry House, 'The Mood of Doubt', in *All in
Due Time* (London, 1955), pp. 94–100.

The obvious illustration of this combined role of heroines is the formidable one of Pompilia in *The Ring and the Book*. Though she is forced to flee her husband, Pompilia, too, is a 'Champion of truth'. And 'because she lies too by my side', Caponsacchi imagines that he will rise on the last day. 'You know this is not love, Sirs,—it is faith, / The feeling that there's God.' But so does her persecutor, Guido, with his last breath, hope to be saved from death by Pompilia. Hostility to a heroine might be said to reach its ultimate, Browningesque extension in Guido; its violence is such that his surrender is postponed to the last moment. Then he calls out to all possible saviours, in ascending order: 'Abate,—Cardinal,—Christ,—Maria,—God, . . . /Pompilia, will you let them murder me?'[30]

With the notable exceptions of Florence Dombey and Lizzie Hexam the connection between the figure of truth and death in the novels of Dickens is far less dramatic, and often suggested in dreamlike details that strike one at first as rather meaningless. The most baffling example is the mysterious well in the church at the end of *The Old Curiosity Shop*. What is the reader supposed to understand by such a well? Little Nell is led to it by the sexton, who in the drawing of the scene by Daniel Maclise suggests, with his crutch, the figure of Time.

'Look in,' said the old man, pointing downward with his finger.
The child complied, and gazed down into the pit.
'It looks like a grave itself,' said the old man.
'It does,' replied the child.[31]

The proverb has it, however, that truth will be found at the bottom of a well, not death. And this is a proverb with which Dickens was familiar, to which he has just alluded in the previous chapter, in the frame for this novel, and elsewhere.[32] But whether one can press this identification of death with truth very far, even with a figure of time hovering nearby, is very doubtful. It is only clear that the well makes some reference to Nell and her imminent death.

[30] *The Ring and the Book*, X, l. 683; VI, ll. 1192–4; XI, ll. 2424–5, in *Robert Browning's Poems and Plays*, vol. III, Everyman's Library (London, 1962).

[31] *OCS*, ch. lv, p. 413. Cf. Shakespeare, *King John* (III, i, 324): 'Old time the clock-setter, that bald sexton time.'

[32] *OCS*, ch. liv, p. 400; *MHC*, p. 11. Cf. *OT*, Preface, p. xvii; *D & S*, ch. xxxii, p. 456; *BH*, ch. i, p. 2; and *The Battle of Life*, *CB*, p. 253. Ironic references to truth in a well are made in *MC*, ch. xvi, p. 263; ch. xliii, p. 668.

'Worn out with her own emotions, and yielding to the silence of the room, [Little Dorrit's] hand slowly slackened and failed in its fanning movement, and her head dropped down on the pillow at her father's side. Clennam rose softly, opened and closed the door without a sound, and passed from the prison, carrying the quiet with him into the turbulent streets.'[33] In the following chapter of *Little Dorrit*, the last in Book I, Clennam will bear the insensible figure of the heroine, Cordelia-like, out of the prison. Earlier he felt 'as if he would have been glad to take her up in his arms and carry her to her journey's end'; and eventually they will go down into the roaring streets in a new relationship. Just after she parts with Clennam in the earlier book, he reflecting on her frailty and thinking to take her in his arms to the journey's end, she encounters the prostitute who mistakes her for a child, and continues in the night to the church outside the Marshalsea. There 'the sexton, or the beadle, or the verger, or whatever he was', gives her the burial register of the parish for a pillow, and Little Dorrit sleeps 'with her head resting on that sealed book of Fate, untroubled by its mysterious blank leaves'. At the very end, at the marriage with Clennam the same official, now denominated the 'clerk', makes a point of re-calling the incident. 'Her birth is in what I call the first volume; she lay asleep on this very floor, with her pretty head on what I call the second volume; and now she's a-writing her little name as a bride, in what I call the third volume.' Even the order chosen for the three registers, making marriage come after death, is peculiar. None of these touches is as obtrusive as the sun that shines on them 'through the painted figure of Our Saviour' in the church window during the ceremony; but they build up to a persistent image of Little Dorrit as dead or as one untroubled by death.[34]

This image is curiously transposed by Dorrit herself so as to include Arthur. Dickens quietly permits his heroine to express her thoughts through the fairy-tale that she invents for Maggie's entertainment, which begins, as requested, with a princess but is really about the 'poor tiny woman spinning at her wheel' in a cottage. This woman, who is obviously Little Dorrit and con-ceivably one of the fates, keeps in her closet 'the shadow of Some

[33] *LD*, Bk. I, ch. xxxv, p. 422.
[34] *LD*, Bk. I, ch. xiv, pp. 173, 176, 177; Bk. II, ch. xxxiv, pp. 826, 825.

one ... who had gone on far away quite out of reach', who is Arthur Clennam. What will happen to the shadow, asks the princess, when she dies? The tiny woman answers, conventionally enough, that 'it would sink quietly into her own grave, and would never be found'. The princess comes every day to see the woman spinning at her wheel, until one day 'the wheel was still, and the tiny woman was not to be seen'. She asks 'why the wheel had stopped, and where the tiny woman was', and of course the tiny woman is dead. But the spinner has taken the shadow with her: 'it had sunk quietly into her own grave, and . . . she and it were at rest together.'[35] The comic version of this tale is that of John Chivery, whose fate is also in the hands of the heroine, but who anticipates her by writing his own epitaph: 'Here lie the mortal remains of JOHN CHIVERY, Never anything worth mentioning, Who died about the end of the year one thousand eight hundred and twenty-six, Of a broken heart, Requesting with his last breath that the word AMY might be inscribed over his ashes, Which was accordingly directed to be done, By his afflicted Parents.'[36] Chivery is the reincarnation of Florence Dombey's victim, P. Toots, Esquire, with his readiness to slide into the silent Tomb.

Little Dorrit's role is very close to Florence's where her father is concerned. She is absolutely loyal to him in spite of his disregard, and in being so she is loyal to a man whose worth is not self-evident. Her office continues, or is resumed, at his death: 'for ten days Little Dorrit bent over his pillow, laying her cheek against his.'[37] But her relation to Clennam takes over and outweighs this relation to her father. It is not as readily seen that Dorrit is an angel of death where Clennam is concerned. To understand how this can be so, there have to be taken into account not merely the scattered hints of her special connection with death, but the kind of action she is involved in with the hero. It is a last action, the final disposition of his life, after which action apparently stops. Just as Agnes Wickfield promises that love and truth will triumph 'in the end', and the ending discovers Agnes pointing upward at the end of David's life, so the marriage of Arthur Clennam to Little Dorrit completes his life. Nothing follows except quiet. Arthur comes to understand this

[35] *LD*, Bk. I, ch. xxiv, pp. 292–5.   [36] *LD*, Bk. I, ch. xviii, p. 220.
[37] *LD*, Bk. II, ch. xix, p. 650.

before Dorrit returns to the Marshalsea: 'Looking back upon his own poor story, she was its vanishing point. Every thing in its perspective led to her innocent figure. He had travelled thousands of miles towards it; previous unquiet hopes and doubts had worked themselves out before it; it was the centre of the interest of his life; it was the termination of everything that was good and pleasant in it; beyond there was nothing but mere waste and darkened sky.' A 'vanishing point', 'the termination of everything that was good and pleasant' are curious propositions, implying that marriage to Little Dorrit is the culmination of the hero's life, but also the end of it. Perhaps they explain why the register of marriages comes after the register of deaths. Surely they explain why Arthur first perceives Dorrit's return as a dream. 'Some abiding impression of a garden stole over him—a garden of flowers, with a damp warm wind gently stirring their scents.' Little Dorrit in person arrives in a black mantle, underneath which is the 'old, worn dress' of so many heroines of love and truth. Her tears drop on the hero 'as the rain from Heaven had dropped upon the flowers'.[38]

Dorrit first appears as a child, as if she were the hero's daughter; she tends her father, and subsequently the hero, as if she were their mother; and finally she marries the hero, as she must in any novel of courtship. Florence Dombey contains within herself the same mixture of generations:

A child in innocent simplicity; a woman in her modest self-reliance, and her deep intensity of feeling; both child and woman seemed at once expressed in her fair face and fragile delicacy of shape, and gracefully to mingle there;— as if the spring should be unwilling to depart when summer came, and sought to blend the earlier beauties of the flowers with their bloom. But in her thrilling voice, in her calm eyes, sometimes in a strange ethereal light that seemed to rest upon her head, and always in a certain pensive air upon her beauty, there was an expression, such as had been seen in the dead boy.

When Florence becomes a mother in her own right, she returns to the father to ask *his* forgiveness. When her child was born, she explains, 'I knew what I had done in leaving you.' 'Unchanged still. Of all the world, unchanged,' she is the spirit of love and truth as well as the hallowed figure with the expression

[38] *LD*, Bk. II, ch. xxvii, p. 733; ch. xxix, p. 755.

of the dead boy.[39] The heroine's relation to death justifies these
multiple roles. In her the generations converge and mitigate
against annihilation. Her relation to death especially justifies her
role as little mother.

'A Child's Dream of a Star' is not misnamed; though the hero
of that dream lives out his life to old age, he moves 'towards the
star as a child' in the end.[40] Nearly every human theory of death
expresses the idea of a return: a return to the earth, a return to
heaven, a return to nothingness; but in definable experience immediately before death, a return to childhood. If the neighbouring human face is essential to the sanity and well-being of the
newborn, it is no less imagined to be essential to the dying. At
least those who are not dying assume that those who are wish
to see and recognize their faces at the last. 'Mama is like you,
Floy. I know her by the face!' The dying Paul seizes upon
Florence as a maternal face. But just as sexuality in a heroine
biologically implies the hero's death as an individual, so an actual
mother would prove that he was indeed born and would therefore die. A little mother offers comfort and security without
these terminal implications of physical life. Nor can an actual
mother magically survive 'unchanged' to inspire the confidence
at the end of life that was essential in its earliest stages. Only a
generalized figure can do this. Thus Walter Pater's hero,
Marius, 'came to think of women's tears, of women's hands to lay
one to rest, in death as in the sleep of childhood, as a sort of
natural want'.[41]

Though she is not the destroying angel, the saving angel also
represents the power of death; the hero must overcome some
natural resistance of one degree or another before he can become reconciled to her love. Erikson observes that a mother, in
the earliest stage of life, 'is all of the comprehensible world, and
therefore becomes, and in many ways remains, the model for
the powers which, because they can give, can also withhold
everything'. In his analysis of Freud's dream of the Three Fates
he finds the implication 'that a pact with maternal women is a
pact—with death'.[42] But the clinical discoveries of psychoanal-
ysis often recall the medicine of an earlier time. A poem of the

[39] *D & S*, ch. xlvii, p. 653; ch. lix, pp. 843–4.   [40] *RP*, p. 390.
[41] *Marius the Epicurean*, Everyman's Library (London, 1934), ch. i, p. 13.
[42] *Insight and Responsibility* (New York, 1964), pp. 179–85.

1870s by W. E. Henley calls Death both 'the mother of Life' and 'the lover of Life', because she lays hold of the lives of the men in a hospital ward one by one.[43] With graver archaism Erikson names wisdom as the virtue associated with the last stage of life—the virtue that enables one to face death. The Victorians were well aware that Wisdom promised immortality to the righteous, and that the house of folly, the stranger who competed sexually with Wisdom, was the house of death.[44] The fourth essay of *Unto This Last*, envisioning the whole of private and public endeavour as the enlistment of individuals on the side of life against death, anticipates the later thought of Freud. There Ruskin argues that the true science of political economy teaches one 'how the service of Death, the Lord of Waste, and of eternal emptiness, differs from the service of Wisdom, the Lady of Saving, and of eternal fulness'.[45]

Ruskin offered three explanations of the treatment of death in the novels of Dickens and other contemporaries, of which he disapproved. The explanations, carefully numbered, are remarkably alike, however: 'the hot fermentation and unwholesome secrecy of the population crowded into large cities'; 'The disgrace and grief resulting from the mere trampling pressure and electric friction of town life'; and 'The monotony of life in the central streets of any great modern city, but especially those of London'. Consequently, 'the ultimate power of fiction to entertain' the city-dweller, the Londoner, 'is by varying to his fancy the modes, and defining for his dulness the horrors, of Death'. He lists in a chart the deaths in *Bleak House*. These deaths 'are all grotesquely either violent or miserable, purporting thus to illustrate the modern theology that the appointed destiny of a large average of our population is to die like rats in a drain, either by trap or poison'.[46] In a sense Ruskin is wrong about the deaths in *Bleak House*: sensational or not each is given a special significance by Dickens's rhetoric. The series of unrelieved deaths in *Mary Barton*, Mrs. Gaskell's first novel, is much more chilling and directly attributable to the industrial city. To make death amazing is one of Dickens's ways of making

[43] 'In Hospital', *Poems* (London, 1921), pp. 14–15.
[44] *Insight and Responsibility*, pp. 132–4. Cf. Proverbs 7: 27; 9: 18.
[45] *Unto This Last*, in *Works*, XVII, 85.
[46] *Fiction, Fair and Foul*, in *Works*, XXXIV, 268–72.

his readers comfortable with it. Ruskin yearned for the stricter poetic justice of Scott; his criticism presumed that literature should be morally idealistic. He would hardly disagree with his own observations that city life produced this sensational concern with the death of 'inoffensive' and 'respectable' persons. He refuses to resign himself to the situation, but acknowledges in more than one harangue that men are dying like rats in a drain.

It was against death in the earthly city, and death in the nineteenth-century city, that Dickens was fending. His main strategy, and that of his contemporaries, was to domesticate death, to wrest it from the city and take it in by the fireside. If he would only think 'of Death, or Home, or Childhood', the heroine of *Martin Chuzzlewit* advises the hero, she is sure that he will be able to forgive Martin senior.[47] Such a trinity of sentiments spells out Dickens's religion at a glance. The annual festival of the hearth, half pagan and half Christian, is Christmas, and 'On Christmas Day, we will shut out from our fireside, Nothing' —not even 'the shadow of the City of the Dead'. The redemptive figure who tends the fire is endowed with powers reminiscent of the domestic religion of Greece and Rome, of Christian salvation and more ancient Wisdom, and these powers are concentrated against death.

[47] *MC*, ch. xiv, p. 242.

12. *Little Nell and the Sexton*, by Daniel Maclise

13. *Time, Death and Judgement*, by George Frederick Watts

XIII

THE NOVEL AND THE END OF LIFE

IT seems incongruous to foist an angel of death on these capacious novels, and disproportionate to oppose the nineteenth-century idea of the city and a bride adorned for her husband by appeal to a single text from the book of Revelation.[1] Yet I am repeatedly driven back to these standpoints; I am persuaded that the angel is not merely a figment of a cultural miscellany that happens to be swept up, along with everything else, into the novels of Dickens. She is generated by the novel itself, which in its classic form in English functions almost as a fable of death. English novels of the late eighteenth and nineteenth centuries nearly always pretend to give the crucial period of the hero's life, the whole of his life that matters, and therefore close when the event that is morally decisive in life has occurred—like the marriage of Tom Jones. We have to ask what these novels that pretend to so much, which are perhaps the main cultural expression of the time, are actually about; and what the decisive event is supposed to accomplish. The connection of the heroine with death that is revealed by Dickens confirms rather than rivals the quasi-providential design of English novels. As for the opposition of this angel and the city, that does not depend on myth or scripture alone,'but on the felt opposition between the enclosed family and the streets that is a fact of modern urban experience.

Moreover, the Revelation of St. John was frequently present to the nineteenth-century imagination.[2] There seems little doubt that the imagery of Revelation has retained some hold on the urban imagination even in the twentieth century, and the

[1] Revelation 21:2; quoted on the title page.
[2] Just as apocalyptic ideas ushered in the Puritan revolution in the seventeenth century, they reappeared in the panic that preceded the reform bill of 1832. See Haller, *The Rise of Puritanism*, pp. 269–87; and Owen Chadwick, *The Victorian Church*, Pt. I (New York, 1966), pp. 35–8.

Victorians found it useful on many occasions. What England needs, according to Carlyle, is 'A new and veritable heart-divorce from the Babylonish woman, who is Jesuitism and Unveracity, and dwells not at Rome now, but under your nose and everywhere'.[3] The book of Revelation lent obscure imminence to the Victorians' frequent references to Time—usually with a capital letter and often conventionally personified. The literature of the period abounds with references to time, which threatens and retreats, creates and resolves anxiety, sanctions and obliterates moral acts.[4] 'Time, with his innumerable horse-power', 'Old Time, that greatest and longest-established Spinner of all', is operative in *Hard Times*[5]—but nearly everywhere else in Dickens as well. For the most part his references are to the end of time, time coming to a stop; and Dickens can be said to have contributed richly to the fictional paradigms of apocalypse that Frank Kermode has discussed in *The Sense of an Ending*.[6] The apocalypse invoked does not have to be a very specific event, or closely tied to the forecasts of Revelation. Whether it derives from satire, renaissance allegory, the Puritan tradition, or all three, the threat and satisfaction inherent in time coming to an end stand in answer to an even less tolerable idea of historicism: the thought of time reaching endlessly before and after human life without stop.

Dickens associated this idea of time—so closely allied to the idea of death—with the city. In the course of introducing *Barnaby Rudge* to the reader, Master Humphrey records a visit to the giant clock in St. Paul's:

Its very pulse, if I may use the word, was like no other clock. It did not

---

[3] *Latter-Day Pamphlets*, No. IV, *Works*, XIX, 196. D. H. Lawrence was so aroused by the part the last book of the Bible seemed to have played in his heritage, that he devoted a book of his own to the subject. Revelation had assisted English popular religion to become a religion of death, in effect. The Christ of John's vision is master of death: 'He holds the keys that unlock death and Hades. He is Lord of the Underworld. He is Hermes, the guide of souls through the death-world, over the hellish stream. He is master of the mysteries of the dead, he knows the meaning of the holocaust, and has final power over the powers below. The dead and the lords of death, who are always hovering in the background of religion down among the people, these chthonioi of the primitive Greeks, these too must acknowledge Jesus as supreme lord.' *Apocalypse* (New York, 1932), p. 39.

[4] See Jerome Hamilton Buckley, *The Triumph of Time: A Study of Victorian Concepts of Time, History, Progress, and Decadence* (Cambridge, Mass., 1966).

[5] *HT*, Bk. I, ch. xiv, pp. 90, 95.

[6] *The Sense of an Ending: Studies in the Theory of Fiction* (New York, 1967).

mark the flight of every moment with a gentle second stroke, as though
it would check old Time, and have him stay his pace in pity, but
measured it with one sledge-hammer beat, as if its business were to
crush the seconds as they came trooping on, and remorselessly to clear
a path before the Day of Judgment.

I sat down opposite to it, and hearing its regular and never-changing
voice, that one deep constant note, uppermost amongst all the noise
and clatter in the streets below,—marking that, let that tumult rise or
fall, go on or stop,—let it be night or noon, to-morrow or to-day, this
year or next,—it still performed its functions with the same dull constancy, and regulated the progress of the life around, the fancy came
upon me that this was London's Heart, and that when it should cease
to beat, the City would be no more.[7]

A similar idea works its way into various descriptions of the
metropolis, particularly of the City of London in its aspects of
money and death. 'The closed warehouses and offices have an air
of death about them, and the national dread of colour has an air
of mourning. The towers and steeples of the many house-
encompassed churches, dark and dingy as the sky that seems
descending on them, are no relief to the general gloom; a sun-
dial on a church-wall has the look, in its useless black shade, of
having failed in its business enterprise and stopped payment for
ever.'[8] The idea behind such passages is common enough; it is
the religious and satiric answer to the commercial commonplace
that, in contrast with the village, 'time is of every consequence
in the city'.[9]

The positive fulfillment of the apocalyptic idea is also reflected in Dickens, in his acceptance of the folk-wisdom that
truth will triumph in the end. Falsely candid men like Mr.
Chester, for example, pay 'an unconscious compliment to Truth
. . . which will turn the laugh against them to the Day of Judgment'.[10] The unveiling of truth by time is suggested by Agnes
Wickfield's repeated hope (which is actually a promise) that
love and truth will triumph 'in the end', and by Jarndyce ad-
vising Richard and Ada to leave everything to 'time, truth, and
steadfastness'. When steadfastness fails Richard, Jarndyce must

[7] *MHC*, p. 107.
[8] *OMF*, Bk. II, ch. xv, p. 393.
[9] Smiles, *George Moore*, p. 66.
[10] *BR*, ch. xxiii, p. 174. Cf. *MC*, ch. li, pp. 782, 783, 787; also Chadband's
travesty of 'the light of Terewth', *BH*, ch. xxv, p. 359.

216216 THE BRIDE FROM HEAVEN

fall back on the narrower formula, 'We must trust to you [Ada] and time to set him right'. Time and truth duly catch up with Richard, too, when Ada kisses him for the last time and he departs for 'The world that sets this right'.[11] The end of narrative time is celebrated by the triumph of the heroine of love and truth; and the institution of the hearth itself, over which the unchanging heroine presides, is an inner fortification of time-lessness. In *Barnaby Rudge* a home is called 'that great altar . . . where the best have offered up such sacrifices and done such deeds of heroism, as, chronicled, would put the proudest temples of old Time, with all their vaulting annals, to the blush!'[12]

Dickens's most obvious domestication of the end of time is *The Chimes*, in which the Bell tells Trotty Veck that his daughter 'bewails the dead, and mingles with the dead', though she is living, and instructs him to 'Learn from her life, a living truth'. Here in Trotty's own words, before he wakes from his dream, are the conclusions to be drawn from the story:

I know that our inheritance is held in store for us by Time. I know there is a sea of Time to rise one day, before which all who wrong us or oppress us will be swept away like leaves. I see it, on the flow! I know that we must trust and hope, and neither doubt ourselves, nor doubt the good in one another. I have learnt it from the creature dearest to my heart. I clasp her in my arms again. O Spirits, merciful and good, I take your lesson to my breast along with her! O Spirits, merciful and good, I am grateful!

The Spirits are the bells that ring out the hours. As if the relation of the heroine to time were still not clear enough, Trotty wakes to find her by the fireside, preparing to adorn herself for her husband. 'She was working with her needle, at the little table by the fire; dressing her simple gown with ribbons for her wedding. So quietly happy, so blooming and youthful, so full of beautiful promise, that he uttered a great cry as if it were an Angel in his house; then flew to clasp her in his arms.' And Dickens has still not completed his picture, for Trotty trips over 'the newspaper, which had fallen on the hearth; and somebody came rushing in between them'. This is Meg's betrothed, who gaily seizes his first kiss of the New Year. The intrusion merely

[11] *BH*, ch. xxiv, p. 339; ch. xliii, p. 592; ch. lxv, pp. 870–1.
[12] *BR*. ch. lxxxi, p. 623.

redoubles Trotty's happiness, since the triangular affair once more symbolizes unchanging love and truth.[13]

The prospect of an end to time contravenes the implication of modern historicism. The new idea of history was that of an endless sequence of events, one moment leading to the next from the limitless past to the limitless future. Primitive ideas of time as analogous to the returning seasons, dynastic ideas of time measured in the generations of kings, the Christian cycle of time from the creation of the world to the day of judgement, were eclipsed by historicism. Time was conceived to be irreversible. Yet this characteristic idea of the nineteenth century had a paradoxical effect on the sense of an ending. Illogically, but not surprisingly, historicism in almost every form renewed the need to envision an ending. *In Memoriam* is closely attuned to the scientific ideas of the age that implied continuing evolutionary change, but the last lines of the poem plead for an end to this process: 'one far-off divine event, / To which the whole creation moves'. The inexorable development of the universe is imagined by Spencer to end in 'perfection'. The Comtean and Marxist versions of history are resolved by no less arbitrary attempts to bring the determined course of events to a halt.[14] In a phrase from Dickens's mature historical novel, *A Tale of Two Cities*, 'Time . . . never reverses his formations.' A prospect of irreversible time, however, merely renews and strengthens the desire to make an end, and a few pages later Sydney Carton assures the young seamstress who accompanies him to the guillotine that they are going to a place where there is 'no Time'. The seamstress is a sort of after-image of Lucie Manette, whose 'golden thread' that binds the past, present, and future is opposed in the novel to Madame Defarge's ceaseless and remorseless knitting.[15]

The response of the novel to this paradox is most amply demonstrated by *The Mill on the Floss*, which rigorously applies each possible implication of historicism to the lives and action that it represents, only to rescue the heroine and hero from history in the end. George Eliot begins by setting her novel in a retrospective, Wordsworthian frame; she searches the family histories of the Tullivers and Dodsons, and looks over the social

---

[13] *CB*, pp. 125, 151–3.
[14] Cf. Eliade, *The Myth of the Eternal Return*, pp. 148–50.
[15] *TTC*, Bk. III, ch. xv, pp. 353, 357.

and economic history of St. Oggs; above all, she studies the development of Maggie Tulliver herself. Natural history is brought in to support this emphasis: the survival of the fittest becomes an ironic motif in the childhood of Tom Tulliver, and sexual selection the serious argument of Stephen Guest. A much firmer historical pressure is felt through the morality of consequences, shared by all the Tullivers and sanctioned by time: 'If the past is not to bind us, where can duty lie?' This deeply historical emphasis is heavy with responsibility and cries out for some sort of resolution. Maggie's past includes, after all, her adventure with Stephen as well as her friendship with her cousin Lucy and with Philip Wakem. The past cannot legislate between conflicting moments of the past. The historicism of the novel is swiftly countered therefore by the image of the stopping of time, the studied apocalypse of the flood that takes the lives of Maggie and Tom—'that awful visitation of God which her father used to talk of'. Even the Darwinian, or Spencerian, essay on the 'gross sum of obscure vitality' in the novel is countered by the expectation that it 'will be swept into the same oblivion with the generations of ants and beavers'.[16] There never was a novel with a more open-ended doctrine of history, nor one that focuses more steadily on the end of the characters' existence. At one point the heroine despairs that 'the end of our lives will have nothing in it like the beginning': but the novel unhistorically construes the end of Maggie's life very like the beginning. Her earliest memory is that of 'standing with Tom by the side of the Floss, while he held my hand', and of course they die in one another's arms: 'living through again in one supreme moment the days when they had clasped their little hands in love, and roamed the daisied fields together'.[17] *The Mill on the Floss*, like so many other novels, clings to the belief that for each beginning there is some appropriate ending. The last book is entitled 'The Final Rescue'; and the final posture of brother and sister is by now familiar to us. Though George Eliot's heroine is one of the most richly, and humorously, drawn in Victorian literature, she is also a figure of truth.

The flood in *The Mill on the Floss* is subordinate to the death

[16] *The Mill on the Floss*, Bk. VI, ch. xiv, p. 329; Bk. VII, ch. v, p. 394; Bk. IV, ch. i, pp. 4–5.
[17] Ibid., Bk. III, ch. vi, p. 376; Bk. V, ch. i, p. 61; Bk. VII, ch. v, p. 400.

of the protagonists. The apocalyptic image magnifies the significance of their death, in order to balance the loss of such rich possibility of life. The care with which George Eliot has traced the growth of the Tulliver children has resulted in a changing, open-ended situation, both personal and communal: a situation additionally charged by the modern temptation of making experience an end in itself. This limitless possibility is brought partially under control by rational argument, then hurriedly stopped by the catastrophe. The 'rescue' conducted by Maggie apparently brings 'a new revelation' to her brother and makes it tolerable for them both to die.[18] The rescue operations conducted by the heroines of Dickens are designed to do much the same thing, though they are rendered permanent by marriage instead of death. Not merely do some Dickensian brides lead sacerdotal lives as representatives of death, but marriage in conventional English novels is the event that regularly precludes further experience or change. Scott, the novelist who contributed so importantly to the rise of historicism, was equally successful in perpetuating the myth that personal and public history came to a halt with marriage—at the end of the account of the hero's adventures and that of entire nations. It was well understood by novelists themselves that novels in which the protagonists live happily ever after end with just as arbitrary finality as *The Mill on the Floss*. 'As his hero and heroine pass the matrimonial barrier,' in Thackeray's phrase, 'the novelist generally drops the curtain, as if the drama were over then: the doubts and struggles of life ended.'[19] Thackeray's purpose is to show that the struggles are not ended; but if he were to develop this observation as a critical insight, he would see that marriage in ordinary novels has this air of finality because the hero's death is implicit in the marriage. Merely the circumstance that the narrative comes to an end makes it difficult for the traditional novelist to conclude without the implication of death. This implication depends on the differences of art and life, and on cultural sanctions borrowed by the English novel in the late eighteenth and nineteenth centuries.

Works of art have a way of slicing in and out of life. They not only select events from a nearly infinite range of possibilities,

[18] Ibid., Bk. VII, ch. v, p. 399.
[19] *Vanity Fair*, ch. xxvi, p. 245.

but start and stop the sequence of events. They organize experience into wholes that have beginnings, middles, and ends; and this is particularly evident in the case of narrative arts in which the beginning and end are delineated in historical time.[20] In his preface to *Roderick Hudson* James gave expression to this difference between art and the material from which it draws. Historically and spatially the relations of life stop nowhere, but the artist must limit them. 'Really, universally, relations stop nowhere, and the exquisite problem of the artist is eternally but to draw, by a geometry of his own, the circle within which they shall happily *appear* to do so.' The novelist, therefore, 'has at once intensely to consult and intensely to ignore'—that is, to break—the 'continuity of things'.[21] Further than this James does not wish to go; he reserves to the artist freedom to start and stop where he pleases. Life is 'all inclusion and confusion', as he says elsewhere, and art 'all discrimination and selection'; the artist revels in the difference.[22]

But it is possible to go further and see what endings novelists have in practice employed. 'If it was not for death and marriage,' E. M. Forster protested, 'I do not know how the average novelist would conclude. Death and marriage are almost his only connection between his characters and his plot.' This is a fair description of the English novel before Forster's time—though he failed to weigh its significance or to answer the question that it poses. His speculation that the novelist loses 'pep' at the end is no more satisfactory than the old notion that endings are pasted on to novels in order to satisfy the naïve wishes of common readers. Forster does not speculate that death and marriage amount to much the same thing at the end of a novel, though his observation that characters 'go dead' and leave a final impression of 'deadness' is not applied exclusively to novels in which the characters literally die.[23] Novelists seem to have been talking around this subject for years without really getting to the bottom of it. At the end of *Waverley* Scott compared the endings of novels to 'the progress of a stone rolled down hill by

---

[20] See Barbara Herrenstein Smith, *Poetic Closure: A Study of How Poems End* (Chicago, 1968).

[21] *Roderick Hudson*, Preface, p. vii.

[22] *The Spoils of Poynton*, Preface, p. v.

[23] *Aspects of the Novel* (New York, 1927), pp. 142–4.

an idle truant boy . . . [that becomes] most furiously rapid in
its course when it is nearest to being consigned to rest for ever'.[24]
The idiom is closer to that which we use for dead persons than
to rolling stones.

In a period in which the novel became an accepted expression
of cultural ideals, British novelists copied their endings from life,
discovering in human institutions something very like an interchangeability of death and marriage. Robert Bage, whose novels
Scott at least partially respected, put it as follows: 'The grand
intervening epoch between a man's coming into life and going
out of it, is his marriage; at which, when a man arrives, however
he may increase his consequence in a small circle, he loses it
amongst the large circle of the young, the beautiful, the single
fair, who consider him as dead—in law.'[25] Bage comes very close
to explaining why marriage is as suitable an epoch as death at
the end of a novel. Though James calls for 'discrimination and
selection' as if there were purely artistic grounds for determining where relations should stop, there are more certain thematic
grounds. In comparison with art life may seem to be all 'inclusion and confusion', but it too is highly organized—effort-
lessly in the minutest perceptions and ultimately by human institutions. Marriage itself is an attempt, of varying success, to
impose an ending on life; the institution is designed to withdraw
the individual from a large circle to a small, and to make him, in
Bage's figure, dead to sexual competition. By marriage he moves
from the present generation to the past: if he is willing to take
this step, he implicitly concedes his eventual death. The marriage
ceremony acknowledges as much in the exchange of vows to be
true until death. In human societies the rites of passage quite
typically impose thoughts of birth and death on the occasions of
initiation and marriage.[26]

In a sense the ceremonies of real life are fictions also. The
stoppages of time by birth and death, initiation and marriage,
merely 'happily *appear*' in life, as they appear in art, since the
continuity of nature and of the species tears along regardless of
institutional efforts to check its momentum and memorialize the

[24] *Waverley*, Centenary Edition (Edinburgh, 1885), ch. lxx, p. 436.
[25] *Man as He Is*, 3rd ed. (1819), quoted by A. A. Mendilow, *Time and the
Novel* (London, 1952), p. 51, n. 14.
[26] Cf. Eliade, *The Sacred and the Profane*, pp. 179–97.

place of individuals. But novels have the advantage over life
here, because they are frankly accepted as fictions. They do not
have to dwell on the unchecked surge of life, the life that escapes
confinement by institutions, unless they wish to be 'realistic';
and they can easily pretend to be realistic by subverting the
standard fiction, by insisting that life does not come to a stop
with marriage to a Dora Spenlow, a George Osborne, or a
Reverend Mr. Casaubon. In life and novels both, marriage is
construed as a permanent relation; but novels make the
permanence more definite simply by coming to a stop. Novels
imply that marriage is the most important epoch in life; they
pretend that the years between coming of age and marriage are
the whole of life; and therefore conceive of marriage as equivalent to death. Like *Waverley* itself, the hero and heroine, and a
good many others, are consigned to rest forever. Nothing more
happens in most English novels. And for that matter, nothing
more happens after the second marriage in *David Copperfield*,
Vanity Fair, and *Middlemarch*. Given a choice of death and
marriage, the novelist ordinarily chooses the ending that will—
to shift James's emphasis—'*happily* appear' to make relations
stop somewhere; he chooses marriage for his ending, and a
permanent relation to the heroine as the last relation.

The overwhelming collection of courtship romances that end
in marriage, since it comprises, by in large, the English novel,
demands some kind of explanation. The cultural explanation,
that the institution of marriage was stiffer and stronger in
England than elsewhere, does not preclude, and may reinforce,
the explanation that I am advancing: namely, that the fiction of
marriage is an acceptable refuge for the fear of death. Either the
English were inordinately fond of reading about licit love, or
marriage is indeed embraced in novels as the end of life, the
purpose of life and its termination. 'Looking back upon his own
poor story, she was its vanishing point. Every thing in its
perspective led to her innocent figure. He had travelled thousands of miles towards it; previous unquiet hopes and doubts
had worked themselves out before it; it was the centre of the
interest of his life; it was the termination of everything that was
good and pleasant in it; beyond there was nothing but mere
waste and darkened sky.'[27] Such a marriage subsumes death;

[27] *LD*, Bk. II, ch. xxvii, p. 733.

the novelist creates in it an answer to the destructive force of death.

By the eighteenth century the institution of marriage in real life had become an important expression of the desire for immortality. The intention of creating a personal posterity is one of the shaping attitudes behind the rise of the modern conjugal family; and it coincides with the weakening of Christian faith in immortality. As Carl L. Becker showed, the secular beliefs of the eighteenth century in some ways parody Christian belief: Diderot wrote, 'La postérité pour le philosophe, c'est l'autre monde de l'homme religieux'.[28] Not only the shifting of economic and political power in modern England, but the natural desire for immortality enhanced the value of a personal estate that survives from one generation to the next. This ambition made itself most obviously felt in the celebration of property as an absolute value by the end of the eighteenth century and in the rise of life insurance, which made it possible for 'provident' heads of families to purchase an estate—of value only after death—with the first down payment and a promise from an insurance company. The same ambition contributed to the classic form of the English novel, of which the denouement characteristically linked love with property, and marriage with an ongoing estate. Real property, and living happily ever after, were pointedly dissociated in the novel from getting and spending, or the aspects of money and death in the earthly city. The immortality conveyed was strictly a passive ideal: the 'deadness' that Forster complains of, and the 'dream of *complete idleness*' that Orwell remarks; the reward that, according to Ruskin, is unmerited by the hero but somehow afforded him by the heroine. Before the marriage of the hero and heroine the action comes to a standstill, and after the marriage and arrangement of the estate are certain, the novel closes. Though the estates of Dickens's protagonists are of modest material proportions, they are in the same way fixed and made permanent by the close of the novel.[29]

Certain novels of Scott and others acknowledge the com-

[28] Quoted by Becker, *The Heavenly City of the Eighteenth-Century Philosophers* (New Haven, 1959), p. 119.
[29] The argument is given in more detail in my study of Scott, *The Hero of the Waverley Novels* (New Haven, 1963), ch. iv and sec. 24.

patibility of happy and unhappy endings by openly providing
two heroines, both of whom have mythic powers over death.
The proper heroine, usually a blonde, conveys the immortality
associated with marriage and property; her absolute propriety
confesses that the hero's continuing estate depends on the per-
manency of legal and social sanctions, which the denouement of
each novel also extends toward the future. The career of her
opposite, usually a dark heroine, is pointedly finite; her
passionate nature burns out, as it were; and her death, exile, or
retreat to the cloister, is almost a warning to heroes to eschew
passion and embrace a heroine like Agnes Wickfield or Laura
Bell. This passionate heroine, however, in her closeness to
nature, often prevents the hero's literal death, by nursing him
back to life, as Rebecca nurses Ivanhoe, or by leading him from
physical harm, as the blind Nydia leads Glaucus in *The Last
Days of Pompeii*. When Dickens, in his late novels, experiments
with physically bringing heroes back to life, he accordingly
turns toward this second heroine. Lizzie Hexam is unmistakably
of this type; she not only rescues Eugene Wrayburn and nurses
him back to life, but by her example teaches Bella Wilfer how
to love—a common function of such heroines.[30] It may be
argued, too, that Lucie Manette is a composite of both types.
When two such heroines are used in conjunction, they openly
represent the double implication of death and marriage at the
end of most English novels written before the twentieth century. *The Mill on the Floss* is a devoted study of a dark heroine,
who is compared in the course of the novel to Scott's Rebecca,
Flora, and Minna Troil, and to Madame de Staël's Corinne.
Philip Wakem's speculation that Maggie may 'avenge the dark
women' of romance, and her own exclamation, 'Poor Minna! I
wonder what is the real end', bring the tradition to bear on this
novel's special concern with endings. The eventual marriage of
Lucy Deane and Stephen Guest supplies the other desired ending. Though George Eliot chose to stress the death of Maggie
and Tom, she did not forgo the English novel's customary implication of continuance and permanence. 'And every man and
woman mentioned in this history was still living—except those

[30] Cf. Scott's Flora MacIvor and Rose Bradwardine; Madame de Staël's
Corinne and Lucy Edgermonde; or even—at the very end—Thackeray's Rebecca
and Amelia Osborne.

whose end we know.'[31] Though *The Mill on the Floss* is a
modern history, in short, relations do come to a stop: some die,
some live ever after, and the novel comes to a close.

The special involvement of heroines with endings seems in-
escapable. To bring another writer's hero back to life, as
Thackeray did in *Rebecca and Rowena*, it is essential to kill the
heroine who has triumphed in the original denouement. Still
more cruel is the prospect of a novelist resurrecting his own
hero, whom he has earlier made to die by living ever after—a
prospect of which Trollope offers a notable instance. The
heroine of *Phineas Finn* is the type of love and truth; betrothed
to the hero, she has contributed nothing to his adventures except
to wait for him in Ireland, while ambition and more tempting
women tempt him in London. Mary Flood Jones: readers will
have forgotten her name; but when Phineas returns to her, 'as
sure of her fidelity as though she were a very goddess of faith
and trust', Trollope records her triumph as if she were a figure
in a renaissance allegory: 'With a woman every former rival is
an added victim to the wheels of the triumphant chariot in
which she is sitting.'[32] Within the first six pages of the sequel,
Phineas Redux, Mary Jones Finn is dead from a miscarriage.
Madame Max Goesler, a dark heroine, is required to oversee
the hero's rebirth and rescue him from the suspicion that he is
capable of murder. Trollope breezily dismissed what he had
done in the first novel as a mistake: *Phineas Finn* 'is all fairly
good except the ending,—as to which till I got to it I had made
no provision. As I fully intended to bring my hero again into
the world, I was wrong to marry him to a simple pretty Irish
girl, who could only be felt as an encumbrance on such a return.
When he did return I had no alternative but to kill the pretty
simple Irish girl, which was an unpleasant and awkward necessity.'[33] One is forced to discount the author's claim that he made
no provision for the ending, since *Phineas Finn* is a typical
Trollope production in respect to its beginning, middle, and
end. Like other novels of courtship it compresses the whole of
life into the period of time between the hero's coming of age

[31] *The Mill on the Floss*, Bk. V, ch. iv, p. 102; ch. i, p. 59; Bk. VII, 'Conclusion',
p. 401.
[32] *Phineas Finn*, Oxford World's Classics (London, 1957), ch. lxxvi, p. 435.
[33] *Autobiography*, p. 273.

and his marriage, and therefore has a perfectly suitable ending—
that is, unless the novelist would bring the hero back to life. As
Trollope's own words suggest, Phineas came into and went out
of the world in the first novel; to bring him back in the sequel
requires an act of violence against his angel.

The endings of English novels can today be seen in historical
perspective, since most serious writers of the twentieth century
have been determined to find different ways of bringing their
narratives to a close.[34] The literary frame within which Dickens
worked was itself not valid for all time. Endings that super-
impose death and marriage correspond in part to universal
needs and in part to the culture of the last century. Dickens
wrote at a time when the Christian myth of history, from the
creation to the last day, though fighting a losing battle against
historicism, was still strong in the popular imagination. The
tenets of religion have since grown less and less specific, and
even the faith in posterity as a form of immortality may be
waning. On the whole, as Kermode has pointed out, 'there is a
correlation between subtlety and variety in our fictions and
remoteness and doubtfulness about ends and origins'. As
Christian eschatology becomes more doubtful or more doubted,
the supply of endings should never altogether run out, however,
since one of the functions of novels is to compel relations to stop
somewhere—even if marriage and death should become meaningless epochs in life. 'Change without potentiality in a novel is
impossible, quite simply; though it is the hopeless aim of the
cut-out writers, and the card-shuffle writers. A novel which
really implemented this policy would properly be a chaos. No
novel can avoid being in some sense what Aristotle calls "a
completed action." This being so, all novels imitate a world of
potentiality, even if this implies a philosophy disclaimed by
their authors.'[35]

What Kermode calls potentiality was continually pumped
into English culture by novels, which still insisted in the nineteenth century that lives had significant endings. Novels
propagandized on behalf of marriage as the purpose of life, and
thematically relied upon marriage for an ending. Literature and
culture conspired together in the belief that individual death

[34] See Alan Friedman, *The Turn of the Novel* (New York, 1966), ch. ii.
[35] *The Sense of an Ending*, pp. 67, 138.

was provided for in advance by this happy ending; the more extravagant flights of Dickens portrayed the bride as an angel of death. Narrative endings, whether superficially happy or unhappy, exploited what comfort there is in the stoppage of time— a comfort enhanced by the discomforts of modern history and of historicism. If it were not for their generally peaceful character, such endings might be portrayed well enough by Kermode's model of the apocalypse. But in the period we have been studying the more obvious model for the end of time is an intimate death. Indeed, it might be argued that the twentieth-century city has felt the more vivid imprint of the apocalypse. References to the end of time in Dickens are metaphors for the end of individual life. 'Time shall show us. . . . only Time shall show us whither each traveller is bound'; the end of time is death, the 'one sure termination' that Dickens invokes over and over.[36] 'Awake, unkind father! . . . The time is flitting by; the hour is coming with an angry tread. . . . Awake, doomed man, while she is near . . . let him look for that slight figure when he wakes, and find it near him when the hour is come!'[37] The apocalyptic suggestion is added to express the urgency of embracing death voluntarily and so of giving it personal value.

The quasi-providential design of many English novels subordinates the experience of the protagonists to their status, whether measured in social class or moral categories. Such novels imply, with something like Puritan logic, that life is not nearly as important as its outcome—the position so happily satirized in the funereal Dodson sisters of *The Mill on the Floss*, but then oddly confirmed by the ending arranged for Maggie and Tom. The heroic immunity to work in Dickens, or the unilateral direction of charity and forgiveness, are not meant to be undemocratic: the selective application of values derives from the hope that while some are bound fast by experience, others can transcend it. The best Victorian novels convey an abundant sense of life, but they do not describe experience for its own sake. They typically strive to set the lives of the protagonists in order, to secure for them a certain social and moral status before it is too late, before the story of their lives is over. When the cult of experience did arise in the nineteenth century, it remained

---

[36] *LD*, Bk. I, ch. xv, p. 179; cf. *OMF*, Bk. IV, ch. xi, p. 751.
[37] *D & S*, ch. xlv, p. 334.

very difficult to define the purpose of experience without going beyond it; witness Pater's obsession with death, or the intrusion of Pompilia's absolute goodness in the relativism of Browning. Victorian novels are about ends: whatever sense of direction or purpose can be salvaged from experience. But the most general means of defining these ends is by recourse to death, which in its threatening aspect is exactly what brings such immense pressure to bear on the search for a purpose. Holy dying must be obtained because unholy dying comes unasked for.

Death, I have argued, is the common ground of the earthly city and of urban statistics in the nineteenth century; and death is what the heroine of hearth and home is prepared to cope with. Man and woman we were created, but only for the survival of the species: the institution of marriage and the institution of the novel deserve credit for so adroitly converting the sexual relation that implies death into a relation that saves from death. For today it is easier to believe that the holy city in the book of Revelation was made to appear like a bride from heaven because of our human trust in brides, than to believe in the divine truth of John's vision.

INDEX

The Index can be used as a bibliographical guide in conjunction with the notes. Titles by Dickens are followed by the year of first publication, in parentheses; other titles are listed selectively under author entries.